KW-266-281

INTERNATIONAL POLITICAL ECONOMY SERIES

General Editor: Timothy M. Shaw, Professor of Political Science and International Development Studies, and Director of the Centre for Foreign Policy Studies, Dalhousie University, Halifax, Nova Scotia

Recent titles include:

Pradeep Agrawal, Subir V. Gokarn, Veena Mishra, Kirit S. Parikh and Kunal Sen
ECONOMIC RESTRUCTURING IN EAST ASIA AND INDIA: Perspectives on Policy Reform

Deborah Bräutigam
CHINESE AID AND AFRICAN DEVELOPMENT: Exporting Green Revolution

Steve Chan, Cal Clark and Danny Lam (*editors*)
BEYOND THE DEVELOPMENTAL STATE: East Asia's Political Economies Reconsidered

Jennifer Clapp
ADJUSTMENT AND AGRICULTURE IN AFRICA: Farmers, the State and the World Bank in Guinea

Robert W. Cox (*editor*)
THE NEW REALISM: Perspectives on Multilateralism and World Order

Ann Denholm Crosby
DILEMMAS IN DEFENCE DECISION-MAKING: Constructing Canada's Role in NORAD 1958–96

Diane Ethier
ECONOMIC ADJUSTMENT IN NEW DEMOCRACIES: Lessons from Southern Europe

Stephen Gill (*editor*)
GLOBALIZATION, DEMOCRATIZATION AND MULTILATERALISM

Jeffrey Hendersen (*editor*), assisted by Karoly Balaton and Gyorgy Lengyel
INDUSTRIAL TRANSFORMATION IN EASTERN EUROPE IN THE LIGHT OF THE EAST ASIAN EXPERIENCE

Jacques Hersh and Johannes Dragsbaek Schmidt (*editors*)
THE AFTERMATH OF 'REAL EXISTING SOCIALISM' IN EASTERN EUROPE, Volume 1: Between Western Europe and East Asia

David Hulme and Michael Edwards (*editors*)
NGOs, STATES AND DONORS: Too Close for Comfort?

Staffan Lindberg and Árni Sverrisson (*editors*)
SOCIAL MOVEMENTS IN DEVELOPMENT: The Challenge of Globalization and Democratization

Anne Lorentzen and Marianne Rostgaard (*editors*)
THE AFTERMATH OF 'REAL EXISTING SOCIALISM' IN EASTERN
EUROPE, Volume 2: People and Technology in the Process of Transition

Stephen D. McDowell
GLOBALIZATION, LIBERALIZATION AND POLICY CHANGE: A Political
Economy of India's Communications Sector

Juan Antonio Morales and Gary McMahon (*editors*)
ECONOMIC POLICY AND THE TRANSITION TO DEMOCRACY: The Latin
American Experience

Ted Schrecker (*editor*)
SURVIVING GLOBALISM: The Social and Environmental Challenges

Ann Seidman, Robert B. Seidman and Janice Payne (*editors*)
LEGISLATIVE DRAFTING FOR MARKET REFORM: Some Lessons from
China

Caroline Thomas and Peter Wilkin (*editors*)
GLOBALIZATION AND THE SOUTH

Kenneth P. Thomas
CAPITAL BEYOND BORDERS: States and Firms in the Auto Industry,
1960–94

Geoffrey R. D. Underhill (*editor*)
THE NEW WORLD ORDER IN INTERNATIONAL FINANCE

Henry Veltmeyer, James Petras and Steve Vieux
NEOLIBERALISM AND CLASS CONFLICT IN LATIN AMERICA: A
Comparative Perspective on the Political Economy of Structural Adjustment

Robert Wolfe
FARM WARS: The Political Economy of Agriculture and the International Trade
Regime

International Political Economy Series
Series Standing Order ISBN 0–333–71708–2 hardcover
Series Standing Order ISBN 0–333–71110–6 paperback
(*outside North America only*)

You can receive future titles in this series as they are published by placing a standing order.
Please contact your bookseller or, in case of difficulty, write to us at the address below with
your name and address, the title of the series and the ISBN quoted above.

Customer Services Department, Macmillan Distribution Ltd
Houndmills, Basingstoke, Hampshire RG21 6XS, England

Foreign Direct Investment in Three Regions of the South at the End of the Twentieth Century

Susan M. McMillan
Senior Researcher
Educational Data Systems
Morgan Hill
California

PP. 10 - 22

First published in Great Britain 1999 by
MACMILLAN PRESS LTD
Houndmills, Basingstoke, Hampshire RG21 6XS and London
Companies and representatives throughout the world

A catalogue record for this book is available from the British Library.

ISBN 0–333–73488–2

First published in the United States of America 1999 by
ST. MARTIN'S PRESS, INC.,
Scholarly and Reference Division,
175 Fifth Avenue, New York, N.Y. 10010

ISBN 0–312–21725–0

Library of Congress Cataloging-in-Publication Data
McMillan, Susan M., 1964–
Foreign direct investment in three regions of the
South at the end of the twentieth century / Susan M.
McMillan.
p.   cm. — (International political economy
series)
Includes bibliographical references and index.
ISBN 0–312–21725–0 (cloth)
1. Investments, Foreign—Developing countries.
I. Title.   II. Series.
HG5993.M384   1998
332.67'3'091724—dc21   98–35610
                                     CIP

© Susan M. McMillan 1999

All rights reserved. No reproduction, copy or transmission of this publication may be made
without written permission.

No paragraph of this publication may be reproduced, copied or transmitted save with
written permission or in accordance with the provisions of the Copyright, Designs and
Patents Act 1988, or under the terms of any licence permitting limited copying issued by
the Copyright Licensing Agency, 90 Tottenham Court Road, London W1P 9HE.

Any person who does any unauthorised act in relation to this publication may be liable to
criminal prosecution and civil claims for damages.

The author has asserted her right to be identified as the author of this work in accordance
with the Copyright, Designs and Patents Act 1988.

This book is printed on paper suitable for recycling and made from fully managed and
sustained forest sources.

10   9   8   7   6   5   4   3   2   1
08   07   06   05   04   03   02   01   00   99

Printed and bound in Great Britain by
Antony Rowe Ltd, Chippenham, Wiltshire

Contents

UNIVERSITY OF PLYMOUTH

Item No.   9003876832

Date   - 4 MAY 1999   B

Class No.   332·673091814 MAC
Contl. No. 0333734882

LIBRARY SERVICES

v

List of Tables

List of Abbreviations

AFRC	Armed Forces Revolutionary Council (Ghana)
ASEAN	Association of South East Asian Nations
BOI	Board of Investments (Philippines)
CACM	Central American Common Market
CMB	Cocoa Marketing Board (Ghana)
CODESA	*Coporacion Costarricense de Desarrollo SA* (Costa Rica)
CSPPA	Caisse de Stabilisation et de Soutien des Prix des Produits (Côte d'Ivoire)
CPP	Convention People's Party (Ghana)
EOI	Export Oriented Industrialization
ERP	Economic Recovery Program (IMF/World Bank)
FDI	Foreign Direct Investment
GDP	Gross Domestic Product
GNP	Gross National Product
Huk	Hukbalahap (Philippines)
IMF	International Monetary Fund
IMR	Infant Mortality Rate
ISI	Import-Substitution Industrialization
MNC	Multinational Corporation
MNE	Multinational Enterprises
MNLF	Mindanao National Liberation Front (Philippines)
NLC	National Liberation Council (Ghana)
NRC	National Redemption Council (Ghana)
NEDA	National Economic and Development Authority (Philippines)
NIC(s)	Newly Industrializing Country(ies)
OECD	Organization for Economic Cooperation and Development
PDCI	Parti Democratique de Côte d'Ivoire
PLN	National Liberation Party (Costa Rica)
PNP	People's National Party (Ghana)
PP	Progress Party (Ghana)
PNDC	Provisional National Defense Council (Ghana)
SOEs	State-Owned Enterprises
TNC	Trans-National Corporation
UGCC	United Gold Coast Convention (Ghana)

UMOA	Monetary Union of West Africa
UNCTAD	United Nations Council on Trade and Development
UNCTC	United Nations Centre for Transnational Corporations
UNCTC	United Nations Council on Transnational Corporations
USAID	United States Agency for International Development
VAR	Vector Autoregression

Preface

The role of international economic forces in domestic political and economic development has been the focus of several waves of social science research since the end of World War II. The number of poor nation-states grew rapidly in the 1960s, and scholars produced sets of competing theories to provide explanations and policy prescriptions for the development of those countries. The theoretical debate eased in the late 1980s and the 1990s, as scholars and policymakers began to converge on a set of policies that were based in part on neoclassical economic theory, and in part on the practical experience of the East Asian newly industrializing countries (NICs). Typical development policies came to be a mixture of state-centred strategies with market-based policies and this included efforts to use international economic ties as tools for development.

Critical questions about the role of international capital flows such as foreign direct investment have become particularly salient again with the end of the cold war and the increasing globalization of the world economy. The currency crisis in Southeast Asia that began in mid-1997 also highlights the effects of global capital flows on developing countries and the development role played by foreign actors. The long-run political and economic consequences of international economic ties between developed and developing countries seem to be mixed; positive in some cases, for some time periods, and negative for other countries or time periods.

The theoretical mix between neoclassical economic thought and state-centred theories of development makes it difficult to predict how foreign capital and domestic context factors interact to produce different patterns of growth, development and political stability. Divergence from expected patterns of development is frequently explained in terms of country-specific policies or constraints. The difficulty is that these country-specific conditions, and how they interact with the international economy, are not spelled out in a systematic fashion. We are now in a position to use at least 40 years' worth of theoretical and empirical developments to re-think the relationship between domestic factors in development, and international capital flows such as foreign direct investment.

The goal of this project is to develop a framework for analysis that specifies the conditions under which one type of foreign economic interaction, foreign direct investment (FDI), produces different patterns of development outcomes in poor countries. The specific outcome variables of interest are economic growth, economic development and political stability. The first chapter begins with a discussion of why FDI is the featured part of the international economy, and then summarizes the previously dominant theoretical explanations for the consequences of FDI. FDI was initially expected to have positive consequences in the 'modernization' studies, negative consequences according to dependency theory, and potentially mixed results according to dependent-development and bargaining analyses of state strength. The rapid growth of the Newly Industrializing Countries (NICs) seemed to support a mix of neoclassical economic theory with arguments related to state strength.

Although the NICs did rely on many market-based policies, the type of state involvement in their economies was not entirely consistent with the modernization approach to development, so theoretical explanations for why some states did relatively well became less clear. Economists have been able to make some head-way in incorporating indicators of economic policy and human capital development as determinants of economic growth (Barro, 1991; Barro and Lee, 1994; Dollar, 1992). But, the difficulty of operationalizing the concept of state strength has made large-scale empirical investigations problematic. Analysis of state bargaining power and the outcomes of FDI continues to be based on case studies without systematic comparison that might yield more general conclusions about how bargaining power and FDI might be associated with clear patterns of domestic development outcomes.

The theoretical framework for analysis developed in this book is based on the bargaining approach to understanding the consequences of FDI in developing host countries. The inductive analysis yields a set of domestic political and economic context conditions that can be compared in order to determine what domestic conditions are likely to interact with FDI to produce different types of development outcomes. There are several analytic advantages to be gained from this strategy. One is that this framework directs attention to why firms would want to invest in some countries versus others, thus providing clues about the most important aspects of bargaining power. It also makes apparent the need to examine the consequences of FDI in conjunction with the motivations firms might have for investing in foreign countries. Finally, the bargaining approach highlights the fact that earlier development outcomes are the context for current and future efforts, so patterns tend to be self-reinforcing. Whether and how FDI fits into those development patterns is investigated in the case-comparisons of Chapters 2 through to 4.

The six countries included in the paired comparative case studies are Thailand and the Philippines in Asia, Ghana and Côte d'Ivoire in West Africa, and Guatemala and Costa Rica in Central America. These country pairs were chosen for several reasons. First, regional representation is important since many development trends follow roughly regional lines (Callaghy, 1993). Second, all of these countries began the post-World War II time period as small political and economic entities that were marginal to the core political, economic and cultural systems (Kirk, 1990:16). Although they have exhibited strong growth at times they were not part of the initial set of NICs. Third, although the countries in each pair are similar in some respects, they present variation in domestic context conditions, their experiences with FDI and development processes.

The principal result of the comparisons is that the domestic context of FDI generates identifiable patterns of development outcomes. FDI, as the indicator of international economic transactions, does interact with the domestic context and so contributes to development patterns, but it is not the primary causal agent in development outcomes. In addition, there is some qualitative evidence for a temporal sequence in which political stability precedes economic growth, and both political stability and economic growth are necessary for further development.

Chapter 5 uses quantitative data to test the temporal patterns of relationships implied by the country comparisons. I use vector auto-regression (VAR) techniques to test for temporal precedence, or Granger causality, among a set of four variables: FDI, economic growth, economic development, and political instability. The results support the contention that FDI is drawn in by a strong bargaining context, but that it is not itself a particularly strong determinant of domestic economic and political outcomes.

The concluding chapter reiterates the findings and discusses the implications for policymakers in developing countries. Among the large set of factors that can produce economic and political change, FDI is one factor over which host country policy-makers may have significant regulatory control. In the context of increasing competition in the global capital market, understanding the complex ways FDI interacts with domestic determinants of development is important for those in the developing countries, as well as actors in the international economy. Despite the focus on FDI, the analysis has broader implications for how other ties to the international economy affect domestic development.

Any project such as this involves assistance and support from many individuals and organizations, and this book is no exception. I would like to gratefully acknowledge the help and encouragement of the faculty members I worked with at the University of Colorado, in particular Steve Chan, Mike Ward, Jim Scarritt, Leslie Anderson and John O'Loughlin. Lonna Atkeson, Kelley Daniel, David Davis, Sean Kelly, Will H. Moore III, Mohan Penubarti, Sheen Rajmaira and Josephine Squires also deserve many thanks for their continuing support of my research efforts.

In addition, J. David Singer and the members of the Correlates of War Seminar at the University of Michigan provided excellent advice for me at critical moments, as did the faculty members of the Penn State Department of Political Science. The Research and Graduate Studies Office and the Department of Political Science at the Pennsylvania State University provided much appreciated financial support for this project. The chapter on Costa Rica and Guatemala was initially a conference paper for the American Political Science Association Annual Meetings in 1994, and the chapter here is dramatically revised. I had excellent research assistance from Jill Blumburg, Jonathan Erikson, Andrew Essig, Brian Grimm, Wendy Holthaus, Timothy Nordstrom and Albert Stemp. Having mentioned all of these people, I must acknowledge that any errors of fact or interpretation are mine alone. Finally, I thank my entire family for their support, especially my long-suffering husband, Doug Cross.

Susan McMillan

1 Theoretical Background and Framework for Analysis

Multiple paths exist through which the international world economy might have an effect on the domestic development processes of poor countries. Trade, portfolio investment, direct investment, commercial loans, and official and private development assistance, all present potential paths for analysis. I have chosen to focus on the consequences of foreign direct investment flows for two primary reasons. First, they are very closely tied to international trade patterns, and so they are strong indicators of other global economic interactions (UNCTC, 1996). As will be discussed further in this chapter, companies which invest directly overseas frequently do so because they expect the investment to yield trade advantages. Stocks of FDI are also closely tied to trade patterns, but the data are very difficult to obtain. Furthermore, because of the way stocks are calculated, they are correlated very highly with flows through time.

The second reason for focusing on FDI is that it involves a degree of foreign control not generally associated with other types of international economic transactions. Direct investment involves a 'lasting interest' in a foreign enterprise, as well as an 'effective voice in the management of the enterprise' (UNCTC, 1983a:26). If the international economy has an influence on domestic development, we can expect to see that influence in relationships where foreign actors exercise some measure of control of capital, production and the related trade patterns.

While the other forms of capital transfers can certainly be seen as tools for domestic development, it is not reasonable to expect their effects to be the same as foreign direct investment. Aid is given primarily for political or altruistic reasons (McKinlay and Little, 1977; and McKinlay and Mughan, 1984), and does not necessarily have the profit motive that is attached to direct investments. Although portfolio investment has become increasingly important for emerging markets, it does not involve the degree of foreign control that comes with direct investment. Finally, commercial loans necessarily involve repayment with interest and for this reason should have different developmental consequences than direct investment. Even so, it is interesting to note that the bargaining process involved in organizing debt relief may be similar to the bargaining involved in attaining direct investments (Lehman, 1993).

The growing importance of FDI flows on a global scale can be seen in the upward trend in flows through time. Table 1.1 indicates that the global flows of FDI grew rapidly during the 1980s, but that much of that growth for the developing countries was concentrated in the East, South and Southeast Asia. FDI inflows to all countries decreased during times of global economic slowdowns, but between 1994 and 1995 inflows increased by 40 per cent (UNCTC, 1996:4). Again, a small group of about ten developing countries retained the highest shares of FDI inflows.

FDI flows form a large part of the international economy, and thus whether and/or how they affect domestic development remains an important question. The review of theoretical arguments that follows here indicates that theoretical and empirical examinations of the problem typically emphasize the outcomes of FDI, without explicitly considering why FDI flows concentrate in some countries. In developing the theoretical framework used in my country comparisons,

Table 1.1   Average Inflows of Foreign Direct Investment to Developing Countries, by Region; selected years

Host Region	(billions of US dollars)		
	1980–4	1986–90	1992
All Countries	49.7	150	126
Developing Countries	12.5	26	40
Africa	1.2	3	2
Latin America and the Caribbean	6.1	9	16
East, South and South-East Asia	4.7	14	21
Oceania	0.13	0.10	0.5
West Asia	0.37	0.5	0.8
Other (includes Malta and Yugoslavia)	0.04	0.05	0.1
Least Developed Countries	0.19	0.17	–

Sources: UNCTC, *World Investment Report 1991: The Triad in foreign direct investment* (New York: United Nations, 1991) p.11; UNCTC (1992) *World Investment Report: Transnational Corporations as Engines of Growth*, p.23; UNCTC (1993) *Transnational Corporations and Integrated International Production*.

I argue that analyzing the problem through the perspective of bargaining power allows us to examine and understand both causes and consequences of FDI flows.

I. THE THEORETICAL BACKGROUND

The theoretical debate on the consequences of FDI in developing host countries is reviewed in more detail elsewhere (Grieco, 1986; Pantojas-Garcia, 1990; Rothgeb, Jr, 1989), but is reiterated here briefly in order to point to differences with the analytical framework used for this project. The modernization and dependency approaches to development of poor countries dominated the early literature, but a more recent 'statist' orientation has lead to a re-emphasis on liberal economic policies implemented by strong developmental states. The three approaches are reviewed here as successive critiques of each other, so the discussion presents each in its most stark and least nuanced form in order to contrast the key points.

Modernization, Dependency and State-led Development

The 'modernization' approach is based on neoclassical economic theories and expects the overall effects of foreign investment to be beneficial for the host-country economy (Healey, 1971; Herrick and Kindleberger, 1983; Todaro, 1985). This framework assumes that a liberal international economy promotes the efficient allocation of resources on a global scale, which in turn is expected to maximize global welfare. Foreign Direct Investment, as one part of the global transfer of resources, is expected to inject funds into the host economy as a supplement to domestic investment and to help alleviate foreign exchange constraints. The added investment boosts the productive capacity of the economy and this leads to higher economic growth rates, provided that the added capital is not simply used to finance consumption. The benefits of that higher growth may initially concentrate in the hands of the wealthy, but then begin to 'trickle-down' to workers at lower levels of income as wages rise in the growing modern sector of the economy. But, even though external economic ties are expected to aid in development, domestic determinants of growth, such as domestic investment and liberal economic policies, are thought to be more important (Rostow, 1971).

The *dependencia* school of thought evolved from the dissatisfaction of Latin American scholars with the inability of the modernization approach to explain continued under-development in that region. The diversity in the dependency literature makes summarizing the perspective difficult, but in general dependency theorists emphasize a relationship of dominance in the international political economy such that developed 'core' countries exploit the relatively underdeveloped 'periphery' (Bauzon and Abel, 1986). Multinational corporations (MNCs), and the direct investments they bring with them, are seen as instruments in maintaining the system of dominance. Early versions of the dependency perspective maintained that, in situations of dependence, development would be arrested, and could not happen as it had in the already industrialized countries (Frank, 1966; dos Santos, 1970).

In later versions of the dependency approach, it is acknowledged that external economic dependence can lead to economic development (Evans, 1979). However, that development will be based on economic growth that is distorted, at least to some extent, by the global interests of the external actors (Cardoso, 1973). In this view, MNCs bring in technology that may not be appropriate for the development goals of the host economy. Furthermore, because of their extensive market networks and more developed production techniques, they make it difficult for domestic firms to compete. The local capitalist class is then coopted into the strategies of corporate growth, and is distracted from, and perhaps even hostile to, national economic growth and development needs.

In addition, FDI is expected to contribute to political and social unrest by concentrating income in the hands of a few, and increasing political tensions between those with 'foreign' interests and those with domestic interests. Even with the possible distortions, the later dependency-type literature allowed a role for the state in regulating and directing foreign economic ties to the domestic economy in ways that could foster dependent development (Cardoso and Faletto, 1979; Evans, 1979).

While the later versions of the dependency approach do allow for external economic ties to lead to economic growth in the short-term, it is essentially a pessimistic outlook for long-term development in poor host countries and did not do well in explaining the rise of the newly industrializing countries (NICs) of Southeast Asia. An approach that may be loosely called 'statist' evolved from the difficulties of dependency theory in explaining the NICs, as well as the re-emphasis that emerged and focussed on state development policies (Deyo, 1987).

This perspective emphasizes aspects of the state as variables that account for the variation in growth and development (Moon and Dixon, 1985: Rueschemeyr and Evans, 1985; Skocpol, 1985; Nordlinger, 1987; Migdal, 1987). In this framework, the autonomy of the state *vis-à-vis* other social actors, the strength of the state, the ideological orientation of the state, the development policies and the structure of the political processes, are expected to be important intervening variables for understanding growth and development in less-developed host countries.

The general expectation is that FDI will have positive economic consequences in relatively strong and capitalist oriented states (Haggard, 1990). The strong capitalist state is expected to boost the economy by intervening in ways compatible with market operations and by implementing policies that are attractive to international economic actors. A strong state can also prevent or control the potential political instability that may accompany rapid economic growth. On the other hand, if economic development is not forthcoming, poor domestic policies tend to be blamed for failure rather than ties to the international system.

Although the fundamental assumptions and causal mechanisms for these three dominant perspectives are quite different, the expectations generated by the later versions of each theoretical perspective seem to have converged on a modified version that combines aspects of the statist and modernization arguments. Early modernization theory would not have expected extensive state intervention in the economy to be an effective means of producing domestic development. However, getting the policies 'right' according to market mechanisms is consistent both with the modernization and statist perspectives. The more recent dependent development theorists also pointed toward state strength as an important factor in regulating foreign economic actors and for capturing domestic benefits from foreign economic ties.

The convergence of expectations from modified theoretical arguments occurred in the face of empirical studies which, taken together, do not unequivocally support any single theoretical framework. The brief review here indicates that some statistical results support the dependency arguments, as do some case studies. On the other hand, some evidence also supports the modernization and neoclassical contentions that international economic ties produce faster economic growth. In addition, there is much evidence to support the argument that state variables are important for determining political and economic outcomes. How influential FDI flows are and how they interact with state variables remain open to question.

Empirical efforts have been concentrated on understanding the effects of FDI on the aggregate outcomes such as domestic economic growth, economic development and political conflict. Several influential studies concluded that when controlling for the level of domestic investment, flows of FDI were positively related to economic growth, while stock of FDI was negatively associated with growth (Bornschier and Chase-Dunn, 1985; London and Williams, 1988). But, Firebaugh (1992) convincingly demonstrated that interpreting the stock as having a negative effect was a misreading of the evidence, and that both stocks and flows of FDI have a positive effect on economic growth in poor countries. On the other hand, Jackman (1982:19) and McGowan and Smith (1978) found that the stock of FDI was unrelated to economic growth in their samples of poor countries.

Domestic economic and political determinants of growth are sometimes downplayed in the effort to tease out the empirical effects of FDI, but it is important to note that in many studies of economic growth, domestic determinants do fairly well in explaining variation. This suggests that the 'engine of growth' is not driven primarily by the international economy. Higher levels of human capital development and higher domestic investment are positively related to growth, while larger government budgets, government induced market inefficiency and political instability have negative effects on growth (Barro, 1991; Barro and Lee, 1994). So, while the effect of FDI may be to increase growth, it is also clear that domestic determinants of growth are at least as important.

Quite a few statistical studies have examined the relationship between FDI and economic inequality which is taken as an indicator of host country development. The evidence indicates a strong and positive relationship between foreign investment penetration and income inequality (Bornschier, 1981; Chan, 1989; London and Robinson, 1989). This finding, though consistent across several studies, does not provide conclusive evidence for or against any single theoretical point of view. Even under the modernization perspective the expectation is that economic growth may lead to higher income inequality in the short run. Furthermore, the effect of FDI on host country development is not as strong when other models and indicators of development are used. For instance, when control variables for the size of the government sector in the economy are added, Bradshaw and Tshandu (1990) found that investment dependence loses its significance for determining Physical Quality of Life Index (PQLI) scores in sub-Saharan African countries.

The empirical evidence linking FDI and political conflict is also not conclusive. The theoretical arguments are more vague on this point, and they generally expect an indirect relationship between FDI and domestic political conflict. Thus, intervening variables such as income inequality, socioeconomic development or government repressiveness are typically the focus of such studies. The relationship between income inequality and political conflict has been studied extensively and is extremely complex. Lichbach (1989:465) reviewed 43 macro-level studies and concluded that 'economic inequality may either have positive, negative, or no impact on dissent.' The circumstances under which inequalities – which may be due in part to FDI – cause domestic political unrest remain unclear.

Studies which focus on testing dependency hypotheses have found some support for the proposition that economic dependency is associated with domestic political unrest. Boswell and Dixon (1990) found that economic penetration and military dependence fuel rebellion through effects on income inequality and government responsiveness. London and Robinson (1989:306) reported that foreign penetration is directly and positively related to political violence, and income inequality becomes insignificant when controlling for foreign penetration. Bradshaw (1985:203) concluded that the stock of FDI is positively associated with state expansion, which is positively related to domestic turmoil. Yet, Arat (1988, 1991) demonstrated that the relationship between foreign economic ties and domestic political unrest depends on the country involved and the time period studied. The mixed findings on this question indicate that state-specific conditions are important for understanding the relationship between FDI and development outcomes, but we have little systematic understanding of how and why.

Studies that specifically include aspects of the state – ideology, structure of the political system, and policy choices – also have found these to be important intervening variables. Hein (1992) found that state policies are important both for attracting FDI and for growth, but that FDI is an insignificant factor in explaining growth. One cross-country study indicated that omission of state fiscal and monetary policies may make the supposed relationship between FDI and growth misspecified (Morisset, 1989). Although Dollar (1992) does not include FDI, he found outward oriented government policies to be a strong determinant of economic growth. In other region or country-specific studies, policy preferences and/or the ability to implement policies are also found to be important for understanding the relationship between external economic ties and domestic outcomes (O'Hearn, 1990; Tugwell, 1974; Watts and Bassett, 1986). In a comparison of six countries, Chan and Clark (1995) conclude that state–society relations and political–economic culture variables help us to understand the consequences of MNCs in Asian countries.

To sum up, the empirical evidence indicates that domestic political and economic variables are very important for determining development outcomes, and this is consistent in some way with each of the development theories that have competed for dominance. But, it is less clear whether and how FDI influences those same outcomes. The theoretical problem revolves around how we draw generalizations about which domestic variables are most important and why, and about how the international economy impinges upon or interacts with those variables.

Since the dominant theories have undergone gradual evolution, the set of domestic conditions to be considered is not always well specified by theory. Inclusion of a variable or factor in the set is more often a function of how well that variable explains results that diverge from earlier expectations. If the state is to be a useful analytic concept in the puzzle of how the international economy affects domestic development, we should be able to identify the important variables and conditions, whether the relationships vary by country and time period, and whether that variation follows identifiable patterns. The bargaining approach discussed below is one method for identifying political and economic context conditions that influence the relationship between FDI and aggregate political and economic outcomes.

II. FIRMS, BARGAINING POWER AND HOST-COUNTRY CONTEXT CONDITIONS

Posing the initial research question in terms of how international economic ties affect domestic development seems to imply a unidirectional relationship. However, as demonstrated by the brief empirical review included here, it may be more instructive to think of the problem as one in which domestic and international factors interact in a more complex fashion. Specifically, if we want to understand the consequences of FDI for domestic development, it helps to begin by considering why firms might wish to invest in one country given all the possible choices of location. Theoretical explanations for firm location and empirical patterns of FDI flows can provide clues about the factors that contribute to host-country bargaining leverage. They can also help us understand why certain countries attract much larger amounts of FDI than others. Recognizing this selection bias at the outset can help map out a general framework under which we can generate specific expectations about whether and how FDI interacts with the domestic conditions to produce patterns of aggregate development outcomes.

Firms and Foreign Direct Investment

Explanations for why firms invest directly in foreign countries revolve around the advantages such investment might provide to the firm. Vernon's (1966) product-cycle theory was an early effort to explain FDI. According to the theory, each stage of production requires a different set of inputs. Countries differ with respect to comparative advantages for those inputs, so firms tend to locate stages of production in countries with the comparative advantage for a particular stage. In the first stage of production for a new product, research and development are critical. These tasks are more likely to be done in an advanced industrialized country because that is where technological innovation and the most advanced R&D facilities are located.

Once the production process has matured, the producer attempts to satisfy overseas demand by first increasing domestic production, then by setting up overseas production facilities where the costs of production are cheaper and transportation costs are lower. Finally, in the standardized-production phase, the initial producer faces stiff price competition from producers copying the product. So, routine production is increasingly shifted to low cost sites, usually in developing countries where labour costs are lower.

Other explanations for firm behaviour compliment the product-cycle theory, but focus on transaction costs that arise from market imperfections. Following Coase (1937) and Hymer (1976), Williamson (1985) argues that firms engage in direct investment as a way of internalizing transaction costs that arise from market imperfections. Similarly, Caves (1982) argues that direct investment abroad is an attempt by firms to lower the transaction costs of production. According to Caves, direct investment in the extractive sectors needs no explanation because it is clear that firms have an interest in extracting particular resources. But, countries with a large local market and a relatively higher level of development would attract more investment in the manufacturing sector than those with small markets and/or a lower level of development.

Dunning (1981, 1985) develops a model of FDI as a function of ownership specific advantages to firms, location specific advantages and incentives for firms to internalize transaction costs. For purposes of understanding what factors draw in foreign investment, the most important part of the model lies in specifying the location specific advantages and how governments might increase or reduce transaction costs. According to Dunning's theory, a country will be a net importer or net exporter of FDI according to its natural resource endowments, size and character of the domestic market, and the economic policies implemented by the government (Dunning, 1981:60). A higher level of economic development in the potential host country can also be a location specific advantage.

The empirical evidence on direct investment decisions by firms demonstrates that many of the theoretical locational advantages – both economic and political – are indeed associated with larger FDI flows (Agarwal, 1980), while Schneider and Frey (1985) found that FDI flows are best modelled with a combination of political and economic variables. Gross National Product per capita had the largest positive impact, but other factors also were important, including: growth of real GNP; rate of inflation; balance of payments deficit; wage cost; presence of a skilled work force; political instability; government ideology; and other international ties, such as bilateral and multilateral aid. These results were supported by Lucas (1993), and by Hein (1992) who provided specific evidence that host-country policies are important for attracting FDI.

There is additional evidence that FDI is involved in a self-reinforcing mechanism so that once a country begins attracting large FDI flows it continues to do so. Wheeler and Mody (1992) conclude that existing stocks of FDI are very important for drawing in new flows, and suggest that this self-reinforcing mechanism 'begins to operate only after a certain development threshold has been reached' (p.71). This helps to explain why the developed economies attract more FDI flows than the developing economies. It also implies that in order to attract FDI, poor countries ought to concentrate on developing better infrastructure, creating a stable investment environment, maintaining stable international relations, and ensuring an expanding domestic market (Wheeler and Mody, 1992:72). These suggestions are consistent with the modernization perspective on how to generate economic growth in the first place.

The potential for a self-reinforcing cycle in which FDI flows are directed to the more developed countries is a frequently neglected piece of the FDI consequences puzzle. As noted above, the outcomes of FDI are often studied in isolation from the reasons firms wish to invest in developing countries. Thus, the potential for a tautological cycle and selection bias is often overlooked. One way to explain the somewhat muddled empirical evidence on the consequences of FDI is to note that countries with strong economies draw in more FDI and are better able to turn it to their advantage, and the weaker countries continue to be unable or unwilling to use the smaller amounts of FDI that they draw in for domestic development. From this point of view, both modernization and dependency-type outcome patterns will result from FDI, but they do not necessarily follow directly from the FDI. In either case, state factors would be found to be important intervening variables for development outcomes, but again, which ones and how they interact with FDI is not easily specified in a general sense.

Bargaining Power of Host Countries

One way to break into the tautology to understand the process by which FDI affects aggregate outcomes in developing host countries is to examine the context conditions – those factors that contribute to host-country bargaining leverage – that shape the host-country response to FDI. The bargaining approach is useful because it helps delineate factors that contribute to the ability and willingness of the host country to use FDI to its own advantage (Grieco, 1985; Moran, 1985 and 1978; Vernon, 1971 and 1977). By focusing on host-country factors that contribute to FDI bargaining outcomes, we can explicitly recognize that they are frequently the same economic and political factors which are jointly significant for drawing in FDI, *and* for determining development outcomes.

For addressing the question of how FDI affects domestic development, the emphasis of the bargaining perspective is on the bargaining power of the host country relative to the foreign investors. Rather than FDI being inherently beneficial or harmful, its effects are seen as dependent on the relative bargaining power of the host country and the potential investors. Thus, the bargaining positions of the key actors determine the distribution of benefits from specific investments or projects. This approach is consistent with the statist inclusion of intervening political variables, but it is broader in scope and includes economic variables as well as state factors.

Because bargaining power can differ across issue areas and through time, a single, simple definition of bargaining power is difficult to pin down. Bergsten, Horst and Moran (1978:369) refer to bargaining power simply as the ability of the host country to 'influence' foreign investors. In discussing the case of the automobile industry in Thailand, Doner (1991:205) argues that 'the bargaining power of host countries is an attribute of the country as such and not simply its government.' Elsewhere, Doner (1991:95) refers to bargaining leverage as the willingness and ability of the host country to mobilize resources to exploit opportunities in a given industry. Making an effort to be very specific, Encarnation (1989:20) cites Lax and Sebenius (1986) to define bargaining power as 'the ability of multinationals, the state, or local enterprises to improve the range of plausible outcomes available to each, and to improve the probability of securing the outcome that each prefers.'

The working definition of bargaining power for this project combines Doner's inclusion of willingness with Encarnation's explanation of what sorts of abilities bargaining power entails. Although any operationalization necessarily depends on value judgments of ability and willingness, the definition offers several analytic advantages. This definition does not exclude the possibility that outcomes of bargaining can be positive-sum rather than zero-sum. Multinational corporation success does not necessarily have to come at the expense of the developing host county, and vice versa. Another closely related point is that the definition allows bargaining power to vary through time. Case studies indicate that developing host countries have been able to gain benefits from MNCs through the bargaining process (Grieco, 1985), but that MNCs are willing and able to fight back against host-country restrictions (Biersteker, 1987). And, another scholar (Thomas) has argued that increasing capital mobility again removes bargaining power from even advanced host countries.

A third reason this definition is useful is that incorporating the willingness to mobilize resources with the ability to improve the range of plausible outcomes provides a means of understanding an apparent paradox. In some cases it seems that a very weak host country has been both willing and able to use weaknesses to build future strengths. For instance, Taiwan as a host country was able to use its initial weakness to exploit a perceived threat to the strategic position of the US, and so gain foreign support and build domestic strength (Chan, 1988). Focusing only on the initial abilities of a host country would not allow us to understand the willingness of the host state to use even strategic weaknesses in order to improve its range of plausible outcomes.

Fourth, this definition of bargaining power does not make the assumption that bargaining power translates directly to economic or political gains in the host country. Rather, bargaining power comes into play as part of a process in which foreign investment interacts with domestic context conditions. As Encarnation (1989:4,30–1) points out, bargaining gains by the host country are not always accompanied by an improved overall economic situation. The domestic division may spread the benefits of investment in such a way that aggregate economic indicators do not improve, and this would closely resemble a dependency-type pattern of outcomes. A strong bargaining position is necessary, but by no means sufficient, for turning FDI into economic growth and development.

Finally, focusing on the ability of the host to increase its policy options and the probability of securing preferred outcomes provides a means of organizing the search for a general set of the most important host-country context conditions, or factors that contribute to bargaining leverage. The essence of a host-country's bargaining strength is that it has something the foreign investor wants: a large domestic market; a cheaper source of labour; a source of an important raw material, and so on. These aggregate factors are precisely those which draw in foreign investment in the first place. One reason why the link between firm investment strategies and aggregate FDI outcomes has not been fully explored is that most studies using the bargaining approach take the relevant outcomes to be the terms negotiated for a specific project, firm or industry (Bennett and Sharpe, 1985; Grieco, 1985; Jenkins, 1987). Similarly, some studies investigate the components of specific strategic bargaining processes, such as negotiations over structural adjustment programmes (Lehman, 1993).

In this project I use the bargaining approach as a means of understanding the aggregate outcomes – political and economic – of FDI in developing host countries. In order to make the transition from firm-level to aggregate-level analysis it is necessary to assume that benefits from individual bargains can be aggregated. This is a plausible assumption because a host country that is strong across many industries should be able to negotiate consistently more beneficial terms with foreign investors than a host country that is weaker on more factors. The more the host country can extract from each bargain, the more resources it has available for development. In order for FDI to have a positive effect on aggregate outcomes, the host country must also be able and willing to harness those resources for domestic development. A weaker host country would not be able to do as well in extracting benefits from foreign investors on as many individual projects. Some projects may enrich the local resource base as expected in the modernization approach, while others might drain the local economy as expected by dependency theorists. The aggregate outcomes of the investments would be mixed, creating a seeming null impact at best, or a negative effect at worst.

One important implication of assuming benefits from specific investment projects can be aggregated up is that climbing down the aggregation ladder is possible as well. That is, we may be able to predict the outcome of specific negotiations from knowing the host-country's aggregate context conditions. In fact, as discussed in more detail at the outset of this section, the theoretical and empirical literature on why firms invest in specific host countries indicates that, in order to attract foreign investors with whom to bargain, a host country needs many of the same conditions expected to contribute to its own bargaining position (Agarwal, 1980; Schneider and Frey, 1985). Given this, the assumption that traces of benefits from specific bargains can be seen in aggregate outcomes does not seem unreasonable.

In most development theories, multinational investors are assumed to present a strong economic force in poor Third World countries. But, specifying the general context, or combination of factors that is likely to produce a host country counter-balance to foreign investors is difficult using the bargaining framework. The bargaining approach is more inductive than the modernization and dependency theoretical perspectives. The conditions that contribute to a strong bargaining position usually are examined on case-specific terms rather than deduced from a theoretical framework, and each case seems to present different components of bargaining power. In other words, bargaining power is over-determined.

Bergsten, Horst and Moran (1978:369–70) argue that the ability of the host to influence the foreign investors is a function of five variables: the ability to monitor investor and industry behaviour; the cost of duplicating, or forgoing, what the investor offers; competition within the industry; vulnerability of the foreigner's assets and earnings to adverse treatment by the host government, and the ability of the host to discount political tension caused by investment disputes. Each of these seems to be a plausible component of bargaining power, but the categories are fairly broad and the concepts can be broken down further into more specific factors.

Bureaucratic unity, the power of the state to implement policies, the presence of a domestic alternative to foreign capital, competition within the industry, and the economic situation and diplomatic skills of the host country are all listed by Bennett and Sharpe (1985:86–90) as contributors to host-country bargaining power. Other factors such as a competent, well educated bureaucracy (Johnson, 1982:305–15), a unified political elite (Deyo, 1981:4), successful mobilization of host-country financial resources (Encarnation, 1989:8), and 'concertation' between the state and local capitalist groups (Doner, 1991:19) are also posited as the most important components of host country bargaining power.

The international context also presents several key factors external to both actors that may contribute to their relative bargaining positions. The nature of the industry, competition for global funds, alternative sources for whatever the host country has to offer, and the condition of the world market for host-country products may all contribute to the bargaining position of either actor. While it is important to note the existence of these factors, they are not the focus of this study simply because they generally are not controllable by either potential investors or host countries. Other conditions that contribute more specifically to host-country bargaining power are the focus here, because it is important for policymakers there to understand which domestic conditions can be used as bargaining chips.

Aside from pointing to variables that affect the willingness and ability of the host country to use resources, the bargaining approach does not provide a mechanism for specifying which of these variables might be necessary or sufficient for a strong bargaining position. One way to address the problem of over-determination would be to analyze all these factors for all developing countries and see what empirical analysis turns up as the most significant conditions. Yet, the sheer bulk of information necessary, and the dubious comparability of data among developing countries makes a full cross-country comparison beyond the scope of this study.

Another way to reduce the list of variables relevant to bargaining power is to divide them into broad categories, and then use those categories as an analytic framework. This latter strategy is followed in this project, and the categories are constructed using variables found to be important in prior studies, as well as those suggested by the literature on why firms invest in developing countries.

Host-Country Conditions that Contribute to Bargaining Power

In this section I combine the discussion of which variables draw in FDI with a more complete discussion of how domestic variables contribute to host-country bargaining power. In order to form a more clear framework for analysis, the variables are categorized into three groups. The first group includes historical background factors, such as colonial history, natural resource endowment, geographic position and infrastructure. The second group includes political and institutional conditions such as political stability, elite unity, the interaction of ideology and state strength, and competence of the bureaucracy. Finally, economic conditions such the size and skills of the labour force, the presence of a domestic capitalist class, and the presence of incentives for rent-seeking behaviour are expected to be important in determining the bargaining position of the host country.

Table 1.2 summarizes the components of host-country bargaining leverage that will be examined for the six countries in this book. The list is not meant to be all inclusive, but it does include many variables found to be important in earlier studies. Thus, it provides a starting point for empirical investigation into the usefulness of the framework. Among each of the categories there is no order of importance implied in the way the variables are listed.

The relative importance of these factors is impossible to determine *a priori* since what is a power resource in a particular situation may

Table 1.2   Summary of Variables Expected to Contribute to Host-Country Bargaining Power

Background	Political	Economic
Geographic position	Elite unity	Size of domestic economy
Natural resources	Mass political stability	Growth of the economy
Low ethnic conflict	Ideology and state strength	Level of development
Initial infrastructure	Competence of bureaucracy	Size and skills of labour force
Initial level of development	Policy implementation	Economic inequality
		Financial autonomy of state
		Domestic capitalist class
		Low rent-seeking incentives

be irrelevant in another (Bennett and Sharpe, 1985:85). Host states may use strengths in some areas to compensate for weaknesses in others, making the variables functional equivalents. Moreover, for any given country bargaining power is over-determined because of the large number of possible contributing factors. For these reasons, the relative importance of specific variables or groups of variables is not derived directly from the bargaining framework. Rather, one of the objectives of the country studies presented in the following chapters is to determine whether a specific order of importance among the variables is evident.

Background context conditions

When examining the background to the bargaining context and outcomes of FDI in specific cases, the time frame necessarily varies by country. For the sake of simplicity here 'background' refers to that time period before FDI became a significant source of funds for the host country. Background conditions such as geographic position, natural resource endowment, colonial history, infrastructure and level of development shape the initial bargaining environment, and provide some host countries more advantages than others *vis-à-vis* foreign investors. A strong position on these background factors, such as high natural resource endowments, a relatively high level of development and a strong and growing economy, can make some countries more attractive to foreign investors and contribute to the level of competition among foreign investors.

A history of low ethnic complexity and/or conflict deserves more explanation as a background factor because of its importance in contributing to mass political stability. Evidence suggests that, at least in African countries, communal political instability is rooted in ethnic plurality and competition (Jenkins and Kposowa, 1992). Since mass political stability is important for drawing in FDI, underlying patterns of ethnic conflict that are more likely to produce instability are expected to make negative contributions to bargaining power.

While having a strong position on background conditions is helpful for a host country, it is not strictly necessary for maintaining a counterbalance to foreign investors. Background factors contribute to bargaining power by providing certain abilities and shaping the willingness to use available tools. They are not the only, or even the primary determining factors, because states can make and enact policies in order to ameliorate the effects of poor background factors.

Furthermore, the bargaining power of the host country and foreign investors is expected to shift through time, so relying on relatively constant background conditions to explain that shift is inadequate.

Political context conditions

Host country context variables in the political category also provide opportunities and motivation for using assets to improve the overall bargaining position. Elite unity presents foreign investors with a higher level of investment certainty when it comes to specific projects or terms of investment. In addition, a unified elite contributes to the ability of the state leaders to formulate development policies, and to the willingness of the elite to push for successful implementation of those policies.

Mass political stability is expected to contribute to host bargaining power before foreign investments are made by increasing investor certainty, and freeing the government from using resources to deal with instability. Mass political *in*stability limits the list of alternatives available to policymakers, and thus their ability to make and implement policy (Jackman, 1993). It also limits the willingness of the state to make policies that bring on, or are perceived to bring on mass instability. The matter is complicated further by the possibility that political *in*stability is itself a potential outcome of FDI. So, if FDI does actually cause mass instability, a process of reciprocal causality is working.

Ideology and state strength, or state capacity (Jackman, 1993), representing political will and ability respectively, are expected to be important for bargaining leverage, particularly as they interact with one another. Ideology shapes the willingness of the elites to undertake economic development policies, as well as their willingness to use FDI as a policy tool. A policy programme based on that ideology must then be backed by a state that is strong enough to carry out the policies suggested by that ideology. Strong policy implementation, a competent bureaucracy and financial autonomy of the host primarily contribute to a state's capacity to implement ideologically based policies. If a state is unable to implement regulation of MNCs, it opens the way for corruption and unrealistic expectations about its capacity (Biersteker, 1987:297). A competent bureaucracy lends credibility to bargains made by the state and thus contributes to a stable investment environment. That stability is attractive to foreign investors, so it adds to the host-country bargaining leverage and allows the host country to implement its own development policies more smoothly (Johnson, 1982).

In sum, strong political conditions allow the state to take an active role in pursuing the obsolescing bargain. A well designed and implemented educational policy, for instance, can be used to increase the skills level of the labour force, making the host more attractive to foreign investors. The state can also endeavor to build up an indigenous capitalist class or strong state-owned enterprises to counter the bargaining position of foreign investors. In the absence of strong political conditions, the host country would have a difficult time maintaining a counter-balance to foreign investors. Again, which of these variables or which combination is most important as a context for FDI is a subject of investigation in the case studies.

Economic context conditions

As with the political context conditions, the economic context conditions listed in Table 1.2 are both determinants of FDI, and factors that contribute to a strong host-country bargaining position. The size of the domestic economy, the history of economic growth, level of development and size and skills of the labour force have all been found to be determinants of FDI flows to developing countries (Schneider and Frey, 1985; Wheeler and Mody, 1992). Because these factors increase the willingness of international firms to invest, they contribute positively to bargaining leverage for the host country that has a strong position on these attributes. Financial autonomy of the host state gives the state leverage over foreign investors by providing other alternatives to financing development (Encarnation, 1989). States which can collect taxes from individuals and firms have a resource base that gives them the opportunity, if not the willingness, to finance development policies independent of FDI.

An indigenous capitalist class and strong state-owned enterprises can also provide specific counter-balances to the bargaining power of foreign investors (Bennett and Sharpe, 1985). A strong domestic capitalist class may balance the strength of foreign investors by decreasing reliance on foreign investors for capital and skills. On the other hand, not all domestic capitalists take national economic development as their goal, and they may simply form an alliance with foreign investors as Evans (1979) argues. Similarly, strong state-owned enterprises may add market inefficiencies and rent-seeking incentives to the economy. Strong domestic capitalists and state-owned enterprises may be double-edged swords in interactions with foreign investors. Nevertheless, they can make plausible contributions to host-country bargaining power. The country comparisons in the next chapters attempt to answer the question of whether SOEs present a clear pattern of positive or negative contributions to bargaining power.

The set of bargaining power determinants summarized in Table 1.2, and the discussion of why firms undertake foreign investment projects again demonstrates a difficult problem in trying to understand the consequences of FDI. Namely, the determinants of FDI and its putative outcomes are integrally related and this presents a problem of tautology. Consequences of FDI at one time point are the determinants of FDI at future time points. For example, FDI is expected to contribute to economic development (even if it is distorted), yet the level of development is also a determining factor of FDI. It is thus extremely difficult to tease out the consequences of FDI from its determinants in any given country.

Moreover, the outcome variables themselves are interconnected in similar ways. Political stability is expected to contribute to economic growth, but rapid growth with slow economic development is often expected to contribute to some sort of political instability (Olson, 1963). So, reciprocal causality among the outcome variables is also plausible. We are left with a complex interaction among international and domestic determinants of economic and political development. Focusing on the context conditions of FDI in the host country contributes to an understanding of how reciprocal causality may reinforce modernization or dependency-type patterns in developing countries.

Initial outcomes – themselves the results of the bargaining process – alter the bargaining position of both host and foreign investors. A host that is gaining bargaining power may use it to strike better deals. Because it does well initially, the country remains attractive to potential investors and individual investment projects are negotiated such that the terms benefit the host as well as the MNC. In such cases, the aggregate results are more likely to be favourable for the host. Thus, I expect that long-term economic growth, development and mass political stability will be seen as consequences of FDI in host countries with context conditions that contribute to relatively high bargaining power. A virtuous cycle – which would tend to support the modernization perspective – would be seen in countries with relatively strong economic factors and with FDI flows that seem to produce continuing strong growth.

On the other hand, countries that are either unable or unwilling, or both, to use domestic and international resources to develop human and physical infrastructure may find they are no longer able to attract beneficial investment deals. A host country that is not improving its bargaining position is likely to stay in a dependent situation and may slide even further back. In this case the vicious cycle expected by dependency theorists is more likely to develop. The cycle would begin in a country with relatively low bargaining power that was unable to turn initial investments into development gains. FDI in this context might contribute to political instability, thus decreasing the future flows of FDI, and perhaps removing all together a potential source of investment capital.

Focusing attention on bargaining conditions also allows speculation concerning the pattern that we may expect regarding the timing sequence for the dependent variables. The three primary dependent variables for this study are economic growth, development and political stability, and they are also key factors in bargaining power for host countries. In the absence of political stability, economic growth is difficult to maintain. Without growth, it is difficult to conceive of long-term sustained economic development. Mass political stability may be necessary, but not sufficient, for growth and growth may be necessary, but not sufficient for economic development.

Host-country bargaining power may also contribute to the presence or absence of trade-offs among the consequences of FDI. For example, the modernization approach expects one of the secondary effects of FDI to be an increased likelihood of social and political unrest due to social mobilization. A host country with a strong bargaining position relative to foreign investors would also have the ability to control the conflict arising from social mobilization. A weaker host country would not have the ability to generate and distribute benefits of FDI as well and would be less able to control mass political unrest.

The country comparisons in the chapters that follow focus on several propositions that can be distilled from the above discussion:

1. The political and economic consequences of FDI will depend on the interaction between host country context conditions and flows of FDI. If the host can counter-balance the interests of the foreign investors, then modernization outcomes are expected to dominate. If not, then dependency outcomes are expected to dominate.
2. Reciprocal causality will tend to reinforce the patterns of association between FDI and its consequences.
3. Political stability is expected to precede economic growth, which in turn is expected to precede economic development.

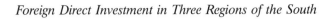

The empirical examination of country-pairs in the following chapters examines the domestic determinants of development as both cause and consequence of FDI flows. Each chapter will examine how FDI contributed to development patterns, whether reciprocal causality can be seen in the process and whether a temporal pattern can be found among political stability, economic growth and development. The chapter on causality addresses this last question more specifically using Granger causality analysis.

2 The Bargaining Context and FDI in Thailand and the Philippines

This chapter presents a comparison of Thailand and the Philippines in the post-World War II era, with specific emphasis on the host-country context of FDI, and how FDI has contributed to the development patterns in these two countries. Until the late 1980s, the Philippines presented a good example of dependency-type development outcomes. It had experienced slow economic growth, low levels of development and a high incidence of mass and elite political instability. During the same time period, Thailand seemed to present a clear case of modernization-type patterns of high economic growth rates, improving levels of development and relatively low levels of mass political instability. Economic growth remained low but improved in the Philippines in the 1990s, but the financial crisis that hit Southeast Asia in mid-1997 will no doubt slow economic growth rates for both countries in the immediate future.

I have chosen to compare these two countries because they are similar on many factors that are important to development theories, and yet they present variation in terms of the putative consequences of FDI. Both countries began the post-World War II period as producers and exporters of raw materials and agricultural products. Both countries have received foreign direct investment, and in fact have encouraged it, although the timing of FDI surges and the primary country of origin have been different. The two countries also have been roughly similar on factors such as size of the domestic market and natural resource endowment. And, both the Philippines and Thailand offer examples of state intervention in the economy in attempts to promote development.

Despite these similarities, the political and economic development patterns in the Philippines and Thailand have been quite different through time. By the early 1990s, Thailand had experienced rapid economic growth and the beginnings of economic development, with relatively few periods of mass political instability. The Philippines had experienced periods of slower economic growth with slow progress in development, and many episodes of mass political instability. The discussion in this chapter compares the patterns of development in these two countries, and how FDI did or did not contribute to those outcomes. The outcome variables of particular interest are political (in)stability, economic growth and economic development. Growth rates of GDP, measures of diversification of the economy- and aggregate socio-economic measures, are the indicators for economic growth and development.

In order to examine how domestic context factors interact with FDI, this chapter first sets the stage for comparison by providing an overview of the background factors for each country in the early post-World War II time period. The political context variables are compared for the entire time period (1950s to early 1990s) in the second section, followed by a discussion of the economic context variables in the third part. The fourth section compares the experiences of these two countries with FDI, and finally the conclusion returns to the research propositions concerning the role of FDI in host-country development processes.

To begin the comparison, Table 2.1 summarizes the context conditions discussed in the text. The table entries indicate the position of

Table 2.1   Status on Factors Contributing to Bargaining Power in the Philippines and Thailand

	Philippines	*Thailand*
Background:		
Colonial History	Spanish/US	None
Land Tenure	Highly unequal (plantation)	More equal (paddy)
Geography	Shipping lanes and cold war interest	Cold war interest
Infrastructure	Poor	Poor
Political:		
Elite Unity	Low	Low
Ideology and State Strength	Low	Medium
Mass Political Stability	Low	Medium
Ethnic Conflict	Low	Low
Competence of Bureaucracy	Medium	Medium
Economic:		
Financial Autonomy	Low	Medium
FDI Policy Implementation	Low	Medium
Domestic Capitalist Class	Fragmented	Coalitional
SOE Rent-seeking Incentives	High	Medium to high

the Philippines and Thailand on the context conditions. When conditions have changed through time, the entries refer to the position that prevailed for the longest period of time.

I. BACKGROUND CONDITIONS

The difference in colonial history of the Philippines and Thailand is sharp, and helps to explain both the ability and willingness of the countries to use FDI for economic growth and development. The Spanish began colonies on the Philippines in 1564 and, except for the Moros on Mindanao, met with little organized opposition from indigenous groups (Hall, 1981:272). National cohesion was lacking, enabling the Spanish to impose political and social structures that created and maintained a highly unequal system of land tenure (Stauffer, 1985:243). Chinese merchants made up the business class, and wealthy Filipinos became large land-owners. The Catholic Church was interdependent with the Spanish colonial government and helped create an educated sector of the landowner elite (Hall, 1981).

The Spanish used Manila as a trading centre, and did little to develop agricultural production in the rest of the islands (Stauffer, 1985:244). When the United States took over as colonial power following the Spanish–American War, it had strong interests in keeping the economy open to free trade, while at the same time obtaining significant concessions for American citizens. Politically, the Americans imposed institutions which allowed the landowner elite to maintain a patronage system that involved mass support for individual politicians (SarDesai, 1981:322). In 1946, the United States demanded that economic autonomy be the price the Philippines had to pay for political independence (Stauffer, 1985:245). The colonial heritage thus produced constraints on the economic policies available to the independent Philippines, as well as the willingness of political elites to redistribute land and thus wealth.

The lack of colonial history was as important for Thailand as was the presence of a colonial history for the Philippines. Thailand maintained formal independence during the colonial period, although it lost some territory to Britain and France, and signed highly unequal treaties with other major Western powers (Wyatt, 1984). Economic independence was compromised by the unequal treaties and Thailand was forced into economic specialization in the world economy, supplying rice, teak wood and tin ore (Suehiro, 1989:274).

In direct contrast to the Philippines, when the Western powers arrived in Thailand they encountered an absolute monarchy and extreme centralization of power in the hands of the king (Stowe, 1991; Suehiro, 1989:278–9). In the mid to late-1800s the monarchy started to develop Western-style institutions in the Thai setting. Institutions such as a parliament, bureaucratic apparatus, political parties and a free press were adopted (see Riggs, 1966). Some important consequences followed from the domestic adaptation of these types of foreign political institutions.

First, although the institutions appeared to have democratic structures, the masses were not involved in politics as they were in the Philippines. The 1932 Revolution against the absolute monarchy was carried out by a group of military officers who tried to make the bureaucracy accountable to political institutions (Laothamatas, 1992:1). The result was that real power simply passed to the bureaucracy, while the institutions remained formalistic (Riggs, 1966:148–9). The state apparatus and the bureaucrats who ran it were quite strong in comparison to the Philippines during the immediate post-war period. Second, the institutions were not imposed by Western powers, so anti-Western nationalism was not as strong as in other developing countries. The result was a greater willingness to consider capital infusions as something other than neo-colonialism.

The difference in colonial history also had a strong impact on the land distribution patterns in the two countries (Hill and Jayasuriya, 1984). Large sugar and coconut plantations made strong economic bases for oligarches in the Philippines, and this helped to perpetuate the patronage system. Benefits of economic growth went to the large landowners rather than a broad base of society. This distribution of economic benefits provided clear disincentives for the economic and political elite to reform the highly unequal system of land tenure.

In Thailand, land holdings were distributed somewhat more equally among the peasants. Rather than large plantations, rice was grown in paddy fields. The benefits of agricultural growth were thus spread in a more equal fashion, although inequalities between rural and urban incomes remained. The Thai economic and political elite had positive incentives to bring economic development to the peasants, as the elite would gain consumers for the market rather than lose one of their bases of power.

The condition of infrastructure also shapes the ability of the host country to bargain with foreign investors and to transform FDI into growth and development. While Table 2.1 indicates that both countries had poor infrastructure as a background condition, Thailand was able to improve rural infrastructure through time more than the Philippines. The Philippine infrastructure had been devastated during World War II and the enormous cost of rebuilding gave the US leverage over the weak Philippine state (Stauffer, 1985:245). In addition, the rebuilding was done primarily in and around Manila, which contributed to further urban–rural economic disparities.

Alliance with the Japanese during World War II did much to protect Thailand's infrastructure from the massive destruction suffered in the Philippines (Neher, 1981:27). Infrastructure was relatively built up in the Bangkok area, but not in the rural areas. During the cold war, particularly during the Vietnam conflict, the United States poured money into economic and military aid, much of it going to build up infrastructure in the rural northeast areas (Wyatt, 1984:271–2). The Thai government also invested in the infrastructure of rural areas, in an attempt to even the spread of benefits from economic growth (World Bank, 1980a).

Geographic position could have added to the Philippines bargaining power in the immediate post-independence period. The country's location on major shipping lines could have been used to attract the attention of foreign firms and thus competition for investment opportunities. The Philippines was also well placed to take advantage of the military needs of the United States during the cold war. The ability to use the geographic assets as bargaining tools was severely constrained by the conditions which had to be accepted for political independence. The US had insisted on equal investment rights for Americans and on the use of Philippine territory for military bases.

Thailand did not have these sorts of constraints on policy and so was able to use its position to get further aid. Thailand is not located on the major shipping lines, a fact which may have helped keep it independent (Silcock, 1967:3). The cold war, however, did give significance to Thailand as a relatively stable anti-communist government in a central position in Indo-China (Silcock, 1967). Since the US did not already have bases there, Thailand was able to use its position and its perceived weakness in the face of neighbouring communists to obtain aid in exchange for military bases. And, as noted above, some of that aid went toward building better infrastructure.

II.   POLITICAL CONTEXT

Elite unity, ideology as it interacts with state strength or capacity and mass political stability are conditions which are expected to be quite important in determining the bargaining power of a host country. Thailand and the Philippines both have had little unity among the elite and may be characterized better by elite fragmentation. The type of elite fragmentation, however and its interactions with the other political conditions differs in the two countries, and produces different development consequences.

Elite Unity

In the Philippines, fragmentation of the elite has contributed to slow policy changes and implementation problems and prevented resolution of anti-government insurgencies. During the 1950s and 1960s, power was concentrated in a small number of elite families, which ran their own private armies and controlled elected representatives and the news media (Neher, 1981:76; Wawm, 1982:73). The sharpness of factional antagonisms weakened the Filipino elite and this prevented them from unifying the nation to face the challenges of economic development (Jayasuriya, 1987:82). Ironically, the one policy the elites have managed to unify on has been prevention of significant land reform policies. The inability of the ruling elite to implement a comprehensive programme for land redistribution led to the strengthening of the Hukbalahap rebellion, which is described in more detail below (see also SarDesai, 1989). Political factionalism did not resolve over time, and Doner (1991:170–1) provides evidence that elite factionalism contributed to implementation problems with economic policies even during the late 1970s and early 1980s.

The ruling coalition under President Marcos, particularly after the imposition of martial law in 1972, was less fragmented although policy implementation was still a problem. The coalition was broad, including foreign investors, their local partners, members of the business community with personal ties to Marcos, local politicians loyal to Marcos, and military officers (Hawes, 1987:14). Close friends of Marcos, or 'cronies', vied for concessions from Marcos that would benefit their own interests. The ruling elites were unwilling to give up the benefits of their position in order to distribute benefits more widely.

The tradition of elite factionalism carried over into the Aquino ruling coalition, which followed the fall of the Marcos dictatorship in

1986. Continued factionalism was demonstrated by frequent party defections and coup attempts. The masses seemed to be firmly behind Aquino, but attempts to redistribute land and improve the economy did not meet with great success (NEDA, 1990). Elite factionalism in politics continued after the election of President Ramos in 1992. This prompted some observers to argue that political bickering among the elite was one of the primary impediments to economic takeoff (Tiglao, 1994). Through time, conditions of political fragmentation among elites have made it difficult for the Philippines to produce a consistent set of policies and then implement them.

Elite factionalism in Thailand has been rampant throughout the time period, partly because the elites have used political positions to reap economic benefits for themselves. The 1932 Revolution against the absolute monarchy began a long chain of *coups d'etat*. Infrequent civilian governments have also experienced many rapid changes in regime. In the three years following World War II, the parliamentary system produced nine administrations, and between 1972 and 1977 six different prime ministers formed governments (Doner, 1991:195–6). The elite fragmentation has not typically involved mass political instability, such as the continuing insurgencies found in the Philippines. SarDesai (1989:224) points out that despite the many coups, political policy changes have not been abrupt or dramatic. The government turnovers have generally indicated a regrouping of a narrow elite, struggling to redistribute the economic benefits of office-holding. But, the more equal distribution of land in Thailand lessens one of the major development policy stumbling blocks faced by the fragmented Filipino elite.

Thai political parties after World War II had little or no base of mass support, they simply reflected factions among the elite (Wyatt, 1984:262–6). The stable policy environment and stability in who makes up the elite have helped increase certainty for foreign investors and thus given the Thai government an advantage in bargaining that was not available to the Philippines. In the 1980s, dissent among the ranks of the elite became more publicized and open (Hewison, 1987). In 1991 a coup ended the government of Prime Minister Chatichai because of what was seen as excessive corruption, but then in 1992 mass political protests called for more democracy. A new constitution – intended to open the system and decrease the power of money in politics – was approved in late 1997. But, the elite politicians remain fractious in their coalitions amid widespread financial crisis and they seem reluctant to make policies that will go against their personal financial interests (see the *Economist*, 25 October, 1997).

Mass Political Stability

While both Thailand and the Philippines have low elite unity, they differ more with respect to mass political stability as a factor in the host-country bargaining context. From the bargaining perspective on FDI and development, mass political stability is both a cause and a consequence of FDI, and this expectation is most similar to the state-led development model. Host countries with stronger context conditions in general, and less political instability in particular, are expected to draw in more FDI and to be able to prevent mass instability that may result from rapid economic growth. The more traditional modernization and dependency approaches tend to focus on an increased likelihood of political conflict as a consequence of FDI. In order to examine how political stability, or lack of it, has interacted with FDI in Thailand and the Philippines, Table 2.2 compares the number of protests, armed attacks against the government, and deaths from domestic political violence in these two countries.

Both the Philippines and Thailand have experienced insurgencies, but as the difference in numbers of armed attacks indicates, they have been more severe and prolonged in the Philippines. The Hukbalahap (Huk) rebellion, started during the Japanese occupation of World War

Table 2.2   Domestic Political Violence, Philippines and Thailand, 1950–93

	Protests	*Armed Attacks*	*Deaths*
Philippines:			
1950–9	25	1 021	9 418
1960–9	34	176	416
1970–9	44	172	3 979
(1972–81)	33	168	3 972
1980–90	88	96	2 861
1991–3	1	1	18
Thailand:			
1950–9	2	22	85
1960–9	3	72	470
1970–9	24	97	1 032
(1973–6)	20	55	799
1980–90	1	11	140
1991–3	15	1	48

Sources: The data are from Taylor and Hudson (1972) and Taylor and Jodice (1983) for 1950 through 1978. The values for 1979 through 1993 were obtained by coding the New York Times Index, using the Taylor and Jodice definitions.

II, posed the first major threat to the independent regime in 1946 (SarDesai, 1989:198). During the war the Huks were able to gain control of central Luzon, and began a land distribution programme. The group did not break up after the war and attracted members from a wide range of society, including peasants, unemployed youth, communist party cadres and professional bandits.

In the election of 1946 the Huks won several seats in the House of Representatives, but they were refused entry, fuelling the rebellion (Hall, 1981:899). The Huks changed their name to the People's Army of Liberation and took total overthrow of the government as their aim (Hall, 1981:950). The Huk rebellion began to come under control during the 1950s, but the inability of the government to carry out significant land reform during the first Marcos regime (1965–71) brought a revival of the Huks, now mainly communist, who managed to attract a wide measure of public approval (Neher, 1981:77).

In addition to the Huk rebellion, an independence movement by the Moros on the south island of Mindanao gained strength through the 1960s (Mercado, 1984). The Moros had only been conquered by the Spanish in 1878, and allegiance to Islam made assimilation with the rest of the Philippines difficult (SarDesai, 1989; Mercado, 1984; Hall, 1981). A 1980 amnesty for guerilla fighters seemed to end the threat, but the resistance movement was revived in 1985 amid massive anti-government protests and demonstrations (SarDesai, 1989:205–7). After the fall of the Marcos dictatorship, efforts were renewed to end the insurgencies, but they remain and also contribute to violent religious conflicts.

As with insurgencies, the Philippines has experienced more episodes of mass protest than has Thailand. The Filipino economic crisis of late 1969 and early 1970 resulted in acceptance of an IMF austerity package and precipitated an upsurge in student and youth militancy (Jayasuriya, 1987:90–1). The government was unable to stick to the austerity policies. Inflation worsened, there was growing labour unrest, a resurgence of left-wing nationalism and the communist movement, and the delegates to the 1972 Constitutional Convention began making radical nationalistic demands (Jayasuriya, 1987:91).

With the support of some sections of the capitalist class, the technocrats and parts of the middle class, Marcos declared martial law in 1972 (Jayasuriya, 1987:90–1). Marcos abrogated the constitution, took all powers for himself, imprisoned prominent members of the political opposition, censored the press, banned strikes in 'essential' industries, and generally curtailed civil liberties (Stauffer, 1985:253; Wawm,

1982:75; Neher, 1981:77). Even with these repressive measures, the level of political protests was not much lower during martial law than in the 1960s.

As noted above, the inequities perpetuated by the Marcos regime refuelled both the communist and Moro insurgencies. The foreign debt crisis and attendant economic difficulties enabled the communists to organize major protests and strikes in urban areas. Martial law was lifted in January 1981 (Wawm, 1982:75), though the president retained all emergency powers. In April 1983, Benigno Aquino, the most prominent opposition leader, returned from exile to Manila, where he was shot as he left the aeroplane (SarDesai, 1989:204). The shooting was widely blamed on the Marcos regime, and provoked further mass protest demonstrations (SarDesai, 1989:205).

In 1986 Marcos called for presidential elections, at the insistence of the US. The elections were criticized for widespread fraud, but Marcos was declared the winner. Corazon Aquino, the leader of the opposing coalition, declared herself the winner and announced a nonviolent active resistance campaign that was supported by large numbers of people. Defections among Marcos supporters and continuing massive demonstrations against his regime forced Marcos to flee the country and Aquino took over as president (SarDesai, 1989:205–7). Although Aquino faced many coup attempts, she managed to stay in power until the 1992 presidential election which was won by Fidel Ramos. President Ramos has made some progress toward political stability by entering talks with the Moro National Liberation Front and by creating a National Unification Committee to help end the communist rebellion (Ching, 1993; McBeth, 1993; Tiglao, 1992).

In contrast to the Philippines, Thailand has experienced insurgencies that were shorter lived and not as threatening to the central government. The large American presence during the Vietnam Conflict in the late 1960s and early 1970s brought exposure to modernization to the whole population rather than just the elite. Rural farm people, particularly in the Northeast, became aware of the disparities of the development process and joined an anti-government insurgency which included the old leftist political opposition and the Thai communist party (Wyatt, 1984).

By 1967, fighting was spreading and an anti-government Muslim insurgency in the south was also becoming more serious (Uthai, 1984). By the late 1960s, the insurgencies were finally linked with mass protests and demonstrations. In 1969 Prime Minister Thanom tried to institute a more democratic system which included a new constitution with an elected legislature (Wyatt, 1984:289–90). Student demonstrations in favour of an even more democratic government, combined with the growing strength of the insurgencies led Thanom to dissolve parliament, ban political parties and rule under an interim constitution (Wyatt, 1984:290). The American presence lent support to the anti-communist authoritarian regime.

When authoritarian measures were met by even more unrest, the king supported the demonstrators and Thanom was forced to resign as Prime Minister. A civilian government was installed, but this did not end domestic political violence (Wyatt, 1984; Neher, 1981). In October 1973 student and popular unrest toppled 25 years of military rule. The 1973–76 period is included as a subset in Table 2.2 to indicate the magnitude of the unrest. This period of violence included a bloody right-wing 'kill communists' campaign. Political assassinations became frequent and public mistrust and suspicion were widespread. In 1976 the army stepped into politics again. The army killed and injured hundreds of student activists, justifying the action by accusing the demonstrators of being left-wing communists (Wyatt, 1984:289–303).

Mass protests and demonstrations entered Thai politics again in May and June of 1992. After the February 1991 coup, the middle class in Bangkok finally became involved in politics and began demanding that the prime minister be an elected member of parliament. However, in April 1991, General Suchinda Kraprayoon resigned all military posts and became prime minister (*Economist*, 1992a,). In May, 1992 protestors demonstrated in Bangkok in crowds of up to 100,000 people. The army sent in police officers, then troops and opened fire on the demonstrators. At least 40 people were killed and 600 injured, and many others were beaten and taken to prison (*Economist*, 1992b,). The demonstrations and the army's reaction, created fears that Thailand would lose its image as a stable country for foreign investors (Friedland, 1992). But, the king supported the pro-democracy protesters, and parliament quickly passed two amendments to the constitution that limited the power of the generals. Protesters again appeared in the wake of the financial crisis of 1997. Finally, in September of 1997 a new constitution made large-scale changes to the electoral system, but the long term consequences are still unclear.

One further factor that may affect mass political stability in developing host countries is ethnic conflict, and so it is also expected to shape bargaining power. Both Thailand and the Philippines have significant Chinese ethnic minorities, and many of the Chinese hold influential positions within commercial businesses. During the 1940s and 1950s the Chinese minority in Thailand experienced discrimination which included tightened immigration (anti-Chinese) laws (Suehiro, 1989:226). After the 1950s, however, efforts to assimilate the Chinese into wider Thai society have been more effective than similar efforts in the Philippines, where attempts to exclude the Chinese were stronger.

Ideology and State Strength

In addition to elite unity and mass political stability, the interaction between ideology and state strength is expected to make a major contribution to the willingness and ability of the host country to counter foreign investors. Ideology is taken to be one indicator of policy preference, while state strength refers to the ability of the state to carry out relatively autonomous policy preferences. Thailand holds an advantage over the Philippines on this political context factor for much of the time period under consideration, although in comparison with other countries the Thai state is also weak.

The ideology of Thailand does not necessarily match the liberal democratic principles of the West, nor is it the strong anti-Western nationalistic ideology that was prevalent in the Third World during the 1950s and 1960s. The ideological basis for society has traditionally revolved around respect for the monarchy, an hierarchical structure of society and an emphasis on Buddhism (Wyatt, 1984:229). The bureaucracy draws legitimacy from doing the work of the monarchy rather than from upholding a specific ideology.

Ideology has rarely been involved in Thai politics, despite references to anti-communism and national security interests (Neher, 1981:31). The Sarit regime (1958–63) invoked traditional ideology, but used the principles of hierarchy and loyalty in order to pursue policies to promote modernization (Wyatt, 1984:281). Anti-foreign feelings flared during the 1973 October Revolution, but those feelings have not been incorporated into a governing ideology. More recently democratic ideals have been supported by the middle class in Bangkok, but again, the outcome remains to be seen.

Adherence to an ideology of order and loyalty provides the Thai state with a certain amount of strength that is lacking in the Philippines. The pre-1932 tradition of an absolute monarchy included loyalty to the bureaucracy. The ideology supports an authoritarian structure by creating a willingness to work within its confines toward development goals established by the state. A strong and competent bureaucracy has contributed to the ability of the state to implement policies, yet authoritarian military rule seemed to be the only way to control the bureaucracy. The absolute monarchs created a bureaucracy, but did not create a constitutional base for controlling that bureaucracy (Riggs, 1966:131). Thus, demands for change have usually been violent.

The relative strength of the Thai state has been exhibited in international relations as well as domestic politics. Thailand was able to use the military and economic commitment gained from the US in 1962 to pursue its own anti-Vietnamese and anti-communist polices (Wyatt, 1984:284). Then, when public discontent was directed toward the US, the civilian government was able to carry out its own policies, even when those policies involved dislodging the US troops and equipment. In 1975, the US was given 12 months to withdraw all troops and equipment from Thailand. With a concession of only a few months from the Thai government, the US was out by July 1976.

The ideology and the ability of the state to carry out preferred policies have been quite different in the Philippines. The ideology at independence was generally supportive of free market economics, strongly anti-communist, and dedicated to a democratic form of government (Hawes, 1987:32). Through the 1950s and 1960s the ideology became more nationalistic, opposing the restraints the US had placed on the economy. In particular, the American military bases were seen as a symbol of US domination (Hall, 1981:951). Despite periodic anti-American sentiment, the governing ideology has remained democratic, with a commitment to free-market capitalism. The ideological tradition does not include a strong sense of loyalty to the state as in Thailand.

The ability of the Filipino government to implement its policy preferences was not strong at independence. Although the bureaucracy was staffed with competent individuals, the state machinery was weak and highly dependent on economic support from the US (Hall, 1981:902; Jayasuriya, 1987:82) As noted above, that support brought with it significant constraints on policymaking. Corruption has been a persistent problem, as the political power structure encourages patronage politics. The state apparatus gained in strength through time, but was still easily manipulated by those in the top positions.

The Philippine government was structured on the US model, but political power was centralized more in the office of the president (SarDesai, 1989:197). For the most part the presidents have not been able to use their power to implement policies successfully. One notable exception was Mr Magsaysay, president from 1953 to 1957. He enjoyed strong popular support and was able to build a coalition that would back reforms of the economic system, including land reform policies (Hall, 1981:950–1). But, following Magsaysay's death in a plane crash, the policy reforms were not implemented.

The disunity among the elite, combined with the popular uprisings and armed rebellions continued to make the Filipino state weak. When Marcos imposed martial law in 1972, it was viewed by the international community as a means of gaining control, and thus of increasing the perceptions of state strength (Jayasuriya, 1987:92). At that time the state apparatus was strong enough to allow Marcos to use repression to quell popular unrest, but strong and decisive rhetoric often covered hesitancy in action (Jayasuriya, 1987:93). Although the state was seen as stronger, the willingness to implement a set of coherent and strong development policies was not present. Marcos was able to manipulate the state apparatus such that members of his regime became the beneficiaries of the system, and programmes such as land reform were generally weak or nonexistent (Hainsworth, 1979:23).

In the post-Marcos era, conflicting political interests have remained. The record for policy implementation, particularly development policies, has been somewhat mixed. While President Ramos managed to dismantle monopolies in industries such as telecoms and cement, the banking industry still was not reformed by the financial crisis of mid-1997. The Ramos regime also had difficulty getting financing for a light rail transportation plan, as well as an anti-tax-evasion measure.

The elite factionalism in the Philippines that has contributed to political instability has also contributed directly to weakness of the state as a whole. No administration has been able to make structural reforms because the agriculturally based oligarchs and the industrial and mercantilist capitalists (often in collaboration with US capital) have dominated the economy, and the economic interests of these groups have often conflicted in the post-independence period (Jayasuriya, 1987:89).

III. ECONOMIC CONTEXT

From the bargaining perspective, the economic conditions of a host country can be seen as both the causes and consequences of FDI.

A strong history of economic growth and higher levels of development are drawing factors for FDI. How the FDI interacts with the host country conditions to produce outcomes is a key theoretical and empirical question. Thailand and the Philippines both began the post-war period with similar levels of natural resources, similar population levels and low levels of economic development. Other economic conditions were quite different in the two countries and the development patterns have also differed dramatically. After reviewing the patterns of economic growth and development, I compare the two countries' policies toward FDI and their implementation, the presence and strength of a domestic capitalist class, and the impact of state-owned enterprises. Finally, I compare their experiences with FDI and examine how FDI contributed to development patterns.

Economic Growth

Thailand and the Philippines were peripheral countries in the world economy at the beginning of the post-World War II period, and that position set the stage for their economic growth and development policies (Dixon, 1991; Hewison, 1985; Kirk, 1990). Both countries began trying to break out of the periphery and both strategies included FDI. Table 2.3 shows figures for average annual GDP growth in Thailand and the Philippines. Economic growth has been stronger recently in Thailand, but these averages mask some important fluctuations. For instance, economic growth was high in the Philippines during the early 1950s, but declines in growth rates set in when the limits of import substitution policies began to be felt (Hill and Jayasuriya, 1984:140).

Table 2.3   Economic Growth, Philippines and Thailand (selected years)

	Philippines	*Thailand*
GDP, Average Annual Growth Rate (%)		
1951–60	6.6	5.5
1961–70	4.9	8.3
1971–80	6.3	6.8
1981–90	1.8	7.5
1991–95	2.2	8.4

Sources: IMF (various years) *International Financial Statistics Yearbook*; NEDA (various years) *National Income Accounts*; and *Statistical Yearbook of Thailand* (various years); UN, *Statistical Yearbook for Asia and the Pacific, 1996*.

The Philippines adopted what amounted to a severe version of import-substitution industrialization (ISI) at the beginning of the 1950s in response to a balance of payments crisis in late 1949 (Jayasuriya, 1987:83; Glassburner, 1985:172–3). One result was import substitution in capital intensive industries. Another result was that ISI policies helped the manufacturing sector grow rapidly during the 1950s, such that by 1960 manufacturing formed nearly 20 per cent of GDP (Lindsey, 1983:490; Wawm, 1982:86).

High commodity prices cushioned the first round of OPEC price increases, but from 1975 the Philippines experienced deteriorating terms of trade (Hill and Jayasuriya, 1984: 137). The prices of the main agricultural exports, sugar and coconut, were declining in conjunction with oil price increases. In the late 1970s the government began to move toward more liberalized export-oriented trade, but the late shift to export-oriented industrialization (EOI) took place in a more competitive export market than in the 1960s when other Asian countries were beginning to make the shift (Hill and Jayasuriya, 1984:147; Lindsey, 1983).

During the 1970s the capital raised by heavy foreign borrowing frequently was used for prestige projects rather than productive investments (Balassa, 1991:166). The economy did not generate enough output to repay loans and in 1983 a debt moratorium precipitated an economic crisis. The debt problems were exacerbated by an increase in capital flight following the assassination of opposition leader Benigno Aquino in 1983 (Hill and Jayasuriya, 1984:149; SarDesai, 1989:204). In 1985 a stand-by agreement with the IMF was reached, and it included liberalization of imports, and reduction of maximum tariff rates from 100 to 50 per cent (Balassa, 1991:166). As indicated in Table 2.3, economic growth rates in the Philippines did improve in the early 1990s, but did not match the growth rates of Thailand.

Although economic growth was much higher in Thailand in later periods, it did not start out strong in the post-World War II period. Inflation was rampant during the late 1940s, and despite state-led development plans, growth in manufacturing was slow in the 1950s (Suehiro, 1989). Problems with the balance of payments and trade in the late 1950s, and pressure from domestic capitalists induced the government to move toward an ISI strategy that was supported by the World Bank (Hewison, 1987:55).

Aggregate economic growth began to increase in the 1960s, led by growth in manufacturing and high rates of domestic investment

(Hewison, 1987:56). The small size of the domestic market began to limit growth under ISI by the end of the 1960s. In 1971, quite a bit earlier than in the Philippines, the Thai government began moving toward an EOI strategy, and implementing incentives for exports (Hewison, 1987:567). High levels of import protection were kept in some areas, however.

Growth accompanied export-oriented policies, yet it was not as high as in the NICs, South Korea, Singapore, Hong Kong and Korea. Despite the emphasis on exports, balance of payments problems continued, contributing to a growing foreign debt and a debt crisis in the 1980s. In contrast to the Philippines, the public sector debt in Thailand was largely incurred by investments of state enterprises in infrastructure projects that helped to support further economic growth (Hewison, 1987:64–5). The IMF and World Bank mediated the debt crisis, but faced high domestic political opposition because of the demands to reform some sectors of the economy (Hewison, 1987). Growth in GDP picked up again after 1985 and continued strong into the early-1990s. But, by mid-1997 exports had dropped, bad debts were swamping the financial sector and Thailand was forced to devalue its currency (Economist, 1997a). This eventually led to problems paying foreign debt and to an IMF bailout package, but growth rates are almost certain to slow.

Economic Development

Economic development, broadly defined, can be examined in terms of diversification of the economy, and/or performance on socio-economic indicators. Table 2.4 provides several indicators of economic development for the Philippines and Thailand. The two countries have been quite similar in terms of adult literacy, life expectancy and infant mortality rates through the time period, although the infant mortality rate for Thailand is probably somewhat higher than these figures due to under-reporting (Krongkaew, 1982).

As expected given its history of higher economic growth, Thailand has had a higher rate of growth in GNP per capita. The Philippines has been losing ground on this indicator relative to other Asian countries as well. In the early 1960s, the per capita income of the Philippines was behind only Hong Kong and Singapore and quite close to Malaysia (Hill and Jayasuriya, 1984:150). By the late 1980s, the only other member of ASEAN lower than the Philippines on per capita GDP was Indonesia (Balassa, 1991:2).

Table 2.4   Indicators of Development in the Philippines and Thailand
(selected years)

		Philippines	Thailand
GNP per capita,	1965–86	1.9	4.0
(US$)	1985–94	1.7	8.6
Percent of GDP from			
Agriculture	1961	31.5	39.2
	1970	36.0	29.6
	1980	26.4	20.6
	1990	26.9	13.7
Manufacturing	1961	18.9	13.1
	1970	18.7	14.9
	1980	25.2	21.7
	1990	25.1	25.0
Life expectancy	1960	51	51
(in years)	1970	57.2	58.4
	1980	61.6	62.2
	1992	66.3	69.0
Adult literacy	1960	71.9	70.8
	1970	82.6	n.a.
	1980	83.3	81.8
Infant mortality rate	1950	101.6	62.4
	1960	73.1	48.9
	1970	66.4	n.a.
	1980	52.2	49.0
	1992	40.8	37.0

Sources: IMF *International Financial Statistics Yearbook* 1980 and 1989; Asian Development Bank (1991), *Key Indicators of Developing Member Countries;* World Bank, *World Development Report* (1988 and 1996), and *World Tables* (1992).

In addition to the problems of slow per capita growth, the Philippines experienced geographically uneven development. For instance, growth in manufacturing jobs was heavily concentrated in Manila (Dixon, 1991:202–3). The highly unequal land distribution also continued to create rural unrest (Dixon, 1991:203), and the incidence of poverty is estimated to have increased to about 60 per cent in the Philippines (Hall and Jayasuriya, 1984:153; see also Hainsworth, 1979). Between 1962 and 1975, the percentage of Thailand's population living below the poverty line was estimated to have fallen from 57 to 33 per cent (World Bank, 1980b:10). The ability of Thailand to spread the benefits of growth in a more equitable fashion is often attributed to the more egalitarian pattern of land distribution (Hill and Jayasuriya, 1984:153).

But, as in the Philippines, economic development in Thailand has been uneven in geographic terms. Rural areas did not benefit as much from economic growth as did urban areas. Industry has been concentrated in Bangkok, although infrastructure projects are underway to reduce the unevenness (Balassa, 1991:186). Economic and educational development produced a predominantly urban middle class, subject to economic fluctuations of the private sector (Wyatt, 1984:288–302). Many of the urban young people are unemployed, yet well educated. One third of the agricultural households remain below the poverty line, and three-quarters of poor households are in the rural northeast. Over the past 15 years the real wage rate for unskilled labour has remained relatively constant (Akrasanee, 1991:83). The state has tried to encourage rural development with infrastructure improvements and tax incentives, but the results have only been mixed (Fairclough and Tasker, 1994).

The pattern of economic diversification in the two countries looks similar in Table 2.3, but some important differences are masked by aggregation. In the Philippines, smallholder agriculture was generally neglected during the ISI programmes. Rice production increased dramatically, but agriculture was not as diversified as in Thailand (Hill and Jayasuriya, 1984). In Thailand agricultural exports were not discriminated against, and they grew in value, although the percentage contribution was declining relative to manufacturing (Balassa, 1991:183). Crops were diversified to include cassava, maize and tapioca in addition to rice. Public and private investment in irrigation and flood control plans and extensions to the road network made the diversification possible (Glassburner, 1985:179; Richter and Edwards, 1973:31).

The Domestic Capitalist Class and State Financial Autonomy

The presence of a strong domestic capitalist class is an important context condition because it may contribute a counter-balance to the bargaining power of foreign investors in a host country. The Philippines has had a growing capitalist class (Yoshihara, 1985; Milne, 1961), but for the most part it has been neither willing nor able to counter balance foreign investors. The domestic capitalist class has not had a single set of interests that it pursued, and when interests of factions can be identified, they do not seem to match national development interests.

Hawes (1987:136–42) identifies four segments of the domestic capitalist class under Marcos: the crony capitalists; the state capitalists, including the technocrats and professional managers; the producers for the local markets; and finally, producers for the international market. The crony capitalists were interested in lining their own pockets, at the expense of national development goals. Joint ventures with foreign investors provided opportunities to pursue their individual interests (see also Hill and Jayasuriya, 1984). Producers for the local markets were interested in maintaining ISI strategies, and producers for the international market were interested in pursuing free trade and EOI policies.

In addition, the domestic capitalist class has seemed unwilling to shift from real estate investment to riskier industrial enterprises (Golay, 1961; Milne, 1961). 'Given the non-elite's limited access to finances, the domestic initiative for industrialization is largely limited to the already affluent' (Lindsey, 1983:490). The already affluent, however, have their economic and political power base in land ownership and are reluctant to move into other areas. Even an authoritarian state has limited ability to 'push rapid industrialization in a capitalist economy if the wealth-owning class does not cooperate' (Lindsey, 1983:492). In the case of the Philippines, the conflicts of interest within the domestic capitalist class have prevented coherent action as a balance to foreign interests.

In Thailand, the economic base of the domestic capitalist class is not so tied to large land holdings, but connections with political power are clearly strong. Private enterprises developed rapidly in response to increasingly laissez-faire policies of the 1960s and after the provision of basic infrastructure (Balassa, 1991:183). The domestic capitalist class is the ruling class in Thailand and members of the business elite play an integral role in Thai cabinets and economic decisionmaking (Doner, 1991:207; Laothamatas, 1992). Indeed, corruption has become extensive as businesspeople have used political offices to gain economic benefits for themselves.

Suehiro (1989:274–6) describes the structure of the Thai domestic capitalist class as a tripod, with each of the three political legs having a strong economic base. The ethnic Chinese minority has been more fully integrated into this structure than in the Philippines. State and public enterprises are based in the infrastructure sectors of the economy, giving the state a relatively autonomous financial base. Multinational enterprises dominate four industrial categories, including resource based industries and manufactured brand name consumer products. Finally, domestic capitalist groups dominate the financial sector, manufacturing of textiles and agro-industry products and export of agricultural products.

Although foreign investors are an important part of the dominant capitalist class, domestic capitalists have retained significant control over the economy. Joint ventures with foreign investors left more control to domestic capitalists and protected them to a certain extent from risks (Hewison, 1987:58). Cohesion among the capitalist class is stronger than in the Philippines, although differences do exist on economic policy matters.

State Owned Enterprises and Rent-Seeking

State owned enterprises (SOEs) present opportunities for rent-seeking, but they may also form a domestic balance to the power of foreign capital (see Clark and Lemco, 1988). On the positive side for national development, SOEs may fill capital investment gaps without long-term drains on the economy from capital repatriation (see Hewison, 1987; Silcock, 1967). On the negative side, SOEs may become a handicap to growth and development if they perpetuate market inefficiencies and contribute to high foreign debt. Incentives for rent-seeking have been strong in both Thailand and the Philippines, but the two countries have used SOEs differently in their development policies.

State owned enterprises pre-existed independence in the Philippines. Despite frequent calls for privatization during the colonial period and in the 1950s, by 1960 there were more than 20 government corporations (Milne, 1961:257). By mid-1985 there were 96 government corporations with 149 subsidiaries. This does not include the takeovers of private sector firms that occurred when Marcos's cronies started going bankrupt following the 1981 financial crisis (Balassa, 1991).

SOEs in the Philippines have frequently been the centre of major corruption scandals and obvious inefficiencies (Milne, 1961). The oligarches have used SOEs as a source of personal economic gain. The masses also have incentives for keeping SOEs operating. The SOEs employ more people than necessary, and those employees oppose privatization because the jobs pay better than the private sector (Milne, 1961:266). These incentives support rent-seeking at the expense of aggregate growth and development.

Thailand has used state enterprises in addition to FDI as a means of filling capital gaps. At the time of the 1932 Revolution, the Thai government was forced to be involved in capital funding for profit making industries, as the Thai people had no other funds available (Suehiro, 1989:280–1; Silcock, 1967:260–1). Between 1932 and 1945, 30 SOEs were established. By 1960, an audit included 100 state enterprises and public companies (Suehiro, 1989:139). The state enterprises functioned as an important economic base for the military. Ethnic Chinese partners managed the enterprises, while the military leaders grew wealthy on the dividends, bonuses and commissions (Suehiro, 1989:281).

In 1958 a policy shift to an emphasis on private enterprise was strong and reflected in a decrease in the number of Thai SOEs. By the 1980s the number of SOEs fell to 68 (Balassa, 1991:186). The shift away from state enterprises was in part a reflection of the negative view taken by the World Bank, but was also a way for the Sarit regime to remove the power base of political rivals (Suehiro, 1989:180). But, SOEs formed a financial base for the Thai state, and in combination with growing strength in the domestic capitalist class, gave Thailand a financial autonomy *vis-à-vis* foreign investors that was not mirrored in the Philippines. The Thai state was able to encourage and facilitate domestic investment, thus providing alternatives to FDI for economic growth and development (Laothamatas, 1992:151). In contrast, the economic base of the oligarchies in the Philippines has been a constant matter for political contention and has not provided as many incentives for the economic elite to engage in extensive domestic investment.

Policies Toward Foreign Direct Investment

In the Philippines, government policies toward FDI have given quite a bit of lee-way to foreign investors (Wawm, 1982). The government established a Board of Investments (BOI) which, between 1967 and 1971, passed several laws intended to clarify investment policy. Foreign ownership up to 30 per cent is permitted freely, but permission from the BOI is needed above that. In pioneer areas, where production is low or nonexistent, 100 per cent foreign ownership is allowed and up to 40 per cent is allowed in some non-preferred areas (Wawm, 1982). In time, if non-pioneer areas are not exploited by Filipinos, they may be wholly owned by foreign interests. Some industries, such as banking and finance, are limited to 25–50 per cent foreign ownership. Government incentives for foreign investors include guarantees against appropriation without just compensation, free repatriation of earnings and capital, and tax and export incentives (Wawm, 1982:86).

The regulations surrounding FDI provide opportunities for rent-seeking activities by the fragmented elite, and implementation has been open to corruption and manipulation by those in power. Even when the state was relatively strong, the incentive structure contributed to uncooperative behaviour from local capitalists. During the

Marcos regime, concessions that bent investment rules could often be gained that would benefit one company at the expense of a given industry (Doner, 1991). High turnover in membership at the Board of Investment also contributed to policy implementation problems (Doner, 1991:170–1).

Thai government regulations of FDI have reflected efforts to maintain a relatively open economy since 1958. Incentives are provided to foreign investors and include guarantees against nationalization, no price controls or competition from state enterprises, temporary import surcharges and bans against competitive imports, and incentives for exports and for investment in zones outside Bangkok (Balassa, 1991; Wawm, 1982:149–50). The Board of Investment has discretionary authority in many areas, including determining the projects eligible for promotion, setting the conditions for the projects, and setting the time limits for the incentives (Balassa, 1991:184–5).

The implementation of regulations and policies looks strong in Thailand when compared to the Philippines, but there are still difficulties. Corruption still causes concerns and implementation problems have been worse in Thailand than in South Korea or Taiwan (Laothamatas, 1992:166). Nevertheless, initial success with FDI seems to have bred success. Economic growth followed foreign capital infusions and the growth seems to have attracted more FDI. Relatively fair implementation of government policies toward FDI contributed to increases in the certainty of the investment environment, as well as to increases in the competition among foreign investors (Doner, 1991:201).

IV. EXPERIENCES WITH FOREIGN DIRECT INVESTMENT

Several dimensions of FDI must be examined when trying to determine the likely consequences. First, the pattern of surges in foreign investment is important. If the bulk of foreign investment comes in prior to independence, the interests of the multinational corporations are more likely to become entrenched because of the weak state and weak indigenous capitalist class. The segments of the capitalist class and the state would be more likely to form an alliance with the foreign investors, leading to the triple alliance characteristic of dependent development (Evans, 1979). Moreover, the timing of FDI relative to the industrialization policies being pursued by the host may channel FDI into certain areas, perhaps producing a difference in outcomes.

Second, flows of FDI may have different effects than stocks of FDI. Increases in aggregate wealth are dependent on capital formation, thus flows of FDI should be expected to increase economic growth. Once a host acquires a large stock of foreign investment, net increases in investment flows may slow down or become negative due to capital repatriation, market saturation, and/or increases in political risk because of high multinational corporation visibility (Bornschier and Chase-Dunn, 1985:82–84). Should high stocks of FDI combine with low net flows, the host country may begin to exhibit the negative pattern of outcomes expected by dependency theory.

Finally, the country of origin can help explain differences in the pattern of investment, because firms from different home countries tend to specialize in different kinds of production (Kojima, 1978). For instance, American firms tend to invest in products for domestic consumption, while Japanese firms concentrate investment in export manufacturing. Japanese firms have also been more willing to go in on joint ventures than American firms.

The Philippines and Thailand exhibit variation in these aspects of FDI. The difference in the timing of surges in FDI flows is particularly striking. Foreign economic penetration of the Philippines began with the Spanish, continued with American colonial rule, and was still strong when the post-colonial government took over after the war (Stauffer, 1985). The number of US direct investments established in the Philippines prior to 1946 was 83, and the value was US$ 243 million (US Department of Commerce, 1960:99). FDI continued flowing in before the newly independent Filipino government was able to consolidate a position from which to bargain. The government was pursuing an economic growth policy based on import substitution, so the FDI was directed towards those sorts of projects. Between 1946 and 1957, 77 more direct investment projects were established, with a value of US$ 52 million (US Department of Commerce, 1960).

The situation in Thailand was quite different, probably because Thailand had not been formally colonized. Although foreign businesses had been operating there since before World War II, Thailand only started receiving large inflows of direct investment during the Sarit regime which came to power in 1958. Total foreign direct investment as reported by Thai government sources was only US$ 3.3 million in 1958, and US$ 3.4 million in 1959 (*Thailand Statistical Yearbook*). Of 144 multinational enterprise affiliates in Thailand by the mid-1980s, 92 were established between 1957 and 1972 (Suehiro, 1989:193).

Table 2.5 compares the net flows (inflows minus outflows) of FDI in the Philippines and Thailand for the period 1960 through 1990.

Table 2.5 Net Foreign Direct Investment to the Philippines and Thailand, 1960–93 (US$ millions, current prices)

	Philippines	*Thailand*
1960	28	2
1961	56	6
1962	−3	7
1963	−4	21
1964	−4	18
1965	−10	42
1966	−15	27
1967	−9	43
1968	−3	60
1969	6	51
1970	−29	43
1971	−6	39
1972	−21	68
1973	54	77
1974	4	189
1975	97	22
1976	126	79
1977	210	106
1978	101	50
1979	7	51
1980	−106	187
1981	172	288
1982	16	189
1983	105	348
1984	9	400
1985	12	162
1986	127	261
1987	307	182
1988	936	1 092
1989	563	1 727
1990	530	2 236
1991	544	1 847
1992	228	1 979
1993	763	1 493

Sources: NEDA, *Statistical Yearbook of the Philippines*, 1976 p.410–411; NEDA, *Philippine Statistical Yearbook*, 1987, pp.378–9; National Statistics Office, *Philippine Yearbook*, 1989, p.1071; and NEDA, *1990 Philippine Development Report*, p.8. IMF, *International Financial Statistics Yearbook* 1989 and 1990; World Bank, *World Tables*, 1995.

Thailand received much higher net flows than the Philippines for much of this time period. The surge in net flows to Thailand came during the 1960s and 1970s at a time when the government was shifting investment to infrastructure and encouraging private investment in industry (Hewison, 1987:58).

Although Table 2.5 indicates a negative net flow of FDI to the Philippines in the 1960s, Table 2.6 makes it clear that the stock of FDI was higher earlier in the Philippines than in Thailand. Lindsey and Valencia (1982:166–8) report that in 1948 Filipinos controlled 52 per cent of the non-financial sectors, while foreigners owned more than 50 per cent of the assets in electricity, mining, commerce and manufacturing.

The different pattern of FDI flows and stocks in these two countries, and the different development outcomes, present an interesting theoretical contrast. The dependency approach would expect the Philippines to have a lower rate of economic growth due to high capital repatriation by foreign investors. In Thailand, the higher flows of FDI could perhaps offset the effects of the smaller stock of foreign investment. Alternatively, the bargaining approach that I have taken would explain the lower flows to the Philippines as the result of lower aggregate growth there in the 1960s. Similarly, the higher flows to Thailand would be a consequence of earlier growth and achievement. In essence, the two views differ with respect to the temporal pattern of causality. The question is somewhat answered by the fact that through

Table 2.6   Year-end Stock of FDI, the Philippines and Thailand (selected years) (US$ millions)

	Philippines	*Thailand*
1967	723	211
1971	830	410
1972	870	490
1973	920	530
1974	1 100	550
1975	1 220	330
1978	1 400	350
1977	1 620	400
1978	1 820	445

Source: UNCTC (1983a) *Salient Features and Trends in Foreign Direct Investment*, p.62.

time, the Philippines also managed to improve its rate of economic growth, and that improvement was met with increased flows of FDI. The chapter on Granger causality will return to the problem of temporal patterns between FDI and development outcomes.

The majority of the foreign investment in the Philippines has come from the United States (see Yoshihara, 1985). In 1986 the cumulative position of US direct investment in the Philippines was 54 per cent of total foreign investment, compared to Japan's 15.7 per cent (Healey, 1991:80). The American emphasis on production for the domestic market strengthened the hand of the oligarchies who supported ISI policies. The foreign support helped maintain that policy orientation and helped make it particularly severe (Glassburner, 1985; Hill and Jayasuriya, 1984).

Direct investment flows into Thailand have been more diversified. As in the Philippines, the US was the home country for the majority of the large multinational firms in Thailand, but in the early 1960s the investment flows from Japan were larger due to the activities of smaller firms (Suehiro, 1989:195; Wawm, 1982). In 1983 the cumulative position of Japanese direct investment in Thailand was 23.1 per cent of the total, versus 8.9 per cent for the US By 1986 the positions were much closer, with Japan's cumulative investment accounting for 20.5 per cent of the total, the US accounting for 19.1 per cent of the total (Healey, 1991:82).

The structure of capital ownership was distinctly different in the firms from Japan and the US. The parent company completely controlled 68 of 83 American and European multinationals. Only four Japanese firms were totally controlled by the parent company, while 30 of the 48 firms were in the joint venture category (Suehiro, 1989:196). Access to joint venture projects has given domestic (mostly ethnic Chinese) Thai capitalists more control than their Filipino counterparts dealing with mostly American firms.

As Southeast Asian countries have grown in the world economy, direct investment has begun flowing from the NICs to the other ASEAN countries. Taiwanese companies invested heavily in the region in the late 1980s and early 1990s, and new investment flows among the other ASEAN countries have been noted (Evans, 1996:6). These capital flows make trade in Southeast Asia increasingly integrated and this could produce interesting new patterns of regional, as well as country specific development.

In summary, the Philippines and Thailand have both experienced quite a bit of fluctuation in FDI flows through time and Thailand has had higher net new FDI flows. The large influx of FDI was earlier in the Philippines, largely from the United States and directed toward import substitution production. The late start in Thailand allowed the state and domestic capital groups to develop. The Japanese emphasis on joint ventures and production for export allowed those domestic groups to retain more control than in the Philippines. This difference is also reflected in the stock data, where the Philippines had higher levels of foreign stock earlier than Thailand.

V. CONCLUSIONS

The comparison of host-country context for FDI in Thailand and the Philippines indicates differences in the context conditions that con-tribute to bargaining leverage, and differences in the patterns of putative outcomes of FDI. The comparison does not allow us to explain easily these two cases in terms of traditional ideologies of development. The modernization perspective maintained that FDI could infuse needed capital for development projects. But the Philip-pines had much earlier FDI and it had slower growth patterns through time. On the other hand, Thailand managed to produce rapid eco-nomic growth once it mixed FDI with its own capital investments and other development policies. The Thai pattern does not allow easy acceptance of the dependency perspective on development, but seems more consistent with state-led development strategies.

Comparing the two countries in terms of their bargaining positions *vis-à-vis* foreign investors allows us to develop an understanding of how FDI interacts with host-country context conditions. Thailand, has not been strong on all conditions at all times, but it was the stronger of the two countries examined here. Despite elite disunity, Thailand was able to counter-balance foreign investors with a combination of a fairly coherent development strategy, state and local capital working together, and an ability to implement economic policies more effect-ively than the Philippines. Success in using foreign investment flows as part of an economic growth and development strategy initiated a virtuous cycle which has been accompanied by relative mass political stability. FDI was part of that cycle, but was not the primary causal factor in determining development outcomes.

The Philippines, the weaker host country, was not willing or able to use FDI in pursuit of national development goals. At times when the state institutions were relatively strong, the incentives for the political and economic elite encouraged efforts to attain personal wealth at the expense of national development goals. The fragmented elite has so far been unable to overcome the limitations imposed by the colonial history and sustained by continued political and economic instability. Mass political instability has been endemic, early high growth rates stagnated and socio-economic indicators have not shown significant improvement. The case of the Philippines supports the argument that a weak bargaining position is a facilitating, if not a sufficient condition for a dependency-type pattern of outcomes that includes political instability, slower economic growth and little progress in development. FDI contributed to the negative pattern, but it was the interaction with domestic conditions that was more important than FDI flows alone.

Teasing out the path FDI takes through the development process is difficult, but these two countries both present a temporal pattern among the outcome variables that revolves around political (in)stability. Such a pattern is consistent with the bargaining focus on the same factors as both cause and consequence of FDI. In both cases, the pattern seems to begin with political (in)stability among the masses that sets the context for what the governing regime is able to do. Once FDI flows into the host country, it interacts with other economic conditions and helps to produce economic growth and development in a strong and stable context, or economic decay in a weak and unstable context.

So, relatively high mass political stability in Thailand has been accompanied by economic growth, even though the elite has remained fractious. Policies remained fairly stable and mass political stability was enforced by authoritarian rule for much of the time period. However, when demands for equity became violent the authoritarian regimes attempted to address them by encouraging development from growth. Insurgency and mass political unrest in the Philippines were accompanied by slow economic growth in comparison with Thailand and little economic development. FDI flows contributed to strengthening the pattern in both cases, but did not drive the underlying political stability or lack of it.

The possible temporal pattern among political stability, economic growth and development presents us with a question about the relative importance of the context conditions in determining the outcome patterns. As it stands, the bargaining approach provides an overdetermined model for understanding the consequences of FDI. Narrowing the list of context conditions by designating necessary or facilitative conditions would help alleviate that problem. One argument that can be made is that strong political conditions are the most critical because they contribute most directly to both ability and willingness of the host country to strike beneficial deals with foreign investors.

In the cases of Thailand and the Philippines, it certainly seems that differences in political context were significant for understanding aggregate outcomes. The ability of the state to formulate and implement policies and the willingness of the elite to aid in the process were stronger in Thailand than in the Philippines. The political context in Thailand provided incentives to economic leaders to participate in investment for growth and development, even if those incentives also involved personal gain. In the Philippines the political context provided incentives for the elite to continue lining their own pockets, but economic benefits did not accrue as quickly in other parts of the society. The comparison supports the proposition that a strong political context is necessary, but not sufficient for favourable outcomes of FDI.

Yet, background and economic factors also played significant roles, and 'secondary' status may not be entirely appropriate. First, the background conditions were very important for shaping both the political and economic context for FDI immediately following World War II. Thailand had fairly well established political patterns before it began experiencing significant flows of FDI. The colonial status of the Philippines produced an inability to consolidate a position *vis-à-vis* foreign investors before significant amounts of FDI began flowing in. Whether FDI then actually prevented the evolution of a stronger bargaining position for FDI is a significant question. If colonial status produces FDI, and FDI produces further signs of dependency, a feedback cycle is involved and it has quite pessimistic implications for further development.

Through time, however, other context conditions seem to be important and may even ameliorate the continuing negative effects of colonialism. The ability and willingness of the economic elite to work with the state in attaining development goals seems to be a key difference between modernization outcomes in Thailand and dependency-type outcomes in the Philippines. Thailand did not have to rely entirely on foreign investment for development. It had domestic private and public economic resources that it incorporated into plans for national development. The Philippines was unable to mobilize domestic resources for investment in domestic development and so foreign investment became dominant for much of the time period.

Instead of producing a set of conclusions about which context conditions are necessary and which are facilitative, the analysis here indicates that a certain amount of complimentarity exists among context conditions. The combination of political and economic context conditions may be more important than either political or economic conditions alone. If this is the case, modernization-type consequences of FDI would result from host-country context conditions that could balance some political weaknesses with economic strengths, or vice-versa. The implication for host-country policymakers is that concentrating on FDI as a policy tool may be less productive than focusing on domestic context conditions which may be improved.

3 The Bargaining Context and FDI in Ghana and Côte d'Ivoire

The discussion in this chapter focuses on the factors that form the bargaining context for FDI in Ghana and Côte d'Ivoire, and examines how those conditions shape the relationship between FDI and aggregate political and economic outcomes. As in previous chapters, the bargaining approach, with its emphasis on the ability and willingness of the host country to counter-balance foreign investors, is used as a means of organizing the comparison of context conditions. The expectation is that FDI in countries with relatively strong context conditions will be associated with modernization-type outcomes such as high economic growth and long-term development. FDI in countries with weaker context conditions is expected to be associated with dependency-type outcomes, such as slow economic growth, political instability and long-term underdevelopment.

Ghana and Côte d'Ivoire present an easy choice of countries to compare in West Africa, particularly in light of the early wager made by the two leaders concerning which choice of development strategy would be best. Both countries are in one of the poorest and least developed regions, and both are certainly peripheral to the world economy. They both had colonial histories that left lasting economic and political constraints on development, and they both were and are primarily agricultural economies. Because of their similarities, these countries present something of a natural pseudo-experiment with respect to FDI and its consequences in very poor countries. Yet, the political and economic policy choices made by the leaders of these two countries have been very different. In the case of Ghana, the policies have differed quite dramatically at different points in time. The economic and political outcomes have also differed, with Côte d'Ivoire seeming stronger until the late 1980s. Then, Ghana seemed to gain ground both politically and economically. By comparing Ghana and Côte d'Ivoire through time, we can gain a better understanding of how FDI interacts with host-country context conditions to produce aggregate outcomes.

The analysis here concentrates on the post-independence period, but I also include background factors from colonial times in order to portray a brief history of the situation. The discussion of political and economic context conditions includes factors which are expected to be both causes and consequences of FDI. Table 3.1 indicates the status of Ghana and Côte d'Ivoire on the context conditions that are discussed in more detail throughout the chapter. Where the status has changed through time, the table entry indicates the status held for the longest period of time. Or, when a clear shift has occurred, the first value given is for the immediate post-independence period, and the second refers to the present.

Table 3.1 Status on Factors Contributing to Bargaining Power in Ghana and Côte d'Ivoire

	Ghana	*Côte d'Ivoire*
Background:		
Colonial History	British	French
Land Tenure System	Smallholder	Smallholder
Geography	Neither country is located on major shipping lanes	
Infrastructure	Poor to very poor	Poor
Labour Force	Large	Medium
Political:		
Elite Unity	Low	High
Ideology and State Strength	Low	Strong
Mass Political Stability	Low	High
Ethnic Conflict	High	Low
Competence of Bureaucracy	High to Low	Low to Medium
Economic:		
Financial Autonomy	Low	Low
FDI Policy Implementation	Low	Medium
Domestic Capitalist Class	Weak	Weak
SOE Rent-Seeking Incentives	High	Medium to High

I. BACKGROUND FACTORS

Although similar in many respects, differences in colonial history and the struggle for independence produced significant differences in the development trajectories of Ghana and Côte d'Ivoire. At independence in 1957, Ghana seemed well placed to become a successful post-colonial country. Yet for much of the post-independence time period it has exhibited a downward spiral of political and economic problems that the government is still struggling to correct. While Côte d'Ivoire was an African success story for much of the time period, it has begun having economic and political difficulties that seem to make its future less certain. A review of the background conditions for these countries illuminates the similarities and differences at independence, and how they shaped the political and economic context for FDI in these two countries.

Colonial rule by the British in Ghana (then the Gold Coast) was established over an area that included several strong societies which had been distinct states, although not all of the included societies had been highly organized previously (Kraus, 1971:35; Pellow and Chazan, 1986:19). The British followed policies of indirect rule, governing through already developed indigenous political institutions (Pellow and Chazan, 1986:19; Grier, 1987:36). The system of indirect rule sustained a fragmented form of social control that relied on the status and power of local patrons (Chazan, 1992:124). British rule had a major impact on land laws, which set up political configurations that lasted into independence (Crook, 1991:219; Grier, 1987:47). Thus, the lines of political cleavage that developed under British rule had a lasting impact on elite factionalism well into the post-independence period, and this will be discussed at length below.

The process of Africanization in the army officer corps also contributed to fragmentation among the elite. The recruitment and promotion policies of the British left the Ghanaian army with southern and more educated officers in charge of northern troops who were less educated (Baynham, 1988:46). This structure led to exacerbated ethnic tensions, as some of the smaller southern ethnic groups were over-represented in the officer corps (Baynham, 1988:46). The lack of coherence in the military tended to lessen the constraints on the military acting in the political sphere (Baynham, 1988:260). To compound these problems, prior to independence chiefs and the growing educated elite considered themselves to be the logical trainees for positions of authority in the post-independence state (Apter, 1972:149).

The struggle for independence also set the stage for continuing political conflict in Ghana. The fight for independence from British rule began as early as 1937, when the Gold Coast Youth Council was formed on nationalist principles (Pellow and Chazan, 1986:26–7). In 1947 the United Gold Coast Convention (UGCC) formed with the goal of attaining self-governance in the shortest period of time, and Nkrumah returned from London to head the organization (Pellow and

Chazan, 1986:27–28). In 1948, demonstrations, strikes and a boycott of foreign firms brought the masses into politics, and Nkrumah split with the more conservative members of the coalition to form the Convention People's Party (Pellow and Chazan, 1986:28).

The Convention People's Party (CPP) won the 1956 election that determined who would rule Ghana at independence in 1957, but it still faced local opposition (Pellow and Chazan, 1986:34). The cocoa farmers had broken with the CPP in 1951 over the question of cocoa marketing strategies (Crook, 1991:227). The early emergence of competitive class strata in Ghana also provided lines of division, and politicized traditional ties (Kraus, 1971:37; Pellow and Chazan, 1986:102). The politicization of these ties in the anti-colonialist fight created a permanent potential for conflict (Crook, 1991:228).

The British left a concern with building bureaucratic institutions and transferring structural-bureaucratic values to the Ghanaians (Amonoo, 1981:6). The Ghanaian civil service was large and well established relative to other African countries at the time of independence (Killick, 1978). The administrative grades of the civil service were 80 per cent Africanized by 1960, the service had developed an institutional identity, and it was connected socially with the educated elite and the university intelligentsia (Crook, 1991:229). The strength of the civil service, however, made it an object of political contestation and through time it became divided by ethnic rivalries (Crook, 1991:229).

French ruled Côte d'Ivoire developed politically in a very different pattern. Independence came in 1960 for Côte d'Ivoire, three years later than in Ghana. Prior to that, the French administered widely disparate societies in the territory that became the country. Until 1945, identification was with those pre-existing societies (Zolberg, 1971:9–10). In contrast to Ghana, Côte d'Ivoire had no large scale political entities at the time of colonial impact, and had little autonomous 'African' civic life, as it had few state-organized identities prior to colonialism (Crook, 1991:218; Zolberg, 1971:11).

The social composition of the managing group was imposed by colonialism, and its members were recruited with the creation and initial maintenance of the colonial system (Bakary, 1984:26). Since colonization had broken the power of ethnic units, the elite group was multiethnic, although some groups near the coast had better access to power (Bakary, 1984:26; Yansane, 1984:7). The lack of strong political cleavage lines among the elite carried over into the post-independence period and initially contributed to the formation of clear state policies that were not blocked by elite factions.

The colonial history in these two countries also contributed to the land tenure patterns that developed through time. The economies of Ghana and Côte d'Ivoire have been dominated by peasant smallholder cultivation of cocoa and coffee for export (Crook, 1991:216) and neither country has had a fully developed landlord class (den Tuinder, 1978; Killick, 1978). Efforts at economic redistribution have not been blocked by a strong landlord class as in the Philippines, but there have not been enough economic benefits to distribute in order to greatly increase the standard of living.

A skilled and plentiful labour force is a background condition that may provide a host country with some leverage in bargaining with MNCs. At independence, Ghana's work force was more skilled than that of Côte d'Ivoire, and Ghana was more densely populated. The British had followed a policy of Africanization of the civil service, but the French had a disinterest in training Africans to manage independent states (Woods, 1988:95). Both Ghana and Côte d'Ivoire experienced a large influx of foreigners looking for work, but the latter had a larger presence of foreigners, both European and African, than did Ghana (Zolberg, 1971:12).

In French colonial Côte d'Ivoire, care was taken to educate the indigenous people such that those who were selected were 'the most diligent agents of colonialism' (Yansane, 1984:19). This meant that in 1965 only 20 per cent of managerial cadres in the civil service were Ivorian and in 1973 the figure was only 52 per cent (Crook, 1991:222). The lack of a skilled indigenous labour force made it necessary to import Europeans in order to promote rapid industrialization in Côte d'Ivoire (den Tuinder, 1978:17). The Ivorian government has worked to maintain a large flow of unskilled labour by encouraging migrants to work on smallholder farms, estates and in urban areas (Hecht, 1983:32). The ruling regime has also controlled the flow of educated personnel into white-collar jobs.

Foreign labour in both countries has become the scapegoat when unemployment is high (Crook, 1991:217–8). In the midst of an economic crisis, Ghana expelled many aliens at the end of 1969 (Rimmer, 1984:14). The public sector in Ghana could not absorb all the graduates of the universities and colleges, as Africanization of the labour force was virtually complete (Crook, 1991:230). Then, in the early 1980s Ghana experienced a 'brain drain' as many teachers and professionals left the country to escape political and economic crises (Chazan, 1992; Kraus, 1991:124). At the same time, over a million Ghanaians were expelled from Nigeria and again unemployment exacerbated economic hardships (Chazan, 1991:27).

In addition to the colonial history, land tenure patterns and labour force, geographic position and infrastructure development may also contribute to a host country's bargaining power. They can increase the competition among MNCs for projects in countries where access is easy, or where the host country is important to Cold War strategies of the Western powers. Neither Ghana nor Côte d'Ivoire is located on major shipping lines, and neither country has been involved in Cold War struggles as have Angola, Zaire, Ethiopia and Somalia. Geographic location does not add to the ability of these host countries to induce competition among foreign investors and thus boost their own bargaining power.

Similarly, relying on excellent infrastructure to attract foreign investors has not been an option for either country. Ghana experienced substantial capital investment and infrastructure expansion through the 1950s, but as economic conditions deteriorated in the 1960s and 1970s, the transport services also deteriorated and became a serious constraint on all of the productive sectors in Ghana (Killick, 1978:7–8; World Bank, 1984a: xxi). Côte d'Ivoire had an good deep water port in Abidjan after 1950, and transportation infrastructure in the south was improved after World War II (den Tuinder, 1978;14). Development projects undertaken in the 1970s involved projects such as feeder roads and bridges, but the infrastructure is not strong by global standards (den Tuinder, 1978:145).

The background variables do not yield a very strong bargaining position for either Ghana or Côte d'Ivoire *vis-à-vis* potential foreign investors. The history of colonialism left each country open to economic penetration long before an independent modern state was in place. The relatively advanced position of Ghana was accompanied by political cleavage lines which had lasting effects on the ability and willingness of the host to bargain with foreign investors. The lack of a skilled labour force in Côte d'Ivoire left few alternatives to continued dependence on foreign labour.

II. POLITICAL CONTEXT

As described above, the political context for FDI in these two countries began to be established before independence. The pattern of political conflict in Ghana continued after independence, but for many years Côte d'Ivoire managed to prevent open conflict. This section examines how the political context factors contributed to the ability and willingness of these two countries to draw in, and then use, FDI for their own benefit.

Elite Unity and Mass Political Stability

Low elite unity, or high fragmentation, can reduce the ability and willingness of the host country to strike beneficial deals with foreign investors. It can also cause policy swings that make foreign investors uncertain about future investment policies. Elite fragmentation may also encourage mass political instability, again decreasing investor interest in the country. Elite (dis)unity and mass political (in)stability have been so closely integrated in Ghana that it is worthwhile to discuss the two context factors together. Table 3.2 presents several indicators of political instability, although it must be considered seriously underreported. The contrast between the two countries is particularly strong in terms of strikes and riots and deaths due to political violence.

The elite in Ghana has been highly unstable, and this has been reflected in a series of coups that also involved demands made by the masses in political protests and strikes. The long series of political conflicts has been accompanied by a spiral of worsening economic

Table 3.2   Domestic Political Violence, Ghana and Côte d'Ivoire, Independence to 1993

	Protests	*Strikes and Riots*	*Deaths*
Ghana:			
1957–9	0	8	1
1960–9	4	9	72
1970–9	2	8	'hundreds'
1980–90	0	1	16
1991–3	1	2	0
Côte d'Ivoire:			
1960–9	0	2	1
1970–9	0	2	0
1980–90	1	3	0
1991–3	0	1	0

Sources: The data are from Taylor and Hudson (1972) and Taylor and Jodice (1983) for 1950 through 1978. The values for 1979 through 1993 were obtained by coding the *New York Times Index*, using the Taylor and Jodice definitions.

conditions. Nkrumah, as leader of the CPP, was in power from independence in 1957 to 1966. Although a one-party state was declared in 1964, the CPP faced key dissent from mobilized professional and ethnic organizations (Chazan, 1992:125). Deteriorating economic conditions and dissatisfaction with the concentration of political power in Nkrumah's hands were the apparent causes of the 1966 coup in which Lt Gen. Ankrah and the National Liberation Council (NLC) took power (Morrison et al., 1989).

The NLC was followed in 1969 by an elected government led by Dr Busia and the Progress Party. The election played heavily on ethnic politics. When Busia attempted to implement economic adjustment policies, they were met with widespread strikes and riots after the devaluation of the currency, the cedi (Rathbone, 1978:27). In addition, the Busia austerity budget included military budget cuts amidst perceived government extravagance and widespread corruption (Morrison et al., 1989:478). In 1972 the army intervened in another coup, and Col Acheampong came to power as the head of the ruling National Redemption Council (NRC).

The Acheampong regime (1972–8) was extremely corrupt, and was associated with further deterioration of the economy. It emphasized ethnic politics in the extreme, alienated large portions of the population, and seemed to do nothing for social welfare conditions (Chazan, 1992:125; Crook, 1991:231). The inability of Acheampong to provide unity and stability led, in 1978, to an internal putsch by Lt Gen. Akuffo (Morrison et al., 1989:478). Akuffo's attempts to reform the economy led to sharp price increases, which were followed by industrial strikes and strikes in the civil service in November 1978 (Morrison et al. 1989:478). As unrest was dying down, and the regime preparing to restore civilian government, Flt-Lt Jerry Rawlings led a bloody coup in June (Chazan, 1992:125; Morrison et al., 1989:478).

Rawlings headed up the Armed Forces Revolutionary Council (AFRC) with the goal of restoring accountability in government (Hutchful, 1989:93). The AFRC led a campaign to punish the corrupt members of previous governments and three former heads of state were executed, along with other senior military officers (Chazan, 1992:125). Rawlings allowed elections to take place, and in 1979 Dr Limann and the People's National Party (PNP) came to power. Attempts to bolster the economy were unsuccessful, and through February and March 1980 teachers, civil servants and industrial workers staged a series of strikes for better wages and working conditions (Morrison et al., 1989:478).

When Rawlings took power in another coup in 1981, he had difficulty building a consensus among his followers in his Provisional National Defense Council (PNDC). The coup was rather narrowly based but attempted to generate a revolution of people's power (Hutchful, 1989:93). Power conflicts among PNDC supporters led to several abortive coup attempts, but Rawlings managed to stay in power (Kraus, 1991:126). A new technocratic and fairly cohesive elite took shape, in addition to the elites linked to the growing informal sector who were not tied to the resources of the state (Chazan, 1991:32–3).

By the early 1990s, the Rawlings regime began setting the stage for a transition to democracy. Presidential elections were held in November 1992 and Rawlings won with approximately 58 per cent of the vote (Joseph, 1993:45). International observers saw no systematic voting irregularities, but all sides acknowledged problems with the voting registers (Ofori, 1993). Outbreaks of violence, particularly in Ashanti where Rawlings' support was weakest, led to the imposition of a curfew for a few days following the elections (Joseph, 1993:45). Furthermore, ethnic violence broke out in the North in 1994, and the government declared a state of emergency in the Northern region.

The cohesive nature of the Ivorian elite stands in stark contrast to the fragmented elite of Ghana. Houphouet-Boigny was the only head of state in Côte d'Ivoire from independence until his death late in 1993. In conjunction with elite stability, mass political stability has been the norm in Côte d'Ivoire. Ethnic ties have not been as politicized in Côte d'Ivoire as in Ghana. Houphouet-Boigny followed a policy of 'ethnic balancing' in representation among the elite (Bakary, 1984:35–7). He also eliminated tribal chiefships as a possible source of opposition by coopting and transforming them such that they have no power (Zartman and Delgado, 1984:3). Some observers maintained that by the early 1970s, ethnic identification among the elite was transcended by interest politics (Woods, 1988:98).

The elite that formed in Côte d'Ivoire was socially pluralistic, drawing members from modest backgrounds, although some were descendants of chiefs (Bakary, 1984:28). Education, rather than land ownership, became the key to the new social status. Most politicians were civil servants who turned to the plantation economy rather than the other way around (Bakary, 1984:29). Houphouet-Boigny made sure those entering the political elite were relatively unknown in their home region so they owed their success only to him (Bakary, 1984:38). Yet, the elite has been expanded as necessary. For instance,

Houphouet-Boigny integrated the military rather than isolating it after a coup attempt in 1973 (Bakary, 1984:46).

The single party in Côte d'Ivoire has been a channel of recruitment and control rather than an agent which mobilized the masses (Zartman and Delgado, 1984:5–6). Prior to independence the Parti Democratique de Côte d'Ivoire (PDCI) faced opposition parties, but gradually PDCI candidates gained a monopoly. In April 1959 all the candidates to the Legislative Assembly were on the PDCI ticket (Bakary, 1984:31). The semi-competitive elections of 1980 provided some legitimization of the elite in power (Bakary, 1984:46). The 'free and fair' elections were a means of choosing among the overproduction of educated young people who could no longer all be assured of positions (Bakary, 1984:49).

Despite the general political stability in Côte d'Ivoire, there have been some crisis points. An apparently serious political crisis occurred between 1962 and 1964 (Zolberg, 1971:15–20; Zartman and Delgado, 1984). Reports of an attempted coup exacerbated conflicts between the first and second political generations. The generational conflict was met with coercion and a round-up of political opponents of the ruling regime in April 1963 (Zolberg, 1971:16). The 'elders' arrested and imprisoned many of the 'youngsters' who were gradually returned to the ranks of the elite throughout the 1960s (Bakary, 1984:40).

In 1969 demonstrations by the unemployed, rent strikes, tax boycotts and student unrest led Houphouet-Boigny to initiate a process of 'dialogue' with different segments of society to come up with a new economic plan for the 1970s (Mytelka, 1984:156). A supposed coup attempt in June of 1973 was followed by the integration of military officers in the Ivorian elite (Bakary, 1984:46; Zartman and Delgado, 1984:4).

It was not until mid-1990 that relations between the Ivorian government, the middle-classes, and the public sector workers collapsed to produce a political crisis (Crook, 1990:666). Middle-class confidence was destroyed by the new structural adjustment programme demanded by the World Bank and IMF (Crook, 1990:666). Trade unions began a series of protest strikes in the public utilities sector, which prompted student and university riots, and strikes by professional associations (Crook, 1990:666–7). In April 1990, violent riots led to the closure of the university for the year, and a new economic plan which cut civil service jobs and added new taxes on foreigners (Crook, 1990:667). Opposition to the regime surfaced over the way the spending cuts had been handled, and following more street riots the regime legalized opposition parties in May 1990 (Crook, 1990:668).

The first multi-party election in Côte d'Ivoire came in 1991, but there were widespread allegations of intimidation by PDCI members, and the PDCI won (Bourke, 1991). Since opposition parties have been allowed, and since Houphouet's death, the elite seems to have fragmented to a greater extent than before. So, while the elite in Ghana has been stabilizing under Rawlings' rule, the elite in Côte d'Ivoire has become more fragmented since Houphouet's death.

Ideology and State Strength

Ideology and the capacity of the state to implement its preferred policies are closely tied with elite unity and mass stability. Together, these political factors shape the willingness and ability of the host state to use FDI for economic growth and development. The combination of ideology and state strength has been quite different in Ghana and Côte d'Ivoire. Since independence, the ideology of successive ruling regimes in Ghana has experienced dramatic changes (Pellow and Chazan, 1986). The African Socialism of Nkrumah was generally opposed to all forms of colonialism, neocolonialism and external interference (Pellow and Chazan, 1986:41–2). The policy strategy involved industrialization, expansion of state intervention in the economy, and diversification of foreign contacts (Pellow and Chazan, 1986:42).

Following Nkrumah, the Busia regime attempted to swing the pendulum toward a more liberal ideology. Busia viewed the state as a regulatory body (Pellow and Chazan, 1986:54). The NRC (1972–8) and Limann (1979–81) regimes have been described as 'pragmatic' rather than ideological (Pellow and Chazan, 1986:63). The PNDC (1981–92) ideology went through phases in ideological orientation (Chazan, 1991). Initially the PNDC rhetoric was strongly populist and radical, but by late 1984 the radical advisors had been replaced with liberal advisors (Ahiakpor, 1985; Pellow and Chazan, 1986:78–9).

The successive regimes in Ghana had difficulty implementing the policies delineated by their ideologies, even though the administrative institutions of the state were quite strong at independence. Relatively well-organized interest groups put pressure on the Nkrumah government from the start, and these interest groups and ethnic organizations were sources of political cleavage (Crook, 1991:233). Thus, the relatively strong state was balanced by a strong civil society, and experienced a consistent loss of state autonomy as a result of conflict between the two (Chazan, 1991:22; Crook, 1991:215). The low state autonomy was accompanied by inability of the state to implement policies (Chazan, 1992:23).

Nkrumah did not trust the civil service as he thought it was dedicated to essentially colonialist norms, regulations and attitudes (Kraus, 1971:58–59). Nkrumah developed a parallel political administration which was responsible to the National Liberation Council party (Amonoo, 1981). Policy implementation was hindered by conflicts between the two sets of bureaucracies (Amonoo, 1981; Pellow and Chazan, 1986:42). The last years of the Nkrumah administration saw deterioration of economic planning and short-term management, the failure of the government to adjust to weaknesses in agricultural and industrial policy, and the disintegration of import programming in 1964 and 1965 (Killick, 1978:337). By 1964 the role of the state was reduced to that of dispenser of patronage (Pellow and Chazan, 1986:45). Institutional capabilities were devastated by the late 1970s and government authority was equally diminished (Kraus, 1991:121).

As the Nkrumah regime lost popular support, it increasingly turned to using the military and police to retain power (Kraus, 1971:59–60). The NLC made major efforts to improve policy implementation, but the achievements in this regard were limited (Killick, 1978:337). Successive regimes were restrained from trying policy options that had already been tried, thus reducing the ability of state structures to control events (Pellow and Chazan, 1986:37). State agencies were weakened by widespread corruption and by 1981 state–society relations had broken down entirely (Chazan, 1991:23).

Ghana was plagued by political strikes even though most labour action was outlawed in 1957 (Rathbone, 1978:24). Government coercion in the 1982–9 time period kept strikes lower, but in the mid-1980s, the urban middle-class, students and trade unions engaged in a series of strikes to express opposition to PNDC policies, particularly economic policies (Chazan, 1992:132; Kraus, 1991:150). The reaction of most of the population to the economic and political chaos in the early 1980s was to withdraw from relations with the government and form their own survival strategies (Chazan, 1992:128). The survival activities centered around provision of basic commodities, and were carried out by social groups such as primary associations, occupational groups, youth and women's organizations, and religious communities; ethnic concerns were not the basis of most of these groups (Chazan, 1992:129).

PNDC efforts at rebuilding a strong Ghanaian state have been somewhat successful. The PNDC was not dependent on the military or the dominant civilian establishment for support, as the coup was a rebellion against the senior military officers and the ruling elites (Chazan, 1992:127). The 1983 decision to undertake economic restructuring on World Bank and IMF terms had the effect of separating economic and political concerns, thus giving the elite some space for policy manoeuvering (Chazan, 1991:28). A national committee for designing a Ghanaian form of democracy was formed, shifting political concerns into 'the realm of thought', while economic concerns shifted to the front (Chazan, 1992:130–131).

During the early phases of the economic recovery programme, the government could control fiscal and adjustment measures, but had to rely on authoritarian measures such as torture and summary executions in order to govern the country with no apparent backing (Chazan, 1991:31). Despite the problems, the Ghanaian state in 1987 was less intrusive and more autonomous than in the past and was more able to implement its policies (Chazan, 1992:133,139). The Rawlings victory in the 1993 presidential election provides some evidence that a broader base of political support has been fashioned, but the depth of the support is unclear (Joseph, 1993:46).

In terms of state strength and ideology, Côte d'Ivoire again provides a stark contrast to the Ghanaian situation for much of the time period under consideration. The prevailing ideology in Côte d'Ivoire, like the elite, has remained fairly consistent, and until the economic crises of the 1980s, the state was able to formulate and implement policy preferences relatively well. The Ivorian governing ideology was based on the 'belief that economic growth achieved by the most effective means, including dominance by foreign personnel and capital, will maximize the regime's capability for distributing material benefits to its population and hence foster support' (Zolberg, 1971:27). A one-party state was considered the best way to organize politics to achieve the economic goals (Zolberg, 1969).

The Ivorian state was not terribly strong at independence, but neither was civil society and the PDCI was able to capture the state fairly smoothly (Crook, 1991:221–2). The weakness and lack of mobilization among societal groups were such that, at independence, the state was fairly free to choose what to crush and what to incorporate (Crook, 1991:224). The state was able to use its machinery to 'maintain and control the conditions for both the expansion and extraction of revenue from the peasant and mercantile economy.' (Crook, 1990:654). These actions were supported by the ruling ideology, while society was weakened by low participation in the system (Crook, 1991:225).

Although the Ivorian state appears strong in this comparison, it is strong only in relation to Ghana or to its own relatively weak civil society. The apparent strength of the state rested on the ability to expand and exploit cocoa production. When poor policy decisions and world market conditions weakened the cocoa marketing system in the 1980s, the inability of the state to lead in economic diversification became painfully obvious. The state has been unable to stop the political unrest that accompanied the economic difficulties of the early 1990s, and calls for political change started to challenge the ruling regime in the late 1980s (Bourke, 1992:67). Tax collection is low, and decreasing as economic activity declines, and fraud and evasion increase (World Bank, 1991:144).

The bureaucracy may contribute to a host country's bargaining power by improving the ability of the state to act and simply by dealing with foreign investors in a competent fashion. The bureaucracy of both Ghana and Côte d'Ivoire has been discussed at different points above, but important differences should be noted. After Nkrumah had set up a dual bureaucracy in Ghana, Busia led a politically motivated purge of the civil service. The bureaucracy lost all independence and access to officials became based on kinship, ethnicity and friendship (Pellow and Chazan, 1986:55). The government decentralized administrative tasks, leading to inefficiency and corruption (Pellow and Chazan, 1986:55). The inefficiency and corruption served to decrease the bargaining power of Ghana by making foreign investors wary and unwilling to take chances dealing with the system.

In Côte d'Ivoire, the French system of prefectoral administration continued almost uninterrupted after independence, but an Ivorian bureaucracy hardly existed. In 1957 there were no Africans in executive positions in the civil service (Crook, 1991:222). The restrictive elite recruitment policies followed by Houphouet only gradually allowed educated Ivorians into the civil service. Institutions are now staffed by highly qualified personnel with expectations that more closely reflect rational career development and technocratic commitment (Crook, 1990:665).

In general, the political context conditions for FDI seem to be stronger for much of the time period in Côte d'Ivoire than in Ghana. The highly politicized cleavages in the Ghanaian elite and society at large contributed to a pattern of elite fragmentation that contributed to weakening of the state and its institutions, as well as to mass political instability. The state was stronger in Côte d'Ivoire, but it must be remembered that it only seems stronger in relation to Ghana or to its own civil society. When the elites and masses became mobilized over declining economic conditions, the state had difficulty in formulating and implementing policies. Both countries continue to struggle with making the transition to democracy, and with implementing more liberal economic policies. The poor economic conditions may provide an explanation for why both countries have also drawn in quite low levels of FDI flows.

III. ECONOMIC CONTEXT

Although the aggregate figures seem to provide an edge to Côte d'Ivoire in terms of economic growth and development, these two countries are really very similar in terms of the economic context variables. Both countries remain quite poor relative to other developing economies, so this comparison highlights the differences between the strategies for economic growth, and the differences with respect to foreign direct investment.

Economic Growth

At the time of independence both Ghana and Côte d'Ivoire exemplified Africa's marginalization in the world economy (Austen, 1987:102). Heavy dependence on primary products as the main exports exposed both countries to dramatic fluctuations in world market prices (Onyemelukwe and Filani, 1983:143). Despite their similar peripheral positions in the world economy, the economic histories of Ghana and Côte d'Ivoire show important differences, and their growth policies varied greatly. The cash economy grew much earlier in Ghana, beginning in the south with cocoa and coffee exports. As early as 1930 cocoa exports provided most of the revenue (Green, 1971; Grier, 1987:34). In contrast, coffee exports did not take off in Côte d'Ivoire until the 1950s, and cocoa production took off during the 1960s and 1970s (Crook, 1991:219).

Although the major exports for both Ghana and Côte d'Ivoire are cocoa and coffee, the economic policies which have been built on revenues from these crops have been dissimilar, as have the results. Table 3.3 presents the average annual real growth rate of GDP for both countries. The table indicates that Côte d'Ivoire initially had comparatively high economic growth, but that situation reversed in the 1988–92 time period. The discussion which follows

Table 3.3 Economic Growth in Ghana and Côte d'Ivoire (selected years)

	Ghana	Côte d'Ivoire
GDP, Average Annual Growth (%):		
1960–9	3.0	8.3
1970–9	2.0	7.4
1980–7	1.2	3.8
1988–93	4.3	−1.0

Sources: Hecht (1983:28) for Côte d'Ivoire from 1961–9. IMF (1989) *International Financial Statistics Yearbook* for Ghana, 1960–6. World Bank, *World Tables, 1988–89* for 1967–7; UNCTAD, *Handbook, of International Trade and Development Statistics, 1994* for 1988–93.

the table outlines the differences in policies pursued by the two countries.

At independence, Ghana adopted a highly centralized economic system based on Nkrumah's ideology of 'African Socialism', and it is often taken as a model of the poor economic consequences of that system (Fieldhouse, 1986:139). The growth strategy from 1961 through 1965 was a complex effort to reduce external economic dependence, and included elements intended to expand the domestic and African markets, expand manufacturing, and expand the role of the state in production (Green, 1971:246–7).

The government's policy was to use the cocoa farmers as the main source of government revenues (Fieldhouse, 1986:145). Ghana followed the British preference for handling the export of crops through marketing boards and the marketing system for cocoa was nationalized relatively early in Ghana (Hecht, 1983:34). The Cocoa Marketing Board (CMB) pursued a rigid strategy of selling a large part of each crop in advance, regardless of world market conditions. When the market was rising, for instance in 1966–9, this policy resulted in large losses (Crook, 1991:236; Killick, 1978:120).

Serious economic difficulties emerged in 1961, when imports and government expenditures exceeded export earnings (Pellow and Chazan, 1986:44). A decline in world cocoa prices between 1960 and 1966, exchange rate policies that produced disincentives for export, declining production in government-owned industrial plants and state farms, and massive expansion of the public sector during the 1960s all combined to create a serious economic downturn (Fieldhouse, 1986:139–40; Jeffries, 1989:76; Pellow and Chazan, 1986:44). GNP growth stagnated from 1960 through to 1966, while the population increased (Fieldhouse, 1986:140).

The economic problems led to an austerity budget and large government borrowing (Pellow and Chazan, 1986:44). The Nkrumah regime had underestimated the time span between fixed investment and GDP growth, and over-dependence on high supplier credit resulted (Green, 1971:249). The Busia government inherited a heavy debt burden from the CPP (Green, 1971:260). The NLC and Busia governments turned to more market oriented policies, and the second military government returned to a command economy (Green, 1971:244,257; Killick, 1978:300). Acheampong's (1972–8) fiscal policies led to increased public demand, but it was not met with increased production. Rapid inflation, an imbalance in external accounts, a rise in debt to cover budget deficits and increases in government expenditures were the results (Rothchild and Gyimah-Boadi, 1986:263).

Foreign and international banks began refusing Ghana credit in 1979 (Rothchild and Gyimah-Boadi, 1986:258). Ghana was unable to raise new capital to sustain development in either industry or agriculture (Fieldhouse, 1986:149). When the PNDC took power at the end of 1981 economic conditions had worsened. Per capita GDP fell by about 3.2 per cent during 1970–81 period, gold and mineral production were down by 47 per cent and 32 per cent respectively, and cocoa production had also dropped relative to the 1968–9 harvest (Kraus, 1991:121). The country experienced 'import strangulation' as a result of export declines, and inflation averaged 50 per cent a year between 1976 and 1981 (Kraus, 1991:121).

In 1983, arrangements were made with the IMF and the World Bank to undertake a stabilization programme. The Economic Recovery Program (ERP) included a series of devaluations of the cedi to move towards a more 'realistic' exchange rate (World Bank, 1991:223). Price and distribution controls were lifted for a wide range of products and interest rates were increased gradually (World Bank, 1991:223). The minimum wage was also raised in an effort to offset erosion in real wages (World Bank, 1991:223). The result of the ERP was the longest period of sustained growth in Ghana. From 1984 to 1989 the average annual GDP growth rate was 6 per cent, although output in cocoa, timber and mining and industry was still low compared with 1970 levels (Kraus, 1991:128).

The high aggregate growth rate prompted some to call Ghana the 'success story' of the 1980s (Kraus, 1992:86), however the growth has been accompanied by other problems. The depreciation of the cedi, price changes, limits on credit and high interest rates combined to produce a liquidity crisis for importers and the industrial sector, and depressed the domestic market (Hutchful, 1989:115). The emphasis on export expansion came at a time when there were large market surpluses of cocoa and a major slump in world prices (Hutchful, 1989:115). Primary export expansion undermined the domestic productive sectors (food, agriculture and manufacturing) by shifting relative prices in favour of cocoa and against food producers (Hutchful, 1989:116–17). The implications for the external debt situation were also problematic, as the ability to maintain payment schedules on IMF stand-by resources emerged as a serious problem (Hutchful, 1989:118–19). These problems indicate that calling Ghana an economic success story may be premature, but certainly aggregate economic growth rates have improved.

Côte d'Ivoire was the African economic success story in the 1960s and 1970s, but that success gave way to economic crisis in the 1980s (Fieldhouse 1986:187). During the first two decades of independence the average annual growth rate was 7.5 per cent, and the peasant based export-oriented agricultural sector led the aggregate growth (Michael and Noel, 1984:78). The Ivorian government supported the agricultural sector through public investment in infrastructure and by maintaining high and stable producer prices (den Tuinder, 1978:5). During the 1970s, world prices for cocoa increased and Côte d'Ivoire experienced a financial boom which was not experienced by Ghana, partly because Ghana's production declined during the 1970s (Gbetibouo and Delgado, 1984:121).

The Ivorian growth strategy differed from that of Ghana by placing far more emphasis on maintaining foreign economic ties. Economic expansion was based on broadening the labour base through labour migration, and welcoming foreign investment (Green, 1971:241). Côte d'Ivoire joined in bilateral trade agreements with the French in 1961, and is a partner of the Lome agreements, so it enjoys duty free treatment of exports to the EEC (Mytelka, 1984:152; Michael and Noel, 1984:85). Côte d'Ivoire is also a member of the Monetary Union of West Africa (UMOA), which centralizes foreign currency reserves, issues a single currency (CFA franc), has a common interest structure and allows free trade within the Union (Michael and Noel, 1984:85). Until 1994, the CFA franc was tied to the French franc by a fixed exchange rate and was fully convertible. These arrangements limited policy options, but the ties with the French franc and treasury were advantages (Michael and Noel, 1984:85). Early in 1994 the French announced that they would no longer support the CFA franc and this resulted in a large devaluation (French, 1994).

Another major policy difference between Ghana and Côte d'Ivoire involves the marketing mechanism for export crops. Marketing of export crops in Côte d'Ivoire is done through private actors, organized by the parastatal Caisse de Stabilisation et de Soutien des Prix des Produits (CSSPPA, or the Stabilization Fund). A fixed price is guaranteed to producers, and licensed exporters are bound to take delivery of the crop and sell at a price approved by the Fund (Hecht, 1984:34). The Stabilization Fund keeps the difference if the actual selling price is higher, and if not, makes up the difference (Gbetibouo and Delgado, 1984:118–20).

During the price boom for cocoa and coffee in the late 1970s, the Fund produced surpluses for the state. The ruling circles in Côte d'Ivoire were seized by 'financial euphoria' which led to substantial inflation in public investments (Faure, 1989). The climate of patronage politics was particularly vulnerable to large and expensive projects such as the sugar industry programme and building of a new capital city in Yamoussoukro (Faure, 1989:68). These expensive policies of infrastructure creation and capital goods purchases increased the foreign debt (Faure, 1989:59).

The continued vulnerability to world market prices became obvious with the sharp collapse of coffee and cocoa prices in 1978. The price collapse coincided with a rise in imports and increasing interest rates, and the IMF was called in for assistance in 1980 (Faure, 1989:59–60). External debt had been relatively low in the 1960s because of the reliance on direct investment rather than loans (Fieldhouse, 1986:199). But, insufficient domestic savings and limited amounts of new foreign investment led to accelerated foreign borrowing in the 1970s (Mytelka, 1984:158). Rising levels of foreign debt began to produce serious constraints in the 1980s.

In 1981 Côte d'Ivoire began an economic stabilization programme initiated with IMF support, but the fiscal targets were not met (Michael and Noel, 1984:86). The drought in 1983 meant that the coffee harvest was only one-third that of the previous year (Faure, 1989:60). This was the trigger for serious recognition of economic crisis by the leadership (Faure, 1989:61). Yet, when cocoa prices fell again in the late 1980s, the decision was made to maintain the producer price of cocoa at 1985–6 levels, and the Stabilization Fund ran up even larger debts (Crook, 1990:659; Kraus, 1992:86). In October 1989 new World Bank and French loans were made to prop up the Fund (Crook, 1990:661; Faure, 1989:61). The high economic growth rates that had made Côte d'Ivoire the African miracle thus gave way to low growth rates in the 1980s and negative growth rates in the early 1990s. Côte d'Ivoire had an early history of stronger economic growth than Ghana, but by the end of the time period considered here, Ghana was producing higher aggregate growth rates.

Economic Development

Economic development is generally interpreted to mean economic growth that is accompanied by widely distributed increases in the standard of living for the masses of people. The case of Ghana may

Table 3.4 Indicators of Development in Ghana and Côte d'Ivoire (selected years)

		Ghana	*Côte d'Ivoire*
GNP per capita,	1967	240	210
(US$)	1970	250	270
	1980	410	1 180
	1990	390	750
GNP per capita growth,			
(%)	1965–86	−1.7	1.2
Average Annual Growth Rate (%)			
Agriculture:	1965–80	1.6	3.3
	1980–7	0.0	1.6
Industry:	1965–80	1.4	10.4
	1980–7	0.1	−2.4
Infant Mortality Rate	1967	114	143
	1977	102	116
	1987	89	95
	1992	81	91
Life Expectancy	1967	48	43
	1977	51	48
	1987	54	52
	1992	56	56
Education (% of age			
group enrolled)	1965	69	60
	1980	73	80
	1986	63	78
	1990	77	69

Notes: Ghana's GDP growth for 1984–88 was over 5 per cent per year, and agricultural growth was also high. Education for 1990 indicates only primary school enrolment ratios.

Sources: Kraus (1992); World Bank *World Tables*, 1992 and 1995; World Bank (1989).

be characterized for much of the time period as one of little growth, accompanied by very little economic development. Côte d'Ivoire experienced higher economic growth rates through the 1970s, with some development, but that development was not strong, and could not sustain the growth. Table 3.4 provides several indicators of development for the two countries, but it is worth keeping in mind that data unreliability makes it difficult to interpret small differences in values.

The growth in GNP per capita was stronger in Côte d'Ivoire than in Ghana, but at only 1.2 per cent between 1965 and 1986, it was not very high by world standards. GNP per capita growth in Ghana was actually negative for that time period, reflecting the general economic deterioration. However, growth in GNP per capita was stronger in Ghana near the end of the period and weaker in Côte d'Ivoire (World Bank, 1989). Neither country demonstrates much evidence of economic development as measured by per capita increase in aggregate income.

Ghana was considered to have a higher level of development than other African countries at the time of independence. In 1957, the average incomes were higher in Ghana than most other black African countries and the educational system supplied relatively skilled labour (Killick, 1978:3–4). School enrolment rates show Côte d'Ivoire surpassing Ghana after 1965, but the French educational system seemed to have little relevance in the Ivorian situation (den Tuinder, 1978). Life expectancy and infant mortality rates have been quite similar in both countries, but Côte d'Ivoire lags behind Ghana, perhaps reflecting the difference in the levels at independence.

The heavy investment programme that was a major part of Nkrumah's plan to diversify Ghana's economy in the early 1960s had distorting and inflationary effects rather than producing GDP growth (Green, 1971:249–50). The growth rates of both agriculture and industry were very low through the 1960s and 1970s. The industrialization which did occur produced few linkages to the other sectors of the economy, and made little contribution to employment (Fieldhouse, 1986:143). Income inequalities between wage and salary workers increased, and urban–rural wage differentials also grew quite large (Killick, 1978:81–2). In addition to these problems, the infrastructure began disintegrating to the point where in the early 1980s truck drivers refused to drive on the road system (Jeffries, 1989:80).

Standard of living indicators have shown some improvement in Ghana in the post-stabilization programme period. Real wages have been rising since 1987, although real urban wages are still lower than 1970 levels (Kraus, 1992:86; 1991:145). User fees introduced in health care have had the effect of reducing output and increasing disease (Kraus, 1991:143). In addition, malnutrition in pre-school children was higher in 1988 than 1961–2 (Kraus, 1991:146). The PNDC made progress in repairing the education system, but the universities have been closed repeatedly due to student unrest (Kraus, 1991:144). Infrastructure and productive capacity are being rehabilitated slowly, in efforts to rebuild economic growth and begin development (Kraus, 1992:86).

The signs of growth in the economy generate serious concerns about economic inequalities that exist between the urban and rural population in Ghana. The urban-rural split is compounded by large disparities in the levels of perceived economic development in the northern and southern regions (Rimmer, 1992:98). Onyemelukwe and Filani (1983:142) maintain that the series of coups and counter-coups in Western African states in general is directly attributable to the general dissatisfaction with living conditions, and the failure of governments to solve the problem of inequity. This argument is consistent with the expectation that conditions contributing to bargaining leverage for a host country reinforce patterns of political and economic development.

Ghana has been struggling to produce equitable economic development from its new growth, while Côte d'Ivoire has been struggling to maintain the level of development achieved by the late 1970s. Early on, Côte d'Ivoire based its economic growth and development programme on proceeds from the sale of export crops. Import substitution and processing of agricultural raw materials have been the base of development for Ivorian industry (den Tuinder, 1978:227).

Efforts to diversify the economy had some success. The share in GDP of the three main exports dropped from 91 per cent in the 1950s, to 78 per cent in the 1960s, indicating that other exports grew rapidly (den Tuinder, 1978:15). Export crops were expanded to bananas, pineapple, coconut and palm oil during the 1960s when the world prices for cocoa and coffee were low, but the newer crops could only be produced in the south (den Tuinder, 1978:17). Yet, from 1969–79, per capita food production decreased by approximately 0.9 per cent, and the country's level of food self-sufficiency continued to deteriorate (Watts and Bassett, 1986:115). The agricultural growth rate slowed in the 1980s, and the growth rate for industry became negative (see Table 3.4).

The peasant farmers of Côte d'Ivoire were the driving force in the economic growth of the 1960s and 1970s, yet they gained only limited benefits (Hecht, 1983:38). Political, administrative and technical elites with close ties to the small Ivorian business community were the chief beneficiaries of economic growth (Green, 1971:242). The increase in official producer prices for the two main export crops during the 1960 to 1979 time period was not passed on to producers, as the real price paid to peasant smallholders remained constant (Hecht, 1983:39).

Côte d'Ivoire shares with Ghana problems of economic inequalities between large urban areas and the rural outlying areas. Abidjan, a modern city, is markedly more developed than the rural regions, particularly the eastern forest and savannah areas (Cohen, 1974:22; Schneider, 1992). The development policies have led to rapid urbanization, serving to heighten tensions among the privileged in the core developed area of Abidjan and the underprivileged in the slums (Onyemelukwe and Filani, 1983:144).

Incomes in the south of Côte d'Ivoire have been relatively equal, but there are large disparities in personal wealth between Northern and Southern regions (Gbetibouo and Delgado, 1984:139). Income inequalities are highest among salaried wage earners, the distribution is more even in the civil service, and agricultural income is much more evenly distributed than income in other sectors (den Tuinder, 1978:132–4). Despite the regional inequalities, Chenery, et al. (1974:8–9) place Côte d'Ivoire (c. 1970) in the low income inequality category, in comparison with Kenya and Senegal in the high inequality group of developing countries.

The Domestic Capitalist Class and State Financial Autonomy

Strong financial autonomy of the host state is expected to contribute to host bargaining power by making financial alternatives to FDI available. In both Ghana and Côte d'Ivoire the financial base for the state has been expropriation of surpluses from agricultural production. This resource base has not been effective in producing financial autonomy. The interests of agricultural producers are too politically sensitive in both countries for expropriation of their surpluses to provide an autonomous financial base for the state.

The domestic capitalist class is one facet of the host country that may form a counter-balance to the bargaining power of foreign investors. On the other hand, the domestic capitalists may form an alliance with the foreign capitalists, and then pursue interests not necessarily consistent with domestic development. Neither Ghana nor Côte d'Ivoire has had a domestic capitalist class which is willing and able to balance foreign investors. Competitive class strata emerged soon after World War II in Ghana, and at independence, a small merchant and professional bourgeoisie, which included top educators and bureaucrats, had developed (Kraus, 1971:36). The middle class was made up of teachers, clerks, cocoa brokers, pharmacists, and small contractors. The lower class was composed of waged labourers (Kraus, 1971:36).

Prior to independence a predominantly state-employed petite bourgeoisie was created with a basis in appropriations from cocoa farmers (Grier, 1987:47). During most of the post-independence time period, the bureaucratic elite and influential businesspeople made up the capitalist class, as the state dominated all capitalist relations (Rathbone, 1978:33). Capital formation by petty commodity production did not lead to a 'real' capitalist class, because such capital was redistributed rather than accumulated (Rathbone, 1978:33). But, during the 1980s the informal sector expanded rapidly, creating a new type of elite which was not associated with the Ghanaian state or dependent on its resources (Chazan, 1992:133–4). That elite has not yet developed into a class with resources capable of forming a balance to foreign investors.

Despite discussions of a politically dominant planter bourgeoisie in Côte d'Ivoire (Amin, 1967, 1973; Campbell, 1978), more recent analysis indicates that in the 1950s there was very little in terms of an organized and educated professional middle class (Crook, 1991:223). The economic base of the elite has been the state which they control, making Côte d'Ivoire a 'republic of civil servants' rather than one ruled by a planter bourgeoisie (Bakary, 1984:44–5). Although some of the bureaucrats are absentee landlords of capital intensive plantations, they also have non-agricultural sources of income in commerce, commodity marketing, construction, transport and shares in foreign firms (Hecht, 1983:26 and 45). The state also serves the interests of bureaucrats through awarding public contracts and government loans (Hecht, 1983:26).

Government policies that extracted resources from smallholder producers dampened the level of capital accumulation in the southern areas and prevented the formation of a peasant elite, or 'rural bourgeoisie' (Hecht, 1983:38). The majority of smallholders have found it difficult to accumulate land and investment capital because during 1960–79 the real price paid to peasant smallholders remained constant (Hecht, 1983:39,43). Private Ivorians have been reluctant to invest in industry because large amounts of capital are needed, they do not want to invest in minority situations where their share is small, and they have been able to recover capital more quickly in other sectors such as real estate (den Tuinder, 1978:51). In addition, Ivorian planters who accumulated capital had few opportunities to invest because the local French and foreign based firms were entrenched in coffee commercialization activities (Mytelka, 1984:168).

State-Owned Enterprises and Rent-Seeking

State-owned enterprises can provide the host with more bargaining power by making it less dependent on foreign capital for industrial development, yet they may also reduce bargaining power by introducing and maintaining market inefficiencies in the host country. In 1989 Côte d'Ivoire had the majority interest in 150 SOEs, and Ghana in 181 SOEs (Katz, 1992:3). These figures are quite a bit lower than Tanzania (420), but higher than other African countries such as Botswana (9) (Katz, 1992).

The incentives for rent-seeking have been high in both countries for much of the time period and this has led to high levels of corruption, particularly in Ghana. In Ghana, state control of the cocoa marketing process became a funding agency for government development plans, a source of public employment and a strong source of patronage politics (Rimmer, 1992:202). The apparatus of controls affecting such areas as allocation of imports and cheap credit also contributed to the practice of selectively allocating economic benefits (Jeffries, 1989; Rimmer, 1992).

An additional problem was that, at the outset, Nkrumah did not demand accountability from managers of state corporations, and the different ministries operated more or less autonomously (Kraus, 1971:62–3). Corruption stemmed in part from the attempt to secure covert funds for CPP operations within the country and internationally (Green, 1971:257). Those in 'managerial' roles had little administrative and policymaking competence and the damage they did in these roles has been judged by at least one observer to be 'worse than the appropriation of funds.' (Green, 1971:257)

During the Acheampong regime (1972–8) the state bureaucracy, parastatals and marketing boards consumed large amounts of fiscal resources, yet were ineffective at delivering necessary inputs and infrastructure to farmers (Rothchild and Gyimah-Boadi, 1986:263). Corruption was so bad that a new term, '*kalabule*', was coined to describe it (Jeffries, 1989:78). Many policies related to international economic transactions, such as import licensing, encouraged corruption (Jeffries, 1989:79). Such high levels of corruption could not have added to foreign investor confidence that projects in Ghana would be seen through effectively.

Other problems with SOEs in Ghana include poor feasibility studies and project planning, shortages of critical staff, over-staffing, inadequate capitalization, political interference, mismanagement and inefficiency (Gyimah-Boadi, 1991:195). The PNDC stressed reform through reorganization, but the programme faced many obstacles such as general weakness of private sector, absence of stock markets and/or facilities for routine trading of shares, organized financial markets from which investment funds could be raised and crucial personnel shortages for committees in charge of the programme (Gyimah-Boadi, 1991:199–200).

As in Ghana, the establishment of SOEs in Côte d'Ivoire was motivated by the desire to diversify, to reduce inequalities and to reduce the dominance of foreign capital. The state was a major partner in 33 state enterprises by 1979 (Fieldhouse, 1986:192–3). In the early 1980s an estimated one-third of agricultural production was dependent on public enterprises, and overall 15 to 20 per cent of GDP was attributed to parastatal enterprises in Côte d'Ivoire (Michael and Noel, 1984:82). The Ivorian parastatal enterprises showed the same problems of inefficiency and corruption that other African SOEs exhibited (Fieldhouse, 1986:193), but corruption in Ghana seemed to be far worse. The major difference was that the cocoa marketing process in Côte d'Ivoire was and is based on private traders, although they work within an official price structure (Crook, 1991:235).

Ivorian SOEs created another problem in terms of the economic context of FDI. A large portion of the investment undertaken by public enterprises has been financed by foreign capital, so 35 to 40 per cent of the public debt is attributed to public enterprises (Michael and Noel, 1984:82). The plan to set up six large, capital-intensive sugar plantations and refineries cost over US\$ 1,000 million in the 1970s and did not produce large returns on the investment (Hecht, 1983:28). High foreign debt created economic difficulties in general that made Côte d'Ivoire less attractive for foreign investors.

Policies Toward Foreign Direct Investment

Policies of the host country toward FDI can contribute to bargaining power by serving to increase investor confidence and certainty about

the investment environment. Consistent implementation of those policies is equally important. The rhetoric of the Ghanaian government at
independence did not always match actions when it came to FDI.
Nkrumah encouraged FDI on the one hand, as he was afraid of a
developing indigenous entrepreneurial class, but he maintained strict
exchange controls in order to prevent 'crippling' ties to foreign countries (Killick, 1978:37–40).

From 1966 to 1972 the National Liberation Council and the Busia
regimes produced rhetoric that sounded more accommodating toward
FDI, but the system of controls remained in place (Killick, 1978:300–
2). When the National Redemption Council took over in 1972, it
announced intentions to reactivate state enterprises and take control
of foreign owned industries (Killick, 1978:317). Despite the controls
on exchange and the anti-FDI rhetoric, between 1962 and 1978 foreign capital increased its share in production, although the ownership
was diluted by partnerships with the Ghanaian state and individuals
(Fieldhouse, 1986:140).

When the PNDC took power in December of 1981, it professed a
radical programme based on dependency theory (Chazan, 1991:25).
Actions were not as drastic as rhetoric implied, although some steps
were taken against foreign owned firms (Rothchild and Gyimah-Boadi,
1986:269–70). The PNDC government forced renegotiation of contracts
with several foreign companies and responsibility for allocating foreign
exchange was a virtual state monopoly (Ahiakpor, 1985:543). Foreign
firms reacted by announcing cuts in operations which generally involved
decreasing employment (Ahiakpor, 1985:548). By 1983 the government
was again organizing attempts to attract foreign investors, but they were
not very successful (Ahiakpor, 1985:549).

In contrast to the variation in Ghanaian policies, Côte d'Ivoire
followed a consistent strategy of encouraging FDI. During the colonial
period, French policies had favoured French capital over indigenous
capital (Mytelka, 1984:151). A division of labour emerged in which
Ivorian capital went to the agricultural sector and foreign capital was
invested in industry (Mytelka, 1984:151). A liberal FDI code was
passed in 1959, even before independence, with incentives for FDI
which included a five year tax holiday, ten years' exemption from
import duties on capital goods and no limit to profit repatriation
(Mytelka, 1984:153). The investment code also guaranteed transfer-
ability of profits and capital, made numerous tax concessions and
guaranteed industrial investments against nationalization (Mytelka,
1984:153).

The strength of the one-party state and the willingness of a unified elite allowed consistent implementation of these policies. In 1975 the Ivorian government held 25 per cent equity in industrial sectors, private Ivorians held 9 per cent and foreigners held the rest (den Tuinder, 1978:152). Even schemes which involved the state as the major investor, such as textiles and sugar, relied heavily on foreign management (Mytelka, 1984:1970).

IV. EXPERIENCES WITH FOREIGN DIRECT INVESTMENT

Sub-Saharan Africa in general is not a region that attracts large amounts of FDI. The share of global flows of FDI going to Africa was 2.4 per cent in 1980–4, and that share actually decreased to 1.9 per cent in 1988–9 (UNCTC, 1991:11; Wubneh, 1992). Although the FDI flows are low relative to other developing countries, Table 3.5 indicates that both Ghana and Côte d'Ivoire experienced positive net flows of FDI for much of the time period under consideration, although data are not available for the early years of independence.

The exact timing of early surges in FDI flows to Ghana and Côte d'Ivoire is difficult to pin down, however foreign economic penetration, in general, took place earlier in Ghana than in Côte d'Ivoire (Amin, 1973; Green, 1971). Europeans were initially attracted to the gold in regions that became Ghana, but the slave trade brought in more Europeans until agricultural products replaced slaves as inputs to British industrialization (Pellow and Chazan, 1986:15). Frankel (1938:158–9) estimates that total foreign capital in the Gold Coast for the time period 1870–1936 was £35.3 million sterling, while during the same time all of French West Africa received only £30.3 million sterling. Although Frankel's total capital estimate contains more than FDI, it is clear that foreign capital had penetrated both countries heavily by the time of independence. Their status as colonies made it virtually impossible for either country to formulate and implement strong policies to control foreign investors before becoming independent.

From 1960 on, the pattern of FDI flows to Ghana and Côte d'Ivoire was roughly similar until the late 1970s. Both countries experienced quite a bit of fluctuation, with some years being dramatically lower or higher than the preceding year. After 1977 flows to Côte d'Ivoire were quite a bit higher than to Ghana, seeming to reflect the continuing political turmoil in Ghana. The bottom dropped out for Ghana in the

Table 3.5   Net Foreign Direct Investment to Ghana and Côte d'Ivoire, 1960–92 (US\$ millions, current)

	Ghana	*Côte d'Ivoire*
1960	3.9	n.a.
1961	−11.3	n.a.
1962	9.9	n.a.
1963	7.4	10.5
1964	14.5	11.7
1965	38.2	19.0
1966	56.1	−1.6
1967	32.6	6.5
1968	15.8	12.2
1969	10.2	12.6
1970	67.8	30.7
1971	30.6	15.7
1972	11.5	18.7
1973	14.4	51.0
1974	10.5	32.6
1975	70.9	69.1
1976	−18.3	44.8
1977	19.2	14.7
1978	9.7	83.3
1979	−2.8	74.7
1980	15.6	94.7
1981	16.3	32.8
1982	16.3	47.5
1983	2.4	37.5
1984	2.0	21.7
1985	5.6	29.2
1986	4.3	70.7
1987	4.7	87.5
1988	5.0	22.2
1989	15.0	25.4
1990	14.8	47.7
1991	20.0	46.1
1992	22.5	49.1

Sources: (IMF) *International Financial Statistics Yearbook*, 1989 and 1991, (n.a. indicates data not available); World Bank, *World Tables*, 1995.

1983–8 period, indicating that foreign investors were simply not willing to deal with the disintegrated state. Flows to Côte d'Ivoire were lower again in 1988 and 1989, perhaps in reaction to the economic difficulties faced by that country during the mid-1980s. In general, the fluctuations in FDI flows to Ghana seem to be driven by global supply of FDI, while domestic factors such as economic growth and political stability are important for explaining fluctuation in flows to Côte d'Ivoire (McMillan, 1995).

The higher FDI flows to Côte d'Ivoire during the 1970s and most of the 1980s are also reflected in the available stock data. The data presented in Table 3.6 indicate that in the early post-independence stage, Ghana and Côte d'Ivoire had quite similar levels of stock of foreign investment. The uncertainty of the Ghanaian situation starts to be reflected in decreasing stocks in about 1975, while the stock of FDI continued to increase through the 1970s in Côte d'Ivoire.

Comparing the country of origin of the FDI for Ghana and Côte d'Ivoire does not yield the major differences seen between Japanese and American firms in Southeast Asia. While FDI from the US typically comes from large multinational corporations, European investments range from quite small projects to large concerns (Rood, 1975). Côte d'Ivoire is tied strongly to French FDI, and although Ghana tried to diversify, most of its investment comes from Europe (OECD, 1990). The mix of small and large investors may give the host country a bit of leverage not available to hosts dominated completely by large MNCs. The smaller investors may not have the means to drive hard bargains like their larger competitors. This possible advantage must be considered small in light of the timing of FDI, or the economic context for FDI. Neither state was able to construct a counter-balance to MNCs prior to independence.

Table 3.6   Stock of FDI in Ghana and Côte d'Ivoire (selected years) (US$ millions)

	Ghana	*Côte d'Ivoire*
1967	260	202
1971	345	300
1972	360	340
1973	410	375
1974	440	400
1975	300	420
1976	280	480
1977	275	500
1978	280	530

Source: UNCTC (1983) *Salient Features and Trends in Foreign Direct Investment*, p.58.

V. CONCLUSIONS

In this project I have drawn a set of important host-country context conditions from the bargaining approach to FDI and development, and used these factors as the starting point for comparing the results of FDI in pairs of host countries. My expectation has been that FDI in host countries which are relatively strong on the context conditions will be associated with outcome patterns which are consistent with modernization-type predictions. FDI in weaker host countries is expected to be associated with outcomes more consistent with dependency-type patterns of slow economic growth and political turmoil.

Both Ghana and Côte d'Ivoire started independence in a situation of dependence on foreign inputs, but they have had very different histories of policies for economic growth and development, and of dealing with foreign investors. Initially Côte d'Ivoire increased certainty in the investment environment by accommodating the wishes of foreign investors, but through time the domestic capitalist class was unable to balance the interests of foreign investors, and incentives for rent-seeking in the state-owned enterprises became fairly high. Once the economic decline of the 1980s became undeniable in the political realm, cracks became apparent in the ability of the state to formulate and implement economic development policies. The political conditions in Côte d'Ivoire were strong enough to turn the initial flows of FDI into slight economic growth, but background and economic conditions were weak, and growth could not be sustained.

In Ghana, the weak background and economic conditions were compounded by weak political conditions. Through most of the time period, Ghana experienced high levels of elite conflict, exacerbated by patterns of ethnic conflict. State institutions became mired in the political conflicts, and the state lost the ability to formulate and implement consistent development policies. The weak context conditions were accompanied by very slow economic growth, reverses in economic development and relatively high levels of mass political instability. But, by the mid-1990s, Ghana had managed to create economic growth and to reduce the high levels of political instability.

The comparison indicates that, even in situations of heavy external penetration, FDI can contribute either to vicious cycles of economic and political decay, or patterns where economic growth is produced in a stable political environment. Host-country policies and political situations feed into cycles which draw in or repel FDI, and those same context conditions also help to determine economic and political outcomes. FDI was not the primary causal factor in outcome patterns in these two countries, but it was important for the ways that it interacted with host-country context conditions. Again, as in the Philippines and Thailand, it seems that a balance between economic and political context conditions is as important for development patterns as how much FDI is flowing into the country.

The experiences of Ghana and Côte d'Ivoire also provide some evidence about which context conditions are most important, and where FDI fits into the temporal sequence of political and economic outcome variables. The cases of Côte d'Ivoire and Ghana seem to support the expectation that political stability precedes economic growth, or at least that political instability precludes growth. For most of the time period Ghana did not have political stability, and growth and development were low or negative. During Rawlings' rule there has been some improvement in political stability, as well as a shift toward greater democracy. Economic growth has followed, but many other factors have also changed, so drawing a simple causal connection is not possible. Côte d'Ivoire had exceptional political stability for most of the time period, accompanied by some growth, but the growth did not drive development. In both cases, mass political instability typically accompanied economic decline, implying that poor economic conditions drive instability. On balance it seems plausible to argue that some feedback exists between political stability and economic outcome variables, but further analysis is necessary to draw strong conclusions about the temporal pattern and about exactly where FDI fits in. The Granger causality analysis contained in Chapter 5 attempts to sort out the plausible causal paths among FDI and the putative outcome variables discussed in this country comparison.

4 The Bargaining Context and FDI in Costa Rica and Guatemala

In this chapter, the bargaining leverage of two small, open-economy countries is examined in order to better understand the factors which determine FDI flows, and the process by which the investment seems to produce different results. The expectation is that FDI will be associated with better development outcomes where it interacts with strong political and economic context conditions that contribute to host-country bargaining leverage. When FDI flows into a relatively weaker host country, it is expected to interact in opposite ways to help perpetuate a vicious cycle of underdevelopment and political instability. The context conditions which contribute to bargaining power *vis-à-vis* foreign investors also contribute to host country ability and willingness to pursue economic development and political stability. Thus, the through-time comparison will provide some leverage on the problem of whether there are feed-back cycles involved in development patterns. Such a comparison will also allow us to examine the possible temporal sequence among the key variables, FDI, political stability, economic growth, and development.

The analysis in this chapter focuses on the aggregate economic and political outcomes in Costa Rica and Guatemala during the post-World War II time period. Background conditions prior to World War II are also examined because they set the initial context for FDI, as well as for the other outcome variables examined here. Country specialists will be quick to note that these two countries are very different on some important background conditions, and that current outcomes simply reflect those differences. For instance, Costa Rica did not start out with a large indigenous population that was subjected to strong colonial rule. The resulting lack of ethnic conflict has contributed to mass political stability, and that has been one factor which allowed Costa Rica to produce Central America's strongest economic development performance. On the other hand, Guatemala had a large indigenous population which was subjugated by colonialists. The ethnic composition of the population in Guatemala has contributed to high levels of political violence, at least since 1954, and this has been accompanied by very little improvement on economic development indicators.

Yet, despite the differences, Costa Rica and Guatemala share similarities that make them interesting cases to compare with respect to bargaining leverage *vis-à-vis* foreign investors. Both countries have economies that were built on agricultural exports, and both have been ideologically open to strong ties with the international economy. In addition, both countries fell well within the sphere of US interest during the cold war. If FDI has played a critical role in producing the different political and economic outcomes in Costa Rica and Guatemala, this comparison should highlight that role.

Table 4.1 summarizes the position on the context factors for Costa Rica and Guatemala. Again, since change through time has occurred, the table entries refer to the condition that has been most prevalent in the post-World War II time period. The first section of this chapter compares the background conditions for these two countries, the second part compares the political factors, the third compares the economic context, and then experiences with FDI are compared.

Table 4.1 Status on Factors Contributing to Bargaining Power in Costa Rica and Guatemala

	Costa Rica	*Guatemala*
Background:		
Colonial History	Spanish	Spanish
Land Tenure	Unequal	Highly unequal
	(Small farmers and Plantations)	(Plantation)
Geography	Both countries within US sphere of interest	
Infrastructure	Poor	Poor
Political:		
Elite Unity	High	Medium to Low
Ideology and State Strength	Strong	Strong/oppressive
Mass Political Stability	High	Low
Ethnic Conflict	Low	High
Competence of Bureaucracy	Medium	Low
Economic:		
Financial Autonomy	Medium	Low
FDI Policy Implementation	Strong	Weak
Domestic Capitalist Class	Medium	Medium
SOE Rent-Seeking		
Incentives	High	Low

I. BACKGROUND CONDITIONS

Costa Rica and Guatemala have several similarities with respect to the background factors expected to contribute to bargaining leverage. Although different in important details which will be examined below, they were both part of the Spanish empire and were drawn into the world economy through mercantilistic rule, but they did not have to fight wars against the Spanish for independence in the 1820s (Woodward, 1985). Both countries spent the first 20 to 30 years of independence in situations of domestic political turmoil. Both economies were and are relatively small, they have been and continue to be very open to the international economy and their economic base is export agriculture, primarily coffee and bananas.

The mineral resource endowment did not give an early advantage to either country in terms of drawing in foreign investment (Grunwald and Musgrove, 1970). Although oil was discovered in Guatemala in the mid-1970s (Karp, 1988:69), it became a drawing point for investment much too late in the time period to be considered an important background condition. The infrastructure did not yield early advantages to either country, as the entire Central American region had only primitive communication and transportation systems during and immediately following the colonial period (Weeks, 1985:12). Finally, they both are in a similar international political situation due to their location in a geographic region which continues to draw the strategic and economic interest of the United States.

Despite these similarities, the differences in colonial and early independence-era land holding and labour patterns are critical for understanding current differences in political and economic developments. Costa Rica was much smaller in terms of population and land, and by the sixteenth century the Indian population had been largely destroyed, so the ruling class did not derive its power from the slave or Indian population (Seligson, 1990). Early in the independence period the government granted land to all people willing to cultivate coffee on it (Seligson, 1990:459–60). Because of labour shortages, wages were relatively high, so even people who lost their land during the expansion of coffee production received some benefits of economic growth (Booth and Walker, 1993:30). The peasants of the central highlands of Costa Rica came to play a major role in early coffee production, even though large estates have always existed (Weeks, 1985:14). The boom in coffee production increased wealth tremendously for both the peasants and the elites, and even helped to solidify the elite class (Gumundson, 1986:77).

The higher concentration of Indians in the highlands of the area that became Guatemala provided a large population that, when forced into slave labour, attracted more colonialists (Weeks, 1985:12). The subjugation of the Indian population continued well into the twentieth century. By 1900, Indian and church lands had been opened to cultivation by large landowners of coffee plantations and the Indians were coerced into being labourers on the plantations through a debt-peonage system (Booth and Walker, 1993:41; Trudeau, 1993:19). The structure of the present social hierarchy was embedded early and was based on European domination of the people of mixed race, and domination and exploitation of the Indians by both of these groups (Perara, 1993:5).

These early social and economic patterns created a persistent problem of unequal land distribution in both countries, but the problem has been worse in Guatemala. Costa Rica began with a much less unequal system, and has pursued slower and steadier land reform efforts than Guatemala (Scofield, 1990:139). The relatively more equal distribution of land in Costa Rica has been pinpointed as an early facilitating factor for the development of democracy (Seligson, 1990; Weeks, 1985). In addition, the openness of the Costa Rican political system, at least since 1948, seems to have contributed to the feeling among the peasants that their complaints will be addressed by the government, thus contributing to less mass political violence (Anderson, 1991).

Because of the highly unequal land tenure system in Guatemala, even moderate economic growth has consistently served to concentrate wealth in the hands of the large land owners (Trudeau, 1989:95). The coffee planters took control of society in 1871, and a dual agricultural system developed in which the plantation owners used coerced Indian labour part of the year for export production. The Indians farmed at subsistence level in the highlands to survive for the rest of the year (Moors, 1988:68). In 1952, President Jacobo Arbenz instituted Guatemala's first, and only, significant effort at land reform measures that expropriated land with some compensation to the large landowners (Scofield, 1990:164). After the 1954 overthrow of the Arbenz regime (which is discussed in more detail below), the land was returned to its previous owners. Further efforts to distribute land to peasants have largely failed, while military officers and members of the elite have been able to purchase large tracts of land at concessionary prices (Scofield, 1990:164).

While Costa Rica and Guatemala are similar on some background factors, the differences between the early political and economic development experiences in Costa Rica and Guatemala provide an interesting contrast in the early bargaining contexts for FDI. Since Guatemala had more land and abundant labour, it seemed to have initial advantages in drawing in settlers and foreign investors. Yet, the critical differences in labour and land tenure patterns are at the heart of many explanations for what eventually went 'right' in Costa Rica, and what went 'wrong' in Guatemala. The political context of FDI, to which we turn in the next section, continually reflects these crucial background differences between the two countries.

II. POLITICAL CONTEXT

The political context for FDI is compared in terms of factors that shape the ability and willingness of the host country to bargain with investors for significant gains. In order for those gains to show up as positive aggregate economic outcomes, the host country also must be able and willing to convert those specific gains into growth and development. FDI is expected to be most attracted to a host country with a welcoming ideology and the ability to implement stable investment policies. At the same time, a strong state with stable policies would seem to be the most likely to be able to implement domestic development policies. So, the causes and consequences of FDI can seem tautological, but the comparison between countries and through time can help to unravel the causal patterns. The specific terms of comparison here are the ideology of the host country government, elite and mass political stability, and the strength of the state with respect to being able to implement development policies.

The most similar of these political context factors between these countries and through time is the ideological acceptance of foreign investment in both Costa Rica and Guatemala. Political processes in both countries were dominated through the 1800s and into the 1900s by competition between ideological Liberals and Conservatives (Woodward, 1985:92). Despite the competition, both the Liberals and Conservatives consistently supported a programme of free-market capitalism, and the political economy reflected an orientation toward external markets (Trudeau, 1993:18). In the early post-independence period, potential investors did not face state-imposed barriers to entry in either country and this situation has continued into the 1990s. The political stability and the ability of the states to use foreign investment for domestic purposes have differed tremendously.

Elite Unity and Mass Political Stability

Table 4.2 demonstrates the large differences with respect to indicators of political instability for Costa Rica and Guatemala since 1950. The difference is particularly apparent with respect to deaths due to political violence. Since these figures do not include armed attacks by guerillas against the government, and since the events are probably under reported, the figures should be taken as approximate. Nevertheless, it is clear that political stability has been the norm for Costa Rica, while political turmoil has been the norm for Guatemala during this time period.

Although recently Costa Rica has been relatively free of both mass and elite political instability, for the first 20 years of independence coups, civil wars and peasant uprisings were the rule rather than the exception (Seligson, 1990:461). However, since most of the Indians had been removed or died early in the colonial period, the conflict was not as strongly split along ethnic lines as in Guatemala. The international arena was also fairly unstable in the post-colonial period, with Costa Rica clashing with Nicaragua and Panama over territory around the proposed transisthmian canal sites (Woodward, 1985:137).

Table 4.2   Indicators of Political Instability in Costa Rica and Guatemala, 1950–93

		Costa Rica	*Guatemala*
Deaths due to political violence:	1950–9	57	219
	1960–9	1	171
	1970–9	0	110
	1980–90	5	1 038
	1991–3	0	101
Number of riots:	1950–9	2	21
	1960–9	1	17
	1970–9	8	7
	1980–90	1	2
	1991–3	0	0

Sources: Taylor and Hudson (1972); Taylor and Jodice (1983) for the 1960 to 1978 time period; computed from coding of the *New York Times Index* for 1979–90.

A critical period for Costa Rican political and economic development began with the 1940 ascension to power of Rafael Angel Calderon Guardia. Calderon instituted many social reforms, supported by an uneasy coalition that included the communist party and the catholic church (Seligson, 1990). The World War II alliance between the US and Soviet Union prevented a strong US protest against the communists in Costa Rica, but the coalition faced domestic opposition from fascist sympathizers. In the election of 1944, Calderon's hand-picked successor – Teodoro Picado – defeated the opposition, and continued expanding the social policies, but the system was perceived as increasingly authoritarian (Weaver, 1994:142). In the context of the early cold war, the communists came under increasing domestic pressure, and a coalition between the land owners and middle-class formed the opposition Social Democrat Party which won the election of 1948 (Seligson, 1990; Weaver, 1994). The election was annulled by the legislature which then made Ulate the president. This precipitated the civil war of 1948, in which Jose Figueres and his Army of National Liberation overthrew the Ulate government (Woodward, 1985:300).

Many of the social reforms remained in place despite the violent overthrow of the government and the political repression of labour. The junta carried out reforms which included: abolishing the army; enfranchising women; a temporary tax on the rich, including a 15 per cent profit tax on United Fruit Company; nationalizing the banks; and continuing to construct a welfare state to address middle-class interests (Carballo, 1993:207; Weaver, 1994:143–4). Figueres turned control over to Ulate in 1949, but along with his National Liberation Party (PLN) regained power in 1953 and continued a programme of social reforms (Vilas, 1995:101–2).

The stability of a firmly entrenched political elite in Costa Rica has been described as critical for the stability of national political life (Dunkerley, 1988:614). The stability can be seen in the fact that transfers of power since the civil war have been peaceful and by regularly scheduled elections (see Ameringer, 1982). Elite unity since the 1948 revolution may be due in part to the abolition of an army which removed an instrument of power of the traditional ruling classes (Vilas, 1995:103), but other factors contributed as well. Although the PLN dominated politics from 1953 to 1986, there was an active opposition which was not terrorized or excluded from politics and which managed to win several presidential elections (Carballo, 1993). Even though some observers find a strongly personalized trait in Costa Rican politics (for example Dunkerly, 1988), the elite have exhibited an ability to compromise instead of becoming polarized (Carballo, 1993:203). The ideology of the elite has converged on a social democratic model of a capitalist system, with state regulation and selective state involvement in the economy (Kendrick, 1988: 246–7). The oligarchy was economically dynamic, but there was very little confrontation between coffee growers and industrialists to create splits within the elite as happened in other Central American countries (Vilas, 1995:102).

For the most part, elite unity and stability have been accompanied by mass political stability in Costa Rica. The mass political unrest which has occurred is not clearly separable from the economic and political instability in the Central American region as a whole in the late 1970s and through the 1980s. Border clashes with Nicaragua and some terrorist activities in 1982 and 1983 contributed to domestic feelings of political insecurity (Kendrick, 1988:251). When the Costa Rican army was abolished, it was replaced by the Civil and Rural Guards which were meant to act as police forces. During the Nicaraguan civil war, the *Contras* began using Costa Rica as a base. The US had a strong interest in using Costa Rica as a training ground and spring board for the *Contras*, and used economic and military aid to the Guards as incentives for Costa Rican compliance (Kendrick, 1988; Dunkerly, 1995). Costa Rican policy makers were unhappy with the pressure from the US, but the economic aid was desperately needed and by the mid-1980s Costa Rica was the second highest recipient of US economic aid per capita (Kendrick, 1988:250). Costa Rican president Oscar Arias Sanchez played a key role in negotiations for a Central American peace plan that eventually helped to resolve conflicts in Nicaragua and El Salvador (see Dunkerley, 1995).

The resolution of the Nicaraguan civil war also resolved some of the tensions within Costa Rica over the *Contras* and the military training of the Guards. However, in the late 1980s and early 1990s, austerity measures taken to address economic difficulties were followed by numerous strikes and demonstrations (Booth and Walker, 1993:121). Even though regional political and economic instability had a direct effect on stability in Costa Rica, for most of the post-World War II time period mass and elite political stability contributed positively to Costa Rica's bargaining leverage with foreign investors, at least relative to other Central American countries. There was no civil war, no ongoing political unrest, and as a stable democracy in an unstable region, the country had the strong backing of the US.

Elite and mass instability in Guatemala provide a direct contrast to the situation in Costa Rica. As noted above, several of the background factors are critical for understanding the political instability that has plagued modern Guatemala. Even though Guatemala had been the seat of Spanish colonial authority, the Guatemalan government just after independence was weak in size and in its ability to penetrate society. The church performed a number of social services, as well as educational services. The Liberals gained control in 1871 and followed a programme of capitalist modernization policies that succeeded in producing economic growth, but they also perpetuated land inequality and political exclusion (Ebel, 1990:502). The feudal structure of the *encomienda* system was the base for the handful of families that maintained oligopolistic control of the most important sectors of the economy (Vilas, 1995:74). After the collapse of the world economy in 1929, Jorge Ubico established a strong conservative dictatorship in 1931 that lasted until the 1944 revolution (Ebel, 1990:502; Woodward, 1985:299).

The revolution came to be known as the October Revolution, and began a period of ten years in which there was an effort to build broad class alliances for the first time (Granados, 1992:89). The regimes of Presidents Arevalo (1945–50) and then Arbenz (1951–4) attempted to implement a multiparty political plan that included efforts to reform land-holding patterns, organize and mobilize the peasants, public investment in infrastructure, and the creation of a market based on domestic consumption (Granados, 1992:92). During this time period, however, unity and stability among the elites were not highly developed. President Arevalo had to put down over 20 attempted coups against his government (Ebel, 1990:503).

Because of perceptions of leftist sympathies in the coalition, when Arbenz was elected as president in 1951, the US became worried about a possible communist take-over (Bulmer-Thomas, 1987:141). The 1952 Agrarian Reform Law had confiscated 26,000 acres of United Fruit Company (a US-based MNC) land, and in combination with a shipment of Czechoslovakian arms in May of 1954, this triggered US aid to a rebel army led by Col Carlos Castillo Armas (Ebel, 1990:503). The CIA arranged the emergence of Castillo Armas as leader of the new government in July 1954, and he quickly overturned the land reform and in general turned back the other reforms of the October Revolution (Bulmer-Thomas, 1987:141; Schlesinger and Kinzer, 1982).

Jonas (1989:134) argues that the rise of a revolutionary movement after 1954 could only be contained through a 'permanently institutionalized counter-insurgency campaign.' The political violence by both the left and right increased dramatically after 1954 (see Carmack, 1988). Among the elite, the dominant classes had trouble establishing stable government alliances because of competing economic interests, with export agriculture producers pitted against large industrialists. A failed military coup in the early 1960s by officers who were unhappy with the level of US intervention provided the impetus for an armed opposition movement to the regime (Granados, 1992:95).

Between the successful coups of March 1963 and March 1982, the army managed to consolidate and institutionalize itself as an authoritarian political force and eliminated electoral opportunities for any opposition, thus fuelling further mass insurgencies (Granados, 1992:95–6). But, consolidating its position did not mean the army was able to eliminate political conflict among the elite. Between 1954 and 1985 Guatemala had four new constitutions, six coups, six provisional presidents or chiefs of state and seven juntas (Granados, 1992:93). A new constitution in 1985 preserved the interests of the existing political structure, but even after the electoral process was opened slightly, there were failed coup attempts in May 1988 and July 1989 (Granados, 1992:106). Widespread corruption in the military led to the erosion of the Serrano regime, dissolving the alliances upon which it was built and sparking a political crisis in 1993 (Dunkerley, 1994:38–9).

The response by the masses to the military's rise to power and extreme repression included armed insurgencies and rebel movements. The economic and political marginalization of the Indians in Guatemala did not allow entry of the peasants into the political process, and the racial and cultural aspects of discrimination against the Indians added a dimension to the instability not seen as clearly in Costa Rica (Davis, 1988:33). Indians had made some gains during the October Revolution period under Arevalo and Arbenz. Forced labour officially ended in 1945, as did unpaid road work, civic duty and military service, although indebtedness was still a primary means of recruiting labour (Moors, 1988:70–1). The policies of the 1954 counter-revolution, however, banned all labour and peasant organizations and many of the moderate to leftist political activists were killed (Moors, 1988:71–2).

Between 1966 and 1974, the government implemented a peasant relocation programme to the El Petan region, and decisions on where they went were based primarily on the land speculation interests of the

bureaucrats (Vilas, 1995:87). The relocation programme had the poss-
ibly unintended effect of providing a way for the Catholic church to
organize community cooperatives that ran programmes such as health
centres, schools, housewives clubs and literacy workshops (Vilas,
1995:88). The cooperatives eventually came into conflict with government policies. Between 1976 and 1978, 168 leaders were murdered
and this fuelled further Indian participation in insurgency movements
(Vilas, 1995:88). The success of the long peace process that concluded
in a cease-fire in 1997 will no doubt depend on how well the country is
able to heal long-standing divisions that are supported by ethnic,
social, political and economic cleavages.

   In addition to inequitable land distribution and ethnic conflict, the
general economic situation has also contributed to mass political
instability. Income distribution was also highly unequal, and the economic growth of the post-World War II time period and the boom
years of the Central American Common Market (CACM) in the 1960s
concentrated wealth even further (Booth and Walker, 1993:105). The
growth also lead to the explosion of middle-and upper-sector interest
groups and each attempted to reserve for itself the right to petition,
strike or demonstrate on behalf of its members (Ebel, 1990:503). From
this brief survey, it is clear that both elite and mass political instability
since 1954 contributed negatively to Guatemalan bargaining leverage
with foreign investors. The elite seemed both unable and unwilling to
turn any economic gains toward broad-based domestic development
efforts and the political instability of the masses was continually met
with harsh repression.

Ideology and State Strength

The ability of the state to use FDI as a tool for domestic development
also depends on the ability and willingness of the state to implement
development policies and Costa Rica and Guatemala again present
very different contexts. The relative political stability in Costa Rica has
been accompanied by the rise of a strong state apparatus that is widely
seen as legitimate. One observer noted that 'The important aspects of
state strength were not in terms of armaments or bureaucratic effi-
ciency, ... Rather, the strength of the Costa Rican state that allowed it
to maintain substantial effectiveness was its widespread legitimacy
(Weaver, 1994:94). Relatively early in the post-World War II period
the state was strong enough to tax the key foreign banana companies
and this provided some financial strength for the state, independent of

the wealthy landowners (Weaver, 1994:94). In addition, the state was both able and willing to use those funds for national development projects (Kendrik, 1988:245). In Costa Rica, it seems that state strength and political stability have been mutually reinforcing through time.

The Costa Rican state has also developed a strong bureaucracy. The constitution written after the civil war created a number of autonomous agencies that were intended to institutionalize social reform and implement development policies, independent of the executive and legislative branches of government (Ameringer, 1982:42). Through time, the consequence has been a highly decentralized system of policy making and implementation that included 182 institutions by 1978 (Ameringer, 1982:42). The large number of these autonomous agencies has made it increasingly difficult to maintain central planning and budgetary control (Seligson, 1990:463). Even so, bureaucratic red tape takes up less time for investors in Costa Rica than the other countries of Central America (Willmore, 1992:95;98).

In Guatemala, the state *has* implemented some of its preferred policies, but only at the expense of many lives. Resorting to the use of force can be taken as an indication of a serious legitimacy problem for the state, and this decreases its capacity to implement other sets of policies (see Jackman, 1993). From the time of independence, the state in Guatemala was larger, more powerful and more authoritarian than that of Costa Rica, because it had to maintain order based on coerced labour (Weaver, 1994:95). Early in the 1900s, the government continued to make deals with the United Fruit Company that clearly favoured the company at the expense of the country. Even though the state was more centralized and more authoritarian than in Costa Rica, the personal interests of those in political power seemed to take precedence over broader development policies (Weaver, 1994:95–6). So, the state in Guatemala has been able to implement its preferred policies, but the priority has been to 'provide police protection to the propertied classes and to apply coercion to the majority of the population in order to guarantee a cheap and docile labour force.' (Jonas, 1989:133).

The ability of the Guatemalan state to carry out other functions appears to have deteriorated through time. Several governmental institutions created between 1944 and 1954, for instance the National Agrarian Department and the Agrarian National bank, were intended to implement agrarian reform. Other institutions were created to promote exports, and still others to carry out programmes for social welfare (Lenter, 1993:49). Many of the institutions were meant to establish connections with international institutions, and help provide stability to attract foreign investment (Lenter, 1993:49). In the late 1960s the implementation of government decisions became more difficult because of inter-institutional coordination problems and duplication of many functions (Lenter, 1993:49). The problems of inefficiency within the state apparatus were accentuated in the 1970s as more complex demands were made on the government. The government did not make clear plans of action, and it ignored or underestimated demands in education, health and welfare in the countryside, thus contributing to continued conflict (Lenter, 1993:49).

Given this review of political context conditions, it seems clear that Costa Rica had a stronger bargaining position relative to foreign investors than Guatemala. From a small and backward part of the Spanish empire, Costa Rica developed a political stability which was rare for the region, and the institutional power to form and implement social and economic reforms. Based on political context, we should expect Costa Rica to be improving in its abilities to draw in and use FDI for domestic development. The state demonstrated an ability and willingness to tax large MNCs, and to use the benefits of initial growth to build the base for a welfare state in which the middle-class and peasants had a perceived interest.

On the other hand, the political context for FDI in Guatemala was such that inflows tended to support the ruling elite, and exacerbate economic and political divisions within an already conflict-ridden society. Guatemala has experienced high levels of political violence in the post-World War II era, and its ability to carry out social and economic reforms has been severely constrained. The roots of these difficulties are found in the early post-independence period, and so it is unclear to this point in the analysis that FDI played a large role in determining political patterns of development. Guatemala's larger land and population resources made it more attractive to the Spanish colonialists and subsequently, perhaps, to foreign investors. Through time, however, the Guatemalan state was unable to turn the advantages into economic development because of the highly skewed pattern of economic, social and political privilege.

III. ECONOMIC CONTEXT

From before independence, the international economy has played a large part in economic growth for both Costa Rica and Guatemala. Spanish mercantilist policies dictated trade patterns for Central

America in the colonial period, then the British dominated trade during the first half of the 1800s (Woodward, 1985:128). From the start, foreign trade has been so important to the economies of these countries that it 'penetrates every aspect of economic life' (Weeks, 1985:59). This section will examine the economic growth and development in these two countries in order to determine whether modernization or dependency-type patterns exist, and how domestic and international factors may have contributed to those patterns.

Economic Growth

Early economic growth was dependent on export agriculture, particularly on coffee and bananas. Costa Rica began regular coffee exports in the 1840s and Guatemala and the other Central American countries followed. By 1889 coffee accounted for 96 per cent of the export earnings for Guatemala, and for 91 per cent of the export earnings for Costa Rica in 1890 (Bulmer-Thomas, 1987:2–3). By the 1920s Costa Rica was already the wealthiest country in the region in terms of GDP per capita because of its head start in developing the export sector (Bulmer-Thomas, 1987:10).

Table 4.3 presents the average annual per cent change of real GDP for Costa Rica and Guatemala from 1921 through to 1993, aggregated at ten year time periods except for the 1980s and early 1990s. In terms of average GDP growth rates, Guatemala grew at a higher rate than

Table 4.3 Economic Growth in Costa Rica and Guatemala, 1921–93
(average annual per cent change of real GDP)
(US$ millions, 1988=100)

	Costa Rica	*Guatemala*
1921–30	2.05	3.76
1931–40	3.43	7.53
1941–50	4.92	1.22
1951–60	7.28	3.83
1961–70	6.78	5.51
1971–80	5.72	5.57
1980–4	−0.02	−0.22
1985–90	4.0	2.37
1991–3	5.4	4.1

Source: Wilkie, 1993:1220 and 1227; Bulmer-Thomas (1987) for 1921–84; IMF data for 1985–90; UNCTAD (1994) for 1991–3.

Costa Rica from 1921 to 1940, and then Costa Rica consistently out-performed Guatemala. Both countries experienced economic crises in the first half of the 1980s.

During the 1960s and 1970s the growth of agricultural output was higher than the growth of population in both countries, and this growth spurt was accompanied by growth in the manufacturing sector in the 1960s (Weeks, 1985:63,65). Growth in manufacturing in the region as a whole was spurred by the creation of the CACM. The formation of the CACM was based on the premise that industrializa-tion had to be fostered at the regional level (Bulmer-Thomas, 1987:172). The formal institutions of the CACM were created in mid-1958 and 1959, but Costa Rica did not join until 1963 (Bulmer-Thomas, 1987:173). When it did join, Costa Rica's level of develop-ment and high output per worker allowed it to produce 'the fastest and the least variable rate of manufacturing growth on an annual basis from 1960–1979.' (Weeks, 1985:65)

Even though it increased growth in manufacturing, the CACM placed fiscal pressures on the member governments because of lost import duty revenues. Costa Rica chose to fill the gap with bank loans and Guatemala chose to cut government spending dramatically (Bul-mer-Thomas, 1987:180–1). Costa Rica borrowed heavily to continue government spending and that spending was positively correlated with economic growth in time series data (Ram, 1986). Table 4.4 compares central government expenditure as a per cent of GDP for the two countries and the difference is clear, even in 1970. The Costa Rican government was spending as much as one-fifth of GDP in 1980 and almost that amount in 1990. In contrast, Guatemala cut government spending from 1980 to 1990. These cuts in government spending were accompanied by much lower socio-economic development in Guate-mala, which will be discussed in more detail below.

Table 4.4   Central Government Expenditure in Costa Rica and Guatemala, 1970–90
(as a per cent of GDP)

	Costa Rica	Guatemala
1970	12.8	9.9
1980	20.8	14.2
1990	19.2	10.9

Source: Wilkie, 1993:1094.

External economic shocks coincided in the early 1980s to create an economic growth crisis in all the Central American countries. The openness of the economies had allowed them to benefit when the world market was expanding and the CACM was stimulating production, but in the 1970s the instability of the world market brought instability to these countries (Weeks, 1985:71). The external shocks included oil price increases, an abrupt increase in real interest rates and a recession among the OECD countries (Cardoso and Fishlow, 1992:202). In addition, Guatemala sustained setbacks caused by an earthquake in February of 1976 (Bulmer-Thomas, 1987:213). The external shocks contributed to a debt crisis in Costa Rica, and Guatemala continued to be unable to improve the already very low standard of living for many of its citizens.

Economic Development

To most analysts, economic development involves more than just aggregate growth rates; it includes some concern with a country's standard of living (Weeks, 1985:43). In the post-World War II period Costa Rica has been much better than Guatemala at raising the standard of living, even though aggregate indicators were quite similar early. Table 4.5 presents several telling indicators of development for both countries. Real GDP per capita in 1950 was marginally higher in Guatemala than in Costa Rica, but by 1960 Costa Rica had taken the lead on that indicator. The other indicators of development also demonstrate a consistent lead for Costa Rica. Costa Rica, with its much smaller population, was able to sustain aggregate growth per capita better than Guatemala for almost the entire post-World War II time period.

Other indicators of social development also show Costa Rica with a higher level of socioeconomic development than Guatemala. More Costa Rican workers have had social security coverage than Guatemalan workers, and Costa Rica has been better at providing coverage to the total population. In 1980 81.5 per cent of the total population was covered in Costa Rica, as compared to only 14.2 per cent in Guatemala (Wilkie *et al.*, 1993:201). Costa Rican social security laws were also passed earlier than those of Guatemala. Costa Rica passed laws covering work injuries in 1924, old age, invalidity and death in 1941, and sickness and maternity in 1941 (Wilkie *et al.*, 1993). In contrast, Guatemala's first law regarding social security coverage of old age, invalidity and death was passed in 1969, and the programme was only initiated in 1977 at national level (Wilkie *et al.*, 1993:203).

Table 4.5   Indicators of Economic Development in Costa Rica and
Guatemala (selected years)

		Costa Rica	*Guatemala*
Population (thousands)	1950	858	2 903
	1970	1 727	5 246
	1990	2 807	9 197
	1993	3 270	10 029
Growth rate of GDP per capita,			
(% per year)	1950–80	3.3	1.8
	1981–90	−0.7	−2.0
	1991–3	2.7	1.2
Real GDP per capita,			
(constant US$*)	1950	1 406	1 514
	1960	2 021	1 641
	1970	2 796	2 003
	1980	3 694	2 540
	1990	3 618	2 077
Total external debt,			
(% of GNP)	1980	59.5	14.9
	1990	69.9	37.5
	1994	47.8	23.4
Infant mortality rates			
(deaths per 1,000 live births)			
	1960	83.1	91.9
	1970	58.3	87.1
	1980	27.5	65.9
	1992**	14.0	62.0
Economically active population			
covered by social security			
(%)	1960	25.3	20.6
	1970	38.4	27.0
	1980	68.3	33.1
	1985–8	68.7	27.0

* Expressed in international prices, base = 1985.
** Infant mortality rates are estimates for 1992.
Sources: UNCTAD (1994); Cardoso and Fishlow (1992); Summers and
Heston (1991); Wilkie, et al (1993); World Bank, *World Development Report*
(various years).

The infant mortality rate (IMR) also presents a stark contrast,
although early in the time period the two countries were quite similar.
In 1960 Guatemala reported only nine more infant deaths per 1,000
live births than Costa Rica. By 1992 the IMR for both countries had

fallen, but the difference between 14 infant deaths per 1,000 live births in Costa Rica and 62 in Guatemala is quite large. Education showed similar differences. All of the Central American governments increased spending on education during the 1950s, but in Guatemala the resources went disproportionately to urban areas. Costa Rica was the only country in which the rural illiteracy rate was comparable to the urban rate, at about 60 per cent, in the early 1960s (Bulmer-Thomas, 1987:170–171).

The data on income inequality are notoriously unreliable, but some figures are discussed here for illustrative purposes. In Costa Rica, household income inequality seems to have improved slightly during the 1960s, from a Gini coefficient for distribution of household income of 0.52 in 1961, to 0.44 in 1971 (Gonzalez-Vega and Cespedes, 1993:45). During the 1970s, however, household income inequality seemed to increase slightly, with the share of the richest 60 per cent of households improving and the share of the poorest 40 per cent declining from 14.7 to 10.9 (*Ibid.*, p.49). In Guatemala, a different measure – income distribution to the economically active population – indicates that in 1971, the poorest 20 per cent of the Guatemalan population received an income share of 5.0 per cent, while the richest 5 per cent received 35 per cent (Weeks, 1985:47). These figures indicate that income inequality continues to be a problem for both of these countries, but perhaps Costa Rica is in a somewhat stronger position.

In addition to improved socio-economic indicators, economic development usually includes some notion of a diversified economy. Export diversification was actively pursued in both countries as a means of improving the productive capacity of their economies. Cotton, beef and sugar were the main export crops developed in an effort to diversify. The new products were controlled by nationals rather than foreign investors (Bulmer-Thomas, 1987:159), yet exports remained primarily agricultural. Costa Rica was not involved in the cotton boom, but in Guatemala, cotton production and exports increased dramatically (Williams, 1986). As the world price of cotton declined, the price of sugar increased, drawing former cotton fields into sugar production (Williams, 1986:67). In addition, a new International Sugar Agreement in 1953 offered the prospect of relatively stable sales and stimulated the industry. By the end of the 1950s Costa Rica had developed a significant surplus for export and Guatemala became a net exporter in the early 1960s (Bulmer-Thomas, 1987:159). But, the diversification strategy began running into trouble when the newer exports became subject to quotas in the developed countries (Bulmer-Thomas, 1987:186).

Domestically, the changes in the export sector of the economy contributed to growth in the number of landless peasants and increased land inequality in both Costa Rica and Guatemala (Bulmer-Thomas, 1987:163, 207; Weeks, 1985:17). Even so, Costa Rica was relatively more successful at alleviating poverty, especially in the rural areas. In 1988, 28 per cent of the rural households in Costa Rica were below the poverty line, as opposed to 75 per cent in Guatemala (Feres and Leon, 1990:143).

In short, the indicators of economic development all point toward a situation of stark contrast between these two countries. Even though Costa Rica has had an unequal land tenure pattern, it was able to turn early economic growth into improvement in terms of socio-economic indicators. Guatemala had a more unequal land distribution pattern and political instability that was compounded by economic and ethnic divisions. In this context, economic growth added to the power of the elite, but growth did not evolve into improved standards of living for most people.

According to theoretical explanations for FDI, foreign investors ought to be more attracted to Costa Rica than Guatemala, and this should give Costa Rica more room for bargaining over the benefits from investment projects. Thus, FDI could plausibly be expected to contribute to a virtuous cycle of growth in Costa Rica. On the other hand, FDI flows into Guatemala's mix of context conditions could contribute to the vicious cycle of economic and political instability.

The Domestic Capitalist Class and State Financial Autonomy

Several factors might provide developing states with financial autonomy relative to international economic actors and that yields the ability to bargain more effectively with foreign investors over the distribution of benefits from the investment. Financial autonomy for the state may come from a strong domestic capitalist class that is both willing and able to invest domestically. The state may also be able to reduce the need for foreign investment by being able to borrow on foreign capital markets and get aid from foreign states. Alternatively, the state may be able to construct and maintain state owned enterprises that form a counter-balance to foreign investors. These factors are discussed below, beginning with how the domestic capitalist class has or has not contributed to bargaining strength for these two countries.

In both Costa Rica and Guatemala the presence of a capitalist class has not been particularly in question, but the willingness to invest domestically has. Table 4.6 indicates that since 1975 at least, the private gross fixed investment as a percentage of GDP has been consistently higher in Costa Rica than in Guatemala. Domestic investment is quite clearly a very important determinant of economic growth (see Cardoso and Fishlow, 1992). Costa Rica has maintained higher investment levels than Guatemala and this may explain a large amount of the difference in outcomes between these two countries.

During the 1930s both governments pursued active policies to pull the countries out of the depression and that activity has been attributed to the presence of a national bourgeoisie tied to the countries' export interests (Bulmer-Thomas, 1987:83–4). Yet, the capitalist class, particularly in Guatemala, seems to have contributed more to capital outflow rather than inflow. Huge outflows of capital, both foreign and domestic, from Guatemala in 1949 and 1952 were almost certainly due to the uncertain political environment that accompanied the army revolt and then the land reform measures (Bulmer-Thomas, 1987:129).

Both Costa Rica and Guatemala experienced capital flight in the 1970s. Capital flight was not restricted by any of the central American countries and it was unclear that domestic capitalists were investing at home anymore than foreign capital reinvested earnings there (Weeks, 1985:95 189). Foreign loans tended to end up enriching individuals in governments, so many of the dollars loaned to central American governments during the 1970s were often redeposited in private foreign accounts (Weaver, 1994:188). On the whole, the high level of political instability in the region seemed unlikely to make

Table 4.6 Private Gross Fixed Investment as a Percentage of GDP in Costa Rica and Guatemala 1975–89

	1975	*1980*	*1985*	*1989*
Costa Rica	14.9	15.4	11.7	16.1
Guatemala	12.5	9.9	7.5	7.1

Source: Pelupessy and Weeks, 1993, p.214, table 1.4; 1989 figures were preliminary.

high numbers of investors, domestic or foreign, willing to venture their capital, regardless of government policies (Weeks, 1985:199).

Commercial loans and foreign economic assistance are two other alternatives states may have for funding development efforts independent of foreign investors. Costa Rica has been more willing to rely on foreign debt to fund development, but this strategy contributed to a debt crisis. As indicated earlier, Costa Rica was heavily indebted to foreigners by the early 1980s (see Table 4.5), while Guatemala remained relatively and absolutely unburdened by foreign debt until the mid-1980s (Weeks, 1985:179).

The debt situation demonstrates an important difference in the willingness and ability of these governments to use alternative sources of development funds in order to reduce their vulnerability to demands made by foreign investors. Costa Rica was both willing and able to fund development with foreign loans, but paradoxically that policy may have made it increasingly difficult to attract new foreign investment. The relatively higher level of development in Costa Rica made production costs much higher. A comparison of labour, energy and water costs for early 1992 in the manufacturing sector as a whole revealed that the minimum monthly wage for Costa Rica was more than twice that of Guatemala – the lowest of the five central American countries (Willmore, 1992:105).

The United States government proved to be another source of funds for both Guatemala and Costa Rica. Both countries, because of their strategic position in Central America and their strong stance against communism, were able to encourage flows of development assistance from the US, although Guatemala was able to obtain more in absolute terms. The deflated (1970=100) total of authorized US economic and military assistance to Guatemala for the 1946–89 time period was US$ 826.5 million, while for Costa Rica it was US$ 746.3 millions, with much of that being provided between 1975 and 1989 (Anders, cited in Wilkie, 1993:538–40). The aid to Guatemala did not lead to large increases in the level of development, probably because Guatemala was so involved in fighting insurgencies.

State-Owned Enterprises

Some developing countries have attempted to increase domestic investment by involving the state as the key entrepreneur in state-owned enterprises. In this way they may potentially form a strong domestic counter-balance to foreign investors. But, the enterprises can also create other difficulties in terms of increased debt and increased opportunities for corruption and rent-seeking. Guatemala has had very few public enterprises, probably because of historically low levels of taxation (Dunkerley, 1994:15). So, state-owned enterprises have not played a large role in the bargaining leverage in Guatemala, but the situation in Costa Rica has been quite different.

In Costa Rica, the state was accustomed to intervening in the economy as required by the model of social democracy, and this meant promoting productive activity through 'expansion of infrastructure, access to credit, and protectionist subsidies' (Gonzalez-Vega and Cespedes, 1993:118). During the 1970s the state became more involved in productive enterprises that competed with the private sector (Gonzalez-Vega and Cespedes, 1993:118). The *Coporacion Costarricense de Desarrollo SA* (CODESA) was established in 1972 by Figueres as an autonomous agency for the development of mixed enterprises, in which the state would contribute two-thirds of the investment and the private sector one-third (Dunkerley, 1993:621). In this way, CODESA served as a source of finance and provided a means of overcoming the limits of local capital accumulation (Dunkerley, 1993:622).

CODESA began to grow rapidly in 1975, with many subsidiaries engaged in activities as diverse as railroads, fertilizer, cement, aluminium smelting, sugar, cotton, agribusiness, forestry, ferries, maritime and urban transport, and drawback export firms (Gonzalez-Vega and Cespedes, 1993:118). But, CODESA's productive activities have not been profitable, evidenced by the estimation that the losses were always more than 25 per cent of sales. None of the 12 principal subsidiaries made a profit in any year during the 1976–83 time period, and all had losses every year (Gonzalez-Vega and Cespedes, 1993:118). CODESA and its subsidiaries came to be a drain on the domestic economy because the unrestricted access to Central Bank credit was used to pay for operational expenses, as well as to service the huge external debt that had been acquired in connection with the creation of the corporations largest subsidiaries. All had the effect of crowding out credit for the private sector and contributed to deterioration of public sector finances (Gonzalez-Vega and Cespedes, 1993:119).

The state-owned enterprises did allow for an immense growth in expenditures and capital formation, but CODESA used foreign financing extensively for its subsidiaries, and this also contributed to the foreign debt crisis of the early 1980s (Lenter, 1993:47). The Central Bank stopped all credit to CODESA and its subsidiaries as part of a

1982 IMF agreement, and the government also promised the IMF it would sell some of CODESA's enterprises (Lenter, 1993:47). In March of 1985, the US Agency for International Development (AID) gave Costa Rica $140 million to pay the corporation's debt in order to make the subsidiaries more attractive for privatization (Gonzalez-Vega and Cespedes, 1993:120). In addition to debt, another barrier to privatization is that the state corporations have strong legal status and political influence (Dunkerley, 1994:15). Although Costa Rica's state-owned enterprises seemed to have contributed to domestic investment, they did so at the cost of contributing to a foreign debt crisis that has perhaps decreased Costa Rica's bargaining leverage with foreign investors.

In sum, the economic bargaining context for FDI has varied in these two countries, both through time and within countries. Both countries exhibited at least moderate aggregate economic growth rates until the crisis of the early 1980s. Guatemala has been unable to use initial FDI and economic growth as a tool for providing domestic development, and this is largely because of the political instability described above. Costa Rica has been able to use the initial growth to contribute to economic development, but the development came at the expense of an external debt crisis, and has made production costs higher in Costa Rica than anywhere else in Central America. The next section of the Chapter explores the FDI patterns in the two countries in an effort to establish whether differences in FDI experiences produced the differences in outcomes described here, and whether a sequence among the key variables – FDI, economic growth, development, political stability – can be established.

IV.   EXPERIENCES WITH FOREIGN DIRECT INVESTMENT

Foreign capital penetration came early to Central America, although in the early post-independence years it took the form of mostly British bond issues and loans rather than direct foreign control. The nineteenth century history of foreign loans and bonds was one of default by Central American countries and fraud by bond issuers (Rippy, 1959). Yet, by 1913 the par value of holdings was £2 million sterling for Costa Rica, and more than £1.4 Sterling in Guatemala (Rippy, 1959:106). German capital investments in Central America were also quite large early, with one estimation placing the value at over 1000 million marks in 1898 (Mikesell, 1962:23).

Foreign bondholders frequently pressed for control over part of the revenues from Central American countries in order to guarantee payment (Bulmer-Thomas, 1987:284–5). Guatemala 'committed coffee export tax under a 1929 debt agreement to provide service payments on a new bond issue' and Costa Rica had foreign bondholders secure a first lien in 1926 and 1927 on both customs and railway revenues for debt service payments (Bulmer-Thomas, 1987:285). By the 1930s all of the Central American republics, except Honduras, had defaulted on their external obligations, which effectively crippled the immediate influence of the creditors (Bulmer-Thomas, 1987).

Direct foreign control entered Central America in banana production, which was dominated by large North American firms (Weeks, 1985:15). Banana production required large amounts of land, and, except in Costa Rica, initially developed in the unpopulated Caribbean. This meant that the MNCs were necessarily involved in infrastructure development. In Guatemala, the United Fruit Company owned the railway to the Caribbean, and in Honduras and Costa Rica it controlled the major rail lines through long-term leasing contracts (Weeks, 1985:16). There were few regulatory laws and they were generally written by the companies themselves. If deemed necessary, the companies simply ignored the law, for instance in labour disputes (Weeks, 1985).

By the early twentieth century, foreign companies, especially from the US, dominated railway transportation, public utilities, banking, and mining and agriculture (Bulmer-Thomas, 1987). Table 4.7 summarizes early US direct investment in Costa Rica and Guatemala. In the first half of the twentieth century, Guatemala attracted more US investment and the book value was consistently higher than for Costa Rica. The larger domestic market in Guatemala, and the larger pool of (sometimes forced) labour were apparently strong drawing factors for FDI in the early twentieth century.

Despite early foreign penetration in the economy, the coffee industry in Costa Rica remained largely under national control (Bulmer-Thomas, 1987:15). However, in Guatemala, German nationals and immigrants came to dominate the coffee industry as a result of the Liberal immigration policies after 1871 (Trudeau, 1993:19). Later, when beef became an important export product, US multinationals came to dominate the meat packing plants, but by the 1980s the usual pattern of investment included a joint venture with local partners (Williams, 1986:104).

Table 4.7   US Direct Investment in Costa Rica and Guatemala, 1897–1955
(cumulative US$ millions, book value)

	Costa Rica	Guatemala
1897	3.5	6
1914	21.6	35.8
1924	13.5	47
1929	22	70
1936	13.5	50
1943	30	87
1950	60	106
1955	61	103

Sources: Ramsaran, 1985 p.72–4 for 1897–1943; Wilkie, 1992, p.11331–2 for 1950–5.

Despite the heavy dominance of US-based MNCs in the fruit sector, a study of 187 US-based MNCs which reportedly accounted for over 80 per cent of all US direct investments abroad indicates that there was little interest in the manufacturing sector until economic integration in Central America was well underway (Willmore, 1976:500). Despite efforts of local industrialists and intellectuals, there were 'virtually no restrictions on foreign investments in manufacturing in any of the five countries' (Willmore, 1976:503). Even though the governmental apparatus was growing in Guatemala in the 1970s, no agency had the specific task of monitoring foreign investment (Lenter, 1993:50).

Since the CACM was unable to establish concrete restrictions on FDI, the member countries ended up competing against one another for attracting FDI with liberal fiscal incentives (Willmore, 1976). By 1957 the large companies had only 24 manufacturing subsidiaries within the CACM, but in the next ten years 96 additional subsidiaries were formed; 45 in Guatemala, and 27 in Costa Rica (Willmore, 1976:500). Again, Guatemala's market size and lower production costs seem to have been important drawing factors for FDI, even following the political instability of the 1944–54 decade. Guatemala had the largest net direct investment flows of any of the CACM countries in the 1960–78 time period (Weeks, 1985:92).

The differences between the policies toward FDI in the two countries are slight and both countries continue to be willing to receive it. Guatemala makes no distinction at all between foreign and domestic investment, while Costa Rica encourages foreign investment by providing preferential access to foreign exchange at the official foreign exchange rate (Willmore, 1992:95). Although there are no restrictions on foreign investment, the time lag in setting up production facilities was longer in Guatemala than Costa Rica. But, the Guatemalan Congress passed a law creating a 'single window' for investment that is meant to streamline the process of setting up production facilities (Willmore, 1992:98).

FDI flows to Latin America declined as a whole in the 1980s as FDI among the developed nations and to the Southeast Asian NICs increased, but the level of flows to Costa Rica and Guatemala increased between 1981 and 1990 (see Fuentes and Alberto, 1992:62–3). Table 4.8 presents the net FDI flows to both Costa Rica and Guatemala from 1960 through 1990 in dollar figures, as well as FDI as a per cent of GDP. Flows to Guatemala were marginally higher during the CACM period, but show marked increases after 1976 and hit a peak in 1988. The FDI flows to Costa Rica increased through the 1970s as well and again after the semi-resolution of the debt crisis in the early 1980s.

Costa Rica attracted a more steady flow of FDI than Guatemala, although the amount of FDI has been fairly similar in the two countries through this time period. The direct comparison of FDI flows seems to present justification for the dependency arguments. Guatemala received larger net FDI flows, and it was the country in the pair that experienced a vicious cycle of underdevelopment and political instability. But, this interpretation does not account for the fact that FDI flows to Costa Rica have been higher as a percentage of GDP for much of the time period. When considering stocks and flows of FDI, both of these countries have been heavily penetrated by foreign investment and for a long period of time. Since the differences in terms of economic and political outcome patterns are so great, it seems unlikely that FDI is the key factor in determining political and economic development.

This is not to say that FDI has been completely unimportant in these two countries. For instance, it may be that foreign investment and influence enabled the Guatemalan elite to continue their oppression, thus contributing to a negative cycle without necessarily producing it. The same effect was not seen in Costa Rica because the land inequalities were not so strong at the outset. In addition, the Costa Rican state was both willing and able to tax foreign firms relatively early on in this time period, and this helped contribute to further financial autonomy of the state.

Table 4.8   Net Foreign Direct Investment Flows to Costa Rica and
Guatemala, 1960–90

	Costa Rica FDI flows, US$ millions	FDI/GDP (%)	Guatemala FDI flows US$ millions	FDI/GDP (%)
1960	1.60	0.31	16.80	1.61
1961	7.00	1.42	7.60	0.71
1962	11.90	2.47	9.30	0.81
1963	14.20	2.76	0.50	0.81
1964	7.90	1.45	6.10	0.47
1965	0.10	0.02	14.10	1.06
1966	14.60	2.26	14.50	1.04
1967	15.70	2.24	24.10	1.66
1968	4.50	0.58	29.20	1.81
1969	22.70	2.66	30.20	1.76
1970	26.40	2.68	29.40	1.54
1971	22.10	2.05	28.60	1.44
1972	25.80	2.08	15.90	0.76
1973	37.70	2.47	34.80	1.35
1974	46.30	2.78	47.40	1.50
1975	69.00	3.52	80.00	2.19
1976	60.70	2.52	12.50	0.29
1977	62.50	2.03	97.50	1.78
1978	47.00	1.33	127.20	2.10
1979	42.40	1.05	117.00	1.69
1980	48.10	1.00	110.70	1.41
1981	66.20	2.52	127.20	2.10
1982	26.52	1.02	77.10	0.88
1983	55.30	1.76	45.00	0.50
1984	52.00	1.42	38.00	0.40
1985	65.20	1.66	61.80	0.64
1986	57.40	1.30	68.80	0.95
1987	75.80	1.67	0.91	1.28
1988	121.40	2.63	329.70	4.20
1989	95.20	1.82	76.20	0.91
1990	108.70	1.91	84.60	1.12

Source: IMF *International Financial Statistics* (various years).

V.   CONCLUSIONS

The comparison of Costa Rica and Guatemala indicates that FDI can
contribute to development patterns, but it is not the primary causal
factor. For both of these countries, the background factors seemed to

play the key role in determining both political and economic outcome patterns. The two countries present a strong contrast with respect to their early political configurations, as well as the economic bases of support for the ruling elite. In both cases, foreign economic penetration may be seen as one method used by the elite to support state policies. The key differences in those policies did not generally involve barring or encouraging FDI; both countries encouraged FDI flows. Rather, the most important differences were found in early ethnic composition and land tenure patterns, political instability that resulted from those patterns, and the ability and will-ingness of the state to devise and implement economic development strategies.

In particular, political stability in Costa Rica was both cause and consequence of state policies to invest in human capital efforts such as education and welfare programmes. These efforts improved the level of economic development, and thus contributed to new flows of for-eign investment. FDI in this relatively strong bargaining context per-haps helped strengthen this virtuous cycle of development, but domestic investment and the level of human capital development were probably more important factors in determining economic growth outcomes.

In Guatemala, the ethnic complexity, the economic system based on forced labour and the lack of political openness, all seemed to con-tribute to political instability that constrained the policy options of later governments. The state, although strong in a military repression sense, was unwilling to force foreign investors to pay for development efforts within the country. The ruling elite was unwilling to undertake meaningful land reform that might have spread around the benefits of economic growth. FDI in this host-country context contributed to a vicious cycle of political and economic instability, but the context conditions were more important causal factors in determining patterns of development outcomes.

One conclusion of this comparison is that the host-country political and economic contexts contribute at least as much to aggregate out-comes as does FDI. This conclusion does not mean that we should give up on investigating the role of FDI, or other forms of external capital flows, in development for the relatively poor countries in the global economy. Rather, it forces a redirection from FDI as a critical variable to FDI as one important variable in a set of variables. Several research questions follow from this analysis. First, the bargaining approach points to very broad groups of important factors, but has not yet developed a generalizable set of variables. Perhaps 'generalizable' sets of variables are not possible, given the nature of development problems in specific countries, but that is an empirical question that should be addressed.

Further, the relative importance of context factors is unclear. That is, are political factors more important than economic, or vice-versa? Or, and this seems more likely, can economic and political factors complement one another in complex patterns? This is a particularly important question for policymakers in developing countries because the answer should point out where they should focus their efforts at economic development. This line of research would necessarily draw on and contribute to the already large literature on the relationship between political structure and economic growth and development. Although FDI is not the critical variable it was once thought to be, its relationship to the domestic variables is not well spelled out and deserves further attention.

The comparison of context conditions for these countries also reveals a certain amount of feedback, or reciprocal causality, among the political and economic context conditions and FDI. In Costa Rica, while growth rates and economic development were maintained, they contributed to the sense of political stability and this drew in relatively stable amounts of FDI. In turn, relatively strong economic factors helped contribute to continuing political stability. Although FDI flows continued to be drawn to Guatemala even when political instability was high, they were not as high a percentage of GDP as in Costa Rica. Political instability and the failure to improve the standard of living for most people went together in a negative pattern of dependency-type outcomes.

The presence of these apparent cycles also provides some leverage on the question of what sequence of political and economic variables is associated with which pattern of development outcomes. One conclusion is that the sequence differs in these two countries, and this may contribute strongly to the different patterns of development outcomes. In Costa Rica, strength on the political context conditions seemed to precede economic growth and then those two factors interacted to produce economic development. Foreign economic penetration was present from independence, but seemed to contribute to a pattern of development already established by the political system. For Costa Rica, state strength, political stability and economic growth preceded economic development and FDI was a relatively constant factor through the sequence.

On the other hand, in Guatemala the highly unequal economic context preceded, or at least went hand-in-hand with political instability. Recurring insurgencies slowed economic growth further and prevented serious political change until the mid-1990s. FDI in this context seemed to shore up the ruling elite, and so can be seen to accompany economic disintegration and political instability. The inability of the state to resolve the political conflicts combined with slower economic growth to produce lower levels of economic development. The causality analysis in the next chapter provides some leverage on questions concerning the temporal patterns among FDI, economic growth, development and political instability in these countries.

5   The Question of Causality: Vector Autoregression Analysis

The preceding chapters have focussed on how the context conditions that shape the bargaining power of six specific host countries have been both the causes and consequences of FDI. In this chapter, Granger causality analysis is employed to further specify the relationships among FDI, economic growth and development, and political stability. One purpose is to explore the possibility that FDI is not strongly exogenous as assumed by the dominant theoretical perspectives on development. Granger causality analysis is an inductive method for determining whether predictions of the dependent variable made using its own past history can be improved by incorporating the past history of the independent variable (Freeman, 1983:327–8). The comparative case studies in earlier chapters raised several questions that Granger causality analysis might help to answer.

First, the comparisons of domestic context conditions in six host countries indicated that one key question involves whether FDI is actually an important factor in determining aggregate economic and political outcomes. Although both the modernization and dependency perspectives on development offer FDI as a key causal variable, the case studies suggest that differences in aggregate outcomes may be better explained by domestic context factors than by FDI. Further, the case studies provide evidence that supports earlier empirical findings that many of those same host-country context conditions help determine FDI flows. This result suggests that FDI may be endogenous rather than exogenous to the development process. Granger causality analysis can help understand the nature of the temporal patterns involving FDI and allow us to determine whether FDI is correctly specified as exogenous in the predominant theoretical perspectives on its outcomes.

The second question directly follows the first and involves the possibility that a temporal pattern exists such that feedback cycles – either virtuous or vicious – can be found among political stability, FDI, economic growth and development. For instance, in Thailand, Côte d'Ivoire and Costa Rica, political stability seemed to precede economic growth, which then led to economic development. In the latter two cases, large flows of FDI penetrated the country very early, while in Thailand the state was more established when FDI flows increased. Early success with FDI and economic growth then seemed to draw in further FDI flows. Granger causality analysis can help establish temporal precedence in order to determine whether such cycles exist in the data, and thus how best to understand the patterns involving these aggregate outcomes. An additional question involves whether we can find some empirical foundation for how long FDI might take to make its effects felt in the host economy.

Finally, the argument presented in earlier chapters attempts to resolve the conflicts among the dominant theoretical perspectives on development by pointing out that each may be correct under certain host-country context conditions. Granger causality analysis offers only an indirect way of testing this argument. The direct means of testing the bargaining power approach would be to construct a bargaining power score for each country, and for its major investors, and then determine whether those scores Granger cause aggregate outcomes consistent with the expectations of the theories. Problems with obtaining adequate data make it very difficult to devise and use country-specific bargaining power scores at this time. In addition, a thorough analysis would require constructing a bargaining power score for the major investors and this task is beyond the scope of this study. These limitations led to the indirect approach of comparing the Granger causality patterns found in the data from countries with different positions on the context conditions. Although the language of the bargaining approach is used, the analysis is an examination of the possible macro-level outcomes of FDI, rather than of specific behaviours and bargaining power within a particular negotiation process.

Granger causality analysis does not offer complete answers to all of the questions raised by the country comparisons, but it has some specific strengths for this type of study. The method of analysis is inductive and simply explores the data for a certain type of empirical pattern in an attempt to generate some 'stylized facts' (see Cooley and LeRoy, 1985). Earlier chapters used an inductive approach to understanding how context conditions shaped the outcomes of FDI, so Granger causality analysis is consistent with the country comparisons. Moreover, it has other strengths that make it useful in this situation (see Freeman *et al.*, 1989:329). First, the number and range of plausible relationships between FDI, economic growth, development, and political instability makes specifying endogenous and exogenous variables difficult. If a variable is improperly specified as exogenous and it is not, then structural equation parameter estimates would be inconsistent. Second, Granger causality analysis provides us with a qualitative understanding of the causal patterns among these variables. Since very often explanations for growth, development and political stability seem to be tautological, Granger causality analysis can help describe the possible temporal patterns among the variables.

I. THEORETICAL DISCUSSION AND RESEARCH PROPOSITIONS

The theoretical argument developed in this book is that the consequences of FDI are shaped in large part by the domestic political and economic context within the developing host country. A strong host-country bargaining position relative to foreign investors both attracts FDI, and makes it more likely to be a contributing factor to economic growth and development, along with continued political stability. In contrast, a host country with a weak bargaining position relative to foreign investors will have more difficulty attracting investment, and in turning the investment flows that do arrive into economic growth and long-term development. In this theoretical framework, the direct impact of FDI on host country political and economic outcomes is expected to be mitigated by domestic context conditions.

This approach to understanding the consequences of FDI differs from the other major perspectives in that it explicitly points to the potential for FDI to be dependent on the putative outcome variables. The conventional wisdom of both the modernization and dependency perspectives is that FDI is an important causal factor in the political and economic development, or underdevelopment, of poor countries. The causal mechanisms in which FDI is presumed to play a part are reviewed very briefly here in comparison in order to set the stage for the propositions being tested using Granger analysis.

In the modernization perspective, FDI contributes to high aggregate economic growth, which then trickles-down into long-run economic development through rising wages in the modern sector of the economy. Economic development is then expected to produce further growth. The time period involved in the 'long-run' is not specified, nor is the length of time it might take for the FDI-growth-development cycle to become apparent. The virtuous cycle may be broken by political instability associated with social mobilization that results from economic development. The relationship between economic growth and political instability is not always clearly specified in the literature, but several alternative mechanisms are possible. Income inequalities arising from rapid economic growth may lead to social tensions, which in turn lead to political unrest (Olson, 1963). Another mechanism may be that growth and development lead to rapid urbanization, which then increases the likelihood of political unrest (Rondinelli, 1980). Yet another possible causal link involves regional disparities that exacerbate ethnic tensions and thus drive political unrest (Cohen, 1974). In any case, the modernization perspective assumes that for strong growth to occur, economic policies must be implemented in a fairly stable political environment.

The statist variation on theoretical explanations for development generates expectations which are generally consistent with those listed above, but with some important caveats (Cummings, 1984; Haggard, 1986). The key assumptions from the statist perspective are that development is generated by a strong, relatively autonomous state which is able to formulate and implement clear development strategies. A further assumption is that the state is oriented by a capitalist development ideology. State intervention in the economy is a means of jump-starting the growth and development cycle. The statist variation also expects the strong state to control any political conflict that might be associated with rapid economic growth and socioeconomic development.

In the dependency perspective, FDI is expected to have long-term negative consequences for political stability, as well as for economic growth and development. Some short-term growth may occur as a result of FDI, but again the time period is unspecified. Long-term growth and sustained development will be precluded by the strong interests of the foreign investors who manage, because of their economic power, to control the local elite and coopt them into supporting policies more consistent with global and/or corporate goals. Political instability may result from FDI because it can produce resentment against foreign investors and their domestic allies. It may also arise in response to the uneven economic growth caused when FDI concentrates capital in the hands of a small, foreign oriented elite. When political instability occurs, it is expected to reinforce slow growth and underdevelopment, and thus help create a vicious cycle of dependency.

We are now in a position to compare the theoretical expectations with the qualitative findings from the earlier chapters in order to develop some research propositions to be tested using Granger causality analysis. The country studies carried out using the bargaining framework indicate that FDI may not be as important as previously thought for determining aggregate outcomes. In Thailand, mass political stability, a moderately strong state and a domestic capitalist class, willing and able to contribute to domestic development, all seemed at least as important as FDI in producing economic growth and development. In contrast, in the Philippines, political instability, the lack of a capitalist class willing and able to contribute to development, and a state that was largely unable to implement development policies seemed to initiate a dependency-type pattern of outcomes. FDI may have enabled the ruling elite to consolidate and maintain power, but it did not seem to be the primary causal factor in underdevelopment.

Similar results were found in the comparison between Ghana and Côte d'Ivoire. In Ghana, the weaker host-country for much of the time period, a cycle of dependency seemed to engulf the country in continued political instability, lower growth rates, and poor performance on socioeconomic indicators. The role played by FDI in this cycle was unclear, just as it was in the more virtuous cycle seen in the aggregate outcomes in Côte d'Ivoire. The comparison between Costa Rica and Guatemala also yielded similar conclusions. FDI in the stronger host country seemed to be associated with modernization results and FDI in the country with weaker context conditions seemed to be associated with dependency-type outcomes. In all of the cases, FDI could be perceived to be correlated with outcomes, but it seemed just as likely that FDI was the result of earlier development patterns. Thus, the first proposition to be tested in this chapter is that FDI is caused by aggregate economic growth, development and political stability. This simple proposition can be tested using the Granger causality methodology which is described in more detail below.

The second proposition is that a feedback cycle exists among the variables and FDI forms one link in the cycle. The stronger countries in the paired comparisons, Thailand, Côte d'Ivoire and Costa Rica, seemed to exhibit a pattern in which political stability, development and growth caused FDI, which then contributed to further growth. The cycle continued when growth was turned into further development and so on. The weaker countries, the Philippines, Ghana, and Guatemala, seemed to have concurrent political and economic difficulties that precluded strong growth. When growth did occur, as in

Guatemala, it was not turned into strong and lasting socioeconomic development. The resulting tautological conclusion, that strong countries do better because they are strong and weak countries are worse off because they are weak, can be better understood if we are able to find a clear temporal cycle among the variables. In the cycles described above, both positive and negative, political (in)stability precedes (low) economic growth, which precedes (under)development.

The expectation for causal patterns is that political stability will cause economic growth and development, and all three of these variables will cause FDI flows. FDI would then help determine the aggregate political and economic outcome variables. One implication of this proposition is that the domestic context conditions are as important as FDI in determining other outcome variables. Because of its explicit emphasis on temporal precedence as the criterion for causality, Granger analysis can help understand which of these variables precedes the others and thus help break open the tautology.

One of the arguments made in this book is that the outcomes of FDI depend on how host-country context conditions interact with flows of FDI. Thus, FDI will have different patterns of consequences, modernization or dependency-type, in stronger or weaker host-country contexts. In principle, both types of cycle should be apparent in Granger analysis, but the direction of impact would differ. Because of the problems with inferring direction of a relationship from Granger causality analysis, this argument cannot be tested directly using the Granger technique. However, we can compare the results from the six different countries in order to see if different patterns among the variables are found in stronger or weaker bargaining contexts. This allows us to use the Granger causality results to help build our qualitative understanding of how FDI does or does not contribute to aggregate political and economic outcomes.

II. METHODOLOGY AND DATA

Granger causality analysis provides a fairly simple means of examining the causal patterns between FDI and aggregate outcomes. In technical terms, Granger causality is 'the idea that a variable X "causes" another variable Y, if by incorporating the past history of X one can improve a prediction of Y over a prediction based solely on the history of Y alone'. (Freeman, 1983:327–8) One-way causality exists if X Granger causes Y only, or if Y Granger causes X only. Simultaneous causation occurs when X Granger causes Y, and Y Granger causes X, and in this case the variables are said to be Granger interdependent. If the past history of X does not improve the prediction of Y, and vice versa, no Granger causality exists and the variables are said to be Granger independent. Thus, Granger causality is one way of testing for exogeneity; a non-Granger relationship is necessary, but not sufficient, for exogeneity (see Sims, 1972).

The statistical technique employed in this chapter is a modification of the direct Granger approach which involves ordinary least squares estimation of the following equations (Freeman and Duvall, 1984:384):

$$X_t = \sum_{i=1}^{\infty} \alpha_i X_{t-i} + \sum_{i=1}^{\infty} \beta_i Y_{t-i} + e_t \tag{1}$$

$$Y_t = \sum_{i=1}^{\infty} \theta_i Y_{t-i} + \sum_{i=1}^{\infty} \phi_i X_{t-i} + u_t \tag{2}$$

For a given number of lags on X and Y, F-tests are used to determine whether the β_is are jointly zero, and whether the ϕ_is are jointly zero (Freeman and Duvall, 1984:384). If both null hypotheses are accepted, then X and Y are Granger independent of one another. If the β_i parameters are found to be significantly different from zero, then Y Granger causes X. If the ϕ_i parameters are significantly different from zero, then X is said to Granger cause Y. If both the β_i and ϕ_i parameters are significantly different from zero, a simultaneous causality relationship exists between X and Y.

Two key assumptions of the direct Granger method are that the time series are stationary, and that the series are jointly covariance stationary (Freeman, 1983:330; Pierce and Haugh, 1977:288). If serial correlation is present, least squares estimates will be consistent, but bias occurs in the estimates of their variances (Pierce and Haugh, 1977:279). Standard Granger techniques use either a logarithmic transformation of the data, or use the first difference of a data series in order to achieve stationarity (Pierce and Haugh, 1977:290). All of the data series used in this analysis are first-differenced, with the exception of the economic growth rates. As expected with a growth rate, the Box-Ljung Q scores for the economic growth series indicate that they are stationary, so they are not differenced. Using the first difference for the data series here means that we must interpret the results in terms of change in the variables rather than their levels.

Omission of significant lags can be a cause of serial correlation (Pierce and Haugh, 1977:288), but the propositions examined in this chapter have no strong theoretical means of specifying how many lags ought to be significant. Determining the lag structure empirically is also very difficult because the relatively short time series available for these countries do not leave many degrees of freedom, once lags have been included for both the dependent and independent variables. Given the data limitations, the results presented in the following section provide a qualitative picture of the causal links in the data by testing for Granger causality including up to four lags of the variables. Four years seems short to be considered 'long-term' but the data simply will not support more lag experimentation. Given all the lagged variables included in a Granger causality regression, multi-collinearity could be a statistical problem making individual parameter coefficients insignificant. The usefulness of the technique, however, is that the F-test still reveals the joint significance of a group of variables (Freeman, 1983:346).

The propositions addressed here are tested using multivariate analysis to control for the expected presence of multiple causal links. The direct Granger method assumes that all relevant information is contained in the past histories of the variables in question (Pierce and Haugh, 1977:291). Missing variables present a problem in interpreting the findings of Granger causality, because the observed relationships might change when additional variables are included in the analysis (Freeman, 1983:336; Hoole and Huang, 1989:147). Yet, it is impossible to include all of the known determinants of economic growth, for instance, in this type of analysis. For this reason, the results here should only be used for heuristic purposes or to generate hypotheses that are testable using structural equation models.

As noted above, another difficulty with the Granger causality approach is that it is not easy to determine the direction, positive or negative, of causal impact. The F-tests merely indicate whether adding the past values of a variable significantly improves prediction of the dependent variable. Yet, for distinguishing between modernization and dependency outcomes we generally need to know whether the causal effect is positive or negative. Granger causality analysis does not yield that information, but if there is no Granger causality then the direction of impact is not relevant. For addressing the propositions developed above, the sign (positive or negative) of the relationship is less important than whether there is a relationship, and which variables temporally precede the others.

The indicators included in the models below were collected on an annual basis for all six countries, but the time span for the Granger causality analysis varies depending on the country. For the Philippines, Thailand, Costa Rica and Guatemala, the time frame is from 1960 to 1992, with the exception of infant mortality rates which go only through to 1990. The data for Ghana cover from 1960 to 1992, except the infant mortality rate which is collected for 1968 through to 1990. The available data series were shorter for Côte d'Ivoire, starting only in 1963 and ending in 1990. As with the other countries, when infant mortality rate is included in the regressions the time frame is even shorter, including only 1968 through to 1990. Again, note that except for growth rates, the data series have been first-differenced in order to achieve stationarity.

Several options exist for measuring FDI; one measure is simply the net flows of FDI per year into each host country. Another more complex measure is an indicator of corporate penetration used by Bornschier and Chase-Dunn (1985). This is a measure of the total capital stock in a country that is controlled by MNCs, and includes controls for the levels of host-country factors of production. Measuring FDI stock is more difficult than flows and frequently FDI flows are simply added over a period of time to approximate the current stock levels. It is also extremely difficult to get reliable FDI stock figures on an annual basis. I have chosen to use net FDI flows as a percentage of GDP in order to have a relatively simple indicator of how important FDI is to the host country economy in a given year. The indicator is constructed by dividing the net FDI flows per year by the GDP of the host country and then dividing by 100 to obtain a percentage.

Aggregate economic growth is measured by the annual growth rate of real GDP per capita, calculated using the data in the Penn World Tables, version 5.6 (Summers and Heston, 1991). Indicators that capture conceptions of socioeconomic development are difficult to use in statistical analysis. Economic development is a complex concept, with meanings ranging from 'growth with equity' (Biersteker, 1987:19), to 'industrialization, urbanization, high educational standards, and a steady increase in the overall wealth of the society.' (Lipset, 1959:86). The concept of development in earlier chapters of this book has also included some notion of increased standards of living. The Physical Quality of Life Index (Morris, 1979), would seem to be an ideal indicator, as it includes infant mortality rate, life expectancy at birth, and adult literacy. The difficulty here is that annual data are not readily available for these countries for all indicators included in the index. In their absence, socioeconomic development is measured simply by the infant mortality rate, although the data are available for only a relatively short time series. The infant mortality rate is assumed to reflect the prenatal health of the mother and the ability to provide health essentials for infants. For the countries included here, the absolute value of the correlations between infant mortality rate and other indicators of development such as life expectancy and literacy rates is consistently above 0.80 for the years with available data. The infant mortality rate is thus used to indicate the level of development in the six developing countries included in this study.

Political stability is a difficult concept to measure, and there are far more indicators of political *instability*. So, in order to capture the potentially disquieting effects of political instability for foreign investors, instability is indicated by the number of deaths due to political violence in each year. This indicator is used by many statistical analysts (Lichbach, 1989:443), although it is not without problems. The category 'deaths due to political violence' does not distinguish between deaths due to elite conflict such as *coups d'etat* and mass political instability. Yet, deaths due to any type of political violence seem likely to be brought to the attention of potential investors. Furthermore, the theoretical expectations regarding what type of political instability is most likely to deter investors are sufficiently vague to warrant using a broad indicator. The data for 1960 through to 1978 are taken from Taylor and Jodice (1983) and coded from the *New York Times Index* for 1979 through to 1992. Unfortunately, it must be noted that events in African countries are significantly under-reported in this source. In fact, no deaths due to political violence were reported in Côte d'Ivoire during the time period for which other indicators are available, so a variable for political instability is not examined for that country.

III. MODEL ESTIMATION AND RESULTS

The multivariate Granger causality analysis results in a set of block F-tests and these are reported here first by country. The general discussion then compares the results of the different countries. Each country table is organized in the same way, with the dependent variable for the regression equations listed in the first column and the independent variables in the second. The indicator for socioeconomic development, infant mortality rate, is abbreviated as IMR. The F-tests are listed in the third column and the Q-statistic listed is for joint covariance stationarity in that equation. Finally, the number in the lags column indicates how many lags of the variables were included in that regression. I experimented with including four lags down to one lag for each dependent variable, and reported the first lag structure which had significant results. If no lag structure yielded significant results, I reported the most that could be included given the number of degrees of freedom.

The null hypothesis for each regression is that the independent variables do *not* Granger cause the dependent variable. If we can reject this null hypothesis, we have evidence of causality in the sense that the past history of change in one variable is helpful in predicting current change in another. Because of the small number of cases for each country and therefore the few degrees of freedom, I have chosen to concentrate on F-tests which are significant at the 0.10 level or better. In general, there are not as many significant F-tests as we might expect based on the theoretical positions outlined earlier. Nevertheless, the results are important for understanding the role of FDI in developing host countries.

Thailand

Thailand provides an example of a host country with relatively strong domestic context conditions for FDI for much of the post-World War II time period. The ability and willingness of the host to counterbalance the interests of foreign investors has been boosted by relative mass political stability, a strong state which has been oriented toward capitalist development strategies, and a domestic capitalist class that has been both willing and able to cooperate with the state to achieve economic development goals. When FDI flows began entering this context in the early 1960s, they seemed to contribute to high economic growth rates, improvement on socioeconomic indicators and continued mass political stability. The Granger causality analysis is thus expected to provide evidence that the strong context conditions drew in FDI, but it is unclear whether FDI was a primary cause of the modernization-type outcomes. The F-tests from the Granger analysis for Thailand are listed in Table 5.1

The results listed for the first regression, with FDI/GDP as the dependent variable, indicate that we cannot reject the null hypothesis that growth and development do not Granger cause FDI with one lagged period included in the regression. The F-tests for growth and development are significant, and the interpretation is that the recent

Table 5.1 Multivariate Granger Causality Results:
Thailand, 1960–92

Dependent Variable	Independent Variables	F-test	Q	Lags
FDI/GDP	FDI/GDP	1.94	18.44	1
	growth	4.32**		
	deaths	1.48		
	IMR	3.13*		
growth	FDI/GDP	0.84	15.68	1–4
	growth	0.85		
	deaths	0.86		
	IMR	1.06		
deaths	FDI/GDP	2.37	15.92	1–2
	growth	2.70*		
	deaths	6.71***		
	IMR	2.02		
IMR	FDI/GDP	0.06	10.34	1
	growth	0.27		
	deaths	0.02		
	IMR	2.90*		

Note: * = significance level of 0.10; ** = significance level of 0.05; *** = significance level of 0.01.

history of economic growth, and the change in infant mortality rates both significantly affect current changes in FDI as a per cent of GDP. The first proposition, that FDI is drawn in by host-country conditions, is supported by this finding in the data for Thailand. Neither modernization nor dependency expectations are supported by these results. Rather than FDI being an engine of growth or a driving force in underdevelopment, it seems that in this case FDI comes into an already strong host-country context because of the strength of the domestic economy rather than the other way around.

The second proposition, that feedback cycles exist among the variables, is not as easily supported with these results. Economic growth is not Granger caused by any of these variables, including its own past history and the infant mortality rate is only Granger caused by itself. Furthermore, low host-country political instability is not a significant drawing factor for FDI/GDP as expected, but the third set of F-tests indicate that political instability is important as a dependent variable. Even when controlling for the strong effect of past deaths due to political violence, the past history of economic growth also Granger causes changes in deaths due to political violence. In this case, domestic growth does significantly affect political stability. But, since political instability does not also Granger cause growth, we have some evidence that if a feedback cycle exists, it does not necessarily begin with political stability.

The results for the growth equation are surprising since none of these variables are found to Granger cause economic growth, not even its own past history. This is very similar to findings using data from Taiwan (Chan, Clark and Davis, 1990). One possible explanation is that in a country with strong context conditions, the indicators of aggregate political and economic outcomes move together through time rather than demonstrate discernable temporal patterns of causation, at least using annual time periods. In this case, the lag specification used here may be either too short or too long to capture the direct effects of these variables on economic growth. These possible explanations for the null findings in the Thai data will be discussed later in comparison to the other countries.

Philippines

The bargaining position of the Philippines fluctuated more through time, but was consistently lower than that of Thailand. At times when the state institutions were relatively strong, the incentive structures made the political and economic elite unwilling to work toward national development goals. Mass political instability remained high for much of the time period, mirroring the fragmentation among the elite. FDI flows into this combination of context factors seemed to be associated with economic growth that stagnated after two decades, little improvement on socioeconomic indicators and continuing mass political instability. In general, this case seemed to be one which supported the dependency argument. Table 5.2 provides the results of the Granger causality analysis of whether such a pattern can be found in the Philippine data.

The results from the first equation using the Philippine data indicate that the past histories of both FDI/GDP and economic growth help to predict current changes in FDI/GDP. The relationship is seen in a longer time-frame than in Thailand, showing up with four lags included in the regression. But, while past values of FDI/GDP are strong predictors of current values of the variable, FDI/GDP is not a significant causal factor in any of the other equations. Again, domestic economic conditions affect FDI, rather than FDI being a significant causal factor in aggregate host-country outcomes.

Table 5.2   Multivariate Granger Causality Results:
Philippines, 1960–92

Dependent Variable	Independent Variables	F-test	Q	Lags
FDI/GDP	FDI/GDP	4.16**	9.51	1–4
	growth	3.77**		
	deaths	1.73		
	IMR	0.85		
growth	FDI/GDP	0.59	4.53	1–4
	growth	3.01*		
	deaths	0.64		
	IMR	0.20		
deaths	FDI/GDP	0.44	5.31	1–4
	growth	0.35		
	deaths	0.42		
	IMR	0.19		
IMR	FDI/GDP	0.44	7.49	1–4
	growth	0.34		
	deaths	0.84		
	IMR	5.82***		

Note: * = significance level of 0.10; ** = significance level of .05;
*** = significance level of 0.01.

One of the most striking things about the Philippine data is the lack of significant Granger relationships. Deaths due to political violence are not Granger related to anything else, and the past history of changes in deaths does not even significantly predict the current changes. The only other significant relationships are that growth and infant mortality rates Granger cause themselves. FDI does not seem to contribute to a cycle of dependency, rather these two key variables are largely driven by their own past histories. Thus, growth rates continue to predict growth rates and changes in infant mortality rates help predict current values of the variable. While this is not evidence of a cycle *among* variables, it provides evidence that the history of change *within* the time series for these two variables remains important. The evidence is consistent with the qualitative description of a vicious cycle of low economic growth and development.

Côte d'Ivoire

The qualitative analysis of Côte d'Ivoire indicated that its bargaining leverage *vis-à-vis* foreign investors was higher than that of Ghana, but in comparison to Thailand, the Philippines, or Costa Rica, its bargaining leverage was quite low. Nevertheless, the politically stable Côte d'Ivoire was able to produce economic growth early in the post-independence period, and that was accompanied by some improvement in GDP per capita and socioeconomic indicators. FDI and other foreign inputs contributed to this pattern, but their relative impact was less clear. In the early 1990s, however, an economic crisis was the immediate cause of political unrest. This situation seemed to indicate that the dependency theorists were right in thinking that the long-term consequences of development based on external economic flows would be negative. Unfortunately, since there were no deaths due to political violence between 1968 and 1990 (the period for which infant mortality rates are available), deaths were not included in this analysis. The Granger causality regression results for Côte d'Ivoire are reported in Table 5.3.

The proposition that FDI is determined by host-country context conditions is again supported by the evidence from Côte d'Ivoire. In addition to its own past history, FDI/GDP is Granger caused by the past changes in the level of development, as indicated by the infant mortality rate. In this case, the significant relationship is found with two lags included in the equation. As in the Philippines, there is no evidence in the regression equations for growth and development to support the conclusion that FDI is a significant causal factor of economic outcomes in this host country.

The other significant relationships in this table provide evidence not so much of a temporal cycle among the variables, but of the

Table 5.3 Multivariate Granger Causality Results: Côte d'Ivoire, 1968–90

Dependent Variable	Independent Variables	F-test	Q	Lags
FDI/GDP	FDI/GDP	7.19***	11.99	1–2
	growth	0.00		
	IMR	4.03**		
growth	FDI/GDP	1.89	7.69	1–2
	growth	0.36		
	IMR	3.38*		
IMR	FDI/GDP	0.06	7.12	1–4
	growth	0.21		
	IMR	5.69***		

Note: * = significance level of 0.10; ** = significance level of 0.05; *** = significance level of 0.01.

importance in the level of development for other aggregate outcomes. In addition to Granger causing FDI/GDP, the infant mortality rate Granger causes itself and economic growth. Since IMR only Granger causes growth, and the causal arrow is not reciprocal so that growth Granger causes IMR, this is not evidence of a feedback cycle. Substantively, we can conclude that the level of development temporally precedes both growth and FDI in Côte d'Ivoire. The modernization-type pattern of outcomes seen in the qualitative analysis cannot be said to begin with FDI, so it is not strongly exogenous to the development process in Cote d'Ivoire. We must keep in mind that the economic processes were taking place within a context of relative political stability that is not included in these quantitative models, but that was found to be important in the qualitative comparison.

Ghana

Ghana presents a case of a weaker bargaining context than the Philippines, Thailand or Côte d'Ivoire. The state in Ghana was initially strong, but became weakened by continued conflict with the highly fragmented and politicized society. Factionalism among the elite made them unwilling to formulate and implement consistent economic development policies. Mass political instability and ideological swings both within and between governing regimes decreased investor confidence. These weak context conditions were accompanied by slow economic growth, declines in socioeconomic indicators and continued mass political instability. The economic changes made in the mid-1980s seemed to create a more stable economic environment for investors into the 1990s, but the country is still very poor and seems to exhibit strong dependency-type outcomes. The results of the Granger causality analysis for Ghana are presented in Table 5.4.

In this quite weak host country, the results from the first equation indicate that economic growth Granger causes FDI/GDP, with two lags included in the regression. This finding is consistent with those from the other countries in providing support for the proposition that domestic context conditions draw in FDI. In addition, the results for equations 2 and 3 indicate that FDI does not cause any of the other putative outcomes, at least in the sense of temporal precedence. As in the case of Thailand, nothing is significant for predicting economic growth, including its own past history.

Table 5.4   Multivariate Granger Causality Results: Ghana, 1960–92

Dependent Variable	Independent Variables	F-test	Q	Lags
FDI/GDP	FDI/GDP	5.59**	10.27	1–2
	growth	2.84*		
	deaths	1.92		
	IMR	0.90		
growth	FDI/GDP	0.71	11.30	1–3
	growth	0.82		
	deaths	0.71		
	IMR	1.20		
deaths	FDI/GDP	0.27	5.42	1–2
	growth	0.20		
	deaths	1.73		
	IMR	2.74*		
IMR	FDI/GDP	1.27	13.84	1–3
	growth	1.19		
	deaths	0.15		
	IMR	6.20**		

Note: * = significance level of 0.10; ** = significance level of 0.05; *** = significance level of 0.01.

The proposition that the data will exhibit feedback cycles among the variables garners only partial support in this case. Political stability, indicated by deaths due to political violence, is Granger caused by changes in infant mortality rates. Prior changes in the infant mortality rate predict current changes in the IMR, but the level of development is not a causal factor for growth. This is consistent with a cycle in which changes in the level of development produce changes in political stability. The difficulty in interpretation comes in not finding a significant relationship between growth and IMR that would form either the beginning or end of this cycle. While we can conclude that growth Granger causes FDI, and IMR Granger causes deaths due to political violence, these results do not link all four variables in a clear temporal pattern. Bits and pieces of potential feed-back cycles seem to exist and it may be that the short time series available simply preclude finding more significant links.

Costa Rica

The bargaining context for Costa Rica has been quite strong during the time period considered here and it has also had some of the strongest outcomes in comparison with the other six countries in this study. It is located in a geographic area of key importance to the United States, it has had a stable and well functioning democracy for much of this century, and the level of economic development since before World War II has been the highest in the Central American region. In this context it seemed clear that the state was able to use its bargaining leverage in order to make FDI an effective part of the development strategy. As in the other countries, qualitative analysis was unclear about whether FDI started the positive cycle or contributed to it. Nevertheless, the expectation is that the Granger results will demonstrate a pattern of relationships that supports a modernization understanding of the mechanism by which FDI produced aggregate outcomes in Costa Rica.

The importance of the host-country level of development as a drawing factor for FDI is seen once again in the results for Costa Rica. Changes in the infant mortality rate Granger cause FDI/GDP, but the relationship is not reciprocal. The causal link is also found to have a relatively short-term effect, since the relationship is only significant with one lag period included in the equation. Changes in the

Table 5.5   Multivariate Granger Causality Results: Costa Rica, 1960–92

Dependent Variable	Independent Variables	F-test	Q	Lags
FDI/GDP	FDI/GDP	1.34	15.50	1
	growth	0.04		
	deaths	0.24		
	IMR	3.90*		
growth	FDI/GDP	0.93	9.21	1–2
	growth	7.60***		
	deaths	2.32		
	IMR	2.66*		
deaths	FDI/GDP	2.66*	14.16	1–4
	growth	4.31**		
	deaths	3.18*		
	IMR	1.34		
IMR	FDI/GDP	1.28	8.99	1–4
	growth	1.29		
	deaths	0.77		
	IMR	0.55		

Note: * = significance level of 0.10; ** = significance level of 0.05;
*** = significance level of 0.01.

IMR also Granger cause economic growth at two lags, even when controlling for the strong effect of the past history of growth. So, in this country with strong context conditions, we can begin to see part of a cycle among the variables that would support a modernization interpretation of development outcomes.

In this cycle, FDI/GDP, growth and past deaths due to political violence, all have a significant effect on deaths due to political violence, and it is a relatively long-term effect. So, the infant mortality rate is not Granger caused by the other variables, but in the short-term it precedes both FDI/GDP and economic growth. Economic growth and FDI/GDP then continue to have an impact on deaths due to political violence for at least four years. In this piece of a cycle, economic factors temporally precede political stability and the level of development precedes both economic growth and FDI.

Guatemala

Primarily because of its ongoing insurgencies during the time period examined here, Guatemala was quite weak on context factors in comparison with the other countries in this study. The country study indicated that foreign investors had been able to take advantage of even the strong and repressive state for reasons that included a political split between the agricultural and industrial elites. The Guatemalan ruling elite was unable and unwilling to pursue a development plan that would redistribute the wealth and contribute to improvement on socioeconomic indicators. This, in combination with long-standing ethnic tensions, fuelled continued political violence.

In this context of political and economic turmoil, FDI seemed to have very little effect on aggregate outcomes, except as it may have enabled the ruling class to consolidate its power. For these reasons, we might expect the data for Guatemala to display patterns consistent with dependency arguments about the dangerous effects of FDI. Table 5.6 provides the results of Granger causality tests for Guatemala and is striking for the absence of strong causal patterns. These results are most similar to those for the Philippines.

The most interesting finding is that again, as in most of the other cases, the economic growth rate Granger causes changes in FDI and the impact is seen when including four lagged periods. Even in this weak host country, the past history of economic growth helps explain changes in FDI, but the relationship is not reciprocal or simultaneous. Although the sign of the relationship between previous economic

Table 5.6 Multivariate Granger Causality Results: Guatemala, 1960–92

Dependent Variable	Independent Variables	F-test	Q	Lags
FDI/GDP	FDI/GDP	1.93	10.64	1–4
	growth	2.97*		
	deaths	1.10		
	IMR	0.21		
growth	FDI/GDP	2.18	12.92	1–3
	growth	2.80*		
	deaths	0.68		
	IMR	0.98		
deaths	FDI/GDP	1.08	10.56	1–4
	growth	1.67		
	deaths	2.21		
	IMR	0.65		
IMR	FDI/GDP	0.07	10.10	1–3
	growth	0.22		
	deaths	0.03		
	IMR	2.78*		

Note: * = significance level of 0.10; ** = significance level of 0.05; *** = significance level of 0.01.

growth and FDI/GDP is unclear from the Granger results, this is an important finding because it indicates that FDI is exogenous to processes of political and economic development in Guatemala.

The null findings for the other relationships in question can be interesting as well in this case. Political instability is not Granger related to any of these variables, including FDI. If foreign investors are as averse to political instability as previous studies suggest, there is no evidence of a direct temporal causal connection in Guatemala. It may simply be the case that throughout the time period, foreign investors who found the political risks too high did not invest, while those willing to accept the high risk did so at a fairly constant rate.

Other important theoretical links are also missing. Economic growth is only Granger caused by itself and IMR is only Granger caused by itself. There is no evidence of a cycle among the variables, rather the economic processes are independent of one another and political instability. The lack of significant relationships among the variables may be an important indication that a dependency-type process is occurring. The typical way dependency arguments are interpreted is that they predict negative relationships between FDI and aggregate economic and political outcomes in the host country.

Another way to think about dependency arguments is that they expect modernization mechanisms to break down for various reasons. For instance, economic growth is not converted to domestic development because of the global interests of foreign investors and the domestic capitalist class. If this latter interpretation is correct, then Granger causality analysis would not be expected to find a temporal cycle among the outcome variables. So, in the case of Ghana and the Philippines, the lack of Granger causality may simply indicate a pattern of broken relationships among the key variables.

IV. DISCUSSION

The results from these six developing countries are not easy to summarize, but some general points can be made regarding the causal patterns among FDI and its putative consequences. The first point is that factors which contribute to the domestic bargaining context are important determinants of FDI and this means that FDI is endogenous to the development process. In all cases, some measure of domestic economic performance, either economic growth or infant mortality rates, Granger causes FDI.

This finding provides support for the arguments drawn from the bargaining approach and the international business literature. The conventional wisdom in both the modernization and dependency perspectives that FDI is a key independent variable is not well supported. In only one case does FDI Granger cause aggregate domestic outcomes, and this is in Costa Rica where it causes changes in deaths due to political violence. The sign of the relationship is unclear from this analysis, but deserves further study since the direction of impact is important for understanding the qualitative nature of the relationship.

Although the proposition that FDI is an important endogenous variable is supported by the evidence, the proposition that there are cycles – either virtuous or vicious – among outcome variables receives only marginal support. My initial argument was that FDI would be Granger caused by domestic context conditions, but that it would then contribute to a cycle in which political stability led to growth, which led to development and then from development back to political stability. The lack of empirical support for such a temporal cycle among variables requires some explanation, particularly in light of the country studies in which FDI did seem to play a significant role in buttressing existing patterns of political (in)stability, economic growth and development.

There are several plausible reasons that FDI was not found to be a significant causal factor in most cases, and the first involves the validity and reliability of data, and the shortness of the data series. As with any study involving quantitative indicators for developing countries, the indicators used here have serious problems which must simply be overlooked in order to carry out quantitative analysis. For example, the infant mortality rate for the Philippines is a fairly standard indicator, but consistent time series for it are difficult to find and those that do exist have disturbing blips in trends. The shortness of the data series for each country and thus the very small number of degrees of freedom, can only be overcome through time as more data points are collected.

Even though there are known problems with the data, where values for indicators exist they are used in many studies of development. At present this is the only way to proceed with quantitative empirical analysis, but we must recognize that it entails problems that can jeopardize results. The strength of combining quantitative analysis with the qualitative country studies is that we are able to gain a larger picture of the processes in which FDI is thought to be involved in developing host countries. Although the Granger causality analysis showed FDI to be a significant causal factor in only one case, there are still opportunities for exploring its potential as a contributing factor to development outcomes.

Aside from poor data availability and validity, another plausible explanation for why FDI is not a strong determinant of political and economic outcomes is that it may have to reach a certain threshold level relative to the host economy before it becomes a significant causal factor. To state the obvious, FDI can have no consequences if it does not flow into a developing country. Similarly, if FDI has not been a large part of the productive resources in these countries, it makes sense that the Granger analysis finds it to be not significant for determining aggregate outcomes. In order to understand whether such a threshold exists, Table 5.7 presents the values per year of FDI as a percentage of GDP for all six countries considered in this Granger analysis.

The data listed in Table 5.7 indicate that FDI as a percentage of GDP was consistently highest in Costa Rica. The FDI was also spread fairly evenly through time in Costa Rica, whereas in the other countries larger FDI/GDP values tended to be bunched up in time.

Table 5.7   Net FDI Flows as a Percentage of Gross Domestic Product, 1960–92

			Country			
Year	Thailand	Philippines	Côte d'Ivoire	Ghana	Costa Rica	Guatemala
1960	0.08	0.41	–	0.32	0.31	1.61
1961	0.21	0.76	–	−0.87	1.42	0.71
1962	0.23	−0.07	–	0.71	2.47	0.81
1963	0.64	−0.08	1.31	0.48	2.76	0.04
1964	0.50	−0.07	1.21	0.84	1.45	0.47
1965	1.04	−0.17	1.96	1.86	0.02	1.06
1966	0.55	−0.23	−1.53	2.64	2.26	1.04
1967	0.83	−0.12	0.58	1.82	2.24	1.66
1968	1.07	−0.04	0.92	0.52	0.58	1.81
1969	0.82	0.07	0.90	3.06	2.66	1.76
1970	0.61	−0.40	2.05	1.27	2.68	1.54
1971	0.53	−0.08	0.99	0.26	2.05	1.44
1972	0.83	−0.25	1.00	0.54	2.08	0.76
1973	0.71	0.50	2.01	0.48	2.47	1.35
1974	1.38	0.03	1.06	0.26	2.78	1.50
1975	0.15	0.61	1.77	1.54	3.52	2.19
1976	0.47	0.69	0.96	−0.32	2.52	0.29
1977	0.54	1.01	0.23	0.20	2.03	1.78
1978	0.21	0.42	1.05	0.08	1.33	2.10
1979	0.19	0.02	0.82	−0.03	1.05	1.69
1980	0.58	−0.30	0.93	0.10	1.00	1.41
1981	0.84	0.45	0.39	0.06	2.52	1.48
1982	0.54	0.04	0.63	0.05	1.02	0.88
1983	0.88	0.30	0.55	0.01	1.76	0.50
1984	0.98	0.03	0.32	0.03	1.42	0.40
1985	0.43	0.04	0.42	0.09	1.66	0.64
1986	0.63	0.41	0.75	0.08	1.30	0.95
1987	0.38	0.89	0.87	0.10	1.67	1.28
1988	1.81	2.46	0.55	0.10	2.63	4.20
1989	2.50	1.33	0.19	0.29	1.82	0.91
1990	2.79	1.21	0.29	0.24	1.91	1.12
1991	1.88	1.20	0.77	0.29	3.06	0.96
1992	1.79	0.43	–	0.33	3.23	0.90
Average:	0.84	0.35	0.83	0.53	1.93	1.25

Note: '–' indicates missing information. The percentages are derived from IMF Yearbook data on net FDI flows and GDP.

The hypothesis that a threshold exists below which FDI has no impact on aggregate outcomes seems reasonable, since Costa Rica is the only country in which FDI Granger caused anything (deaths). Thailand and the Philippines only began receiving consistently larger FDI flows relative to the domestic economy in the late 1980s and early 1990s, and Côte d'Ivoire and Ghana received larger amounts in the 1960s and early 1970s. Guatemala had the second highest average, but had several blocks of time in which FDI/GDP was quite low.

The null findings of the Granger analysis regarding the causal impact of FDI in five of the six countries point toward an important area for future research. Further investigation is required in order to determine whether a larger sample of countries would provide evidence of a threshold effect, and to determine the extent to which it might be relatively constant or vary according to time and place. An additional question involves whether FDI must be a consistently high proportion of domestic resources for a long period of time before it has a direct effect on aggregate outcomes. If this is the case, and policy-makers wish to use FDI as a tool for development, they will need to recognize that attracting only a few major investment projects will not necessarily be adequate to create a long-term effect on aggregate outcomes.

The proposition that a cycle of Granger causality exists among the dependent variables did not simply break down at the point where FDI was expected to contribute. Political stability was expected to lead to growth and development, and all three of these were expected to Granger cause FDI, as well as feed back into each other. The results of the Granger causality analysis for these six countries provide very little evidence of such complete cycles, however, parts of this cycle were found in several cases. The analysis did not uncover a general temporal pattern among the variables, but the significant links found can help us begin to map out the relationship between these aggregate political and economic outcomes.

The first part of the expected cycle, that political stability would Granger cause economic growth is not found for any country, although the political indicator was not included for Côte d'Ivoire. In addition, no evidence was found for the second part of the cycle in which economic growth was expected to Granger cause development. In the expected third stage, political stability was generally unrelated to FDI/GDP, but as discussed above, either growth or infant mortality rates Granger caused FDI/GDP in all six countries. Also as discussed above, FDI/GDP did not Granger cause anything except growth in Costa Rica. In short, the first parts of the hypothesized temporal pattern were not found among the key variables in these six countries.

Yet, there was some evidence that feedback among the variables did occur, but the evidence is not strong and consistent across countries.

The evidence is summarized here, before discussing how we might use it as a building block for future research. First, economic growth Granger caused deaths in Thailand, indicating that economic processes precede political change rather than the other way around. In Côte d'Ivoire, changes in infant mortality rates Granger cause growth, or put another way, changes in the level of development temporally precede economic growth. Changes in infant mortality rates are also important in Ghana where they Granger cause deaths due to political stability. Again, the economic process causes changes in political stability, at least when causation is defined as temporal precedence. In the Philippines and in Guatemala there is no evidence that the level of development, economic growth, and political instability are causally related.

Costa Rica is the only case where more pieces to the puzzle fall into place. In perhaps the clearest case of an expected feedback loop, infant mortality rates and economic growth Granger cause further growth in Costa Rica. Then deaths, FDI/GDP, and growth Granger cause deaths due to political violence in Costa Rica. The cycle seems to begin with changes in the level of development, which causes both growth and changes in FDI/GDP. They in turn cause changes in political stability.

Even though direct evidence of cycles is slim, some of the variables Granger cause themselves, and this supports the implication – inherent in the concept of cycles – that once a trend begins, its own past history is the best predictor of current values. For instance, in the data examined here, IMR Granger causes itself in all countries except Costa Rica. Growth Granger causes itself in the Philippines, Costa Rica and Guatemala. FDI/GDP Granger causes itself in the Philippines, Côte d'Ivoire and Ghana. Finally, deaths Granger cause themselves in Thailand and Costa Rica, the two countries with the least overall amount of political instability.

The partial evidence for cycles supports the conclusion from the country studies that the factors which contribute to the domestic bargaining context, rather than the FDI flows, are important in producing different development patterns. Countries with relatively stronger bargaining contexts, such as Costa Rica and Côte d'Ivoire, demonstrate some (minimal) evidence of feedback among the variables. With the exception of infant mortality rates causing deaths in Ghana, the weaker countries show almost no causal connections among growth, IMR or political instability. Poorer and weaker host countries are less able to turn economic growth into development, while the wealthier and stronger host countries show some evidence that they are more able. The results of this Granger analysis indicate that the poor remain poor, and the wealthier have an easier time becoming developed, but FDI is not a strong causal variable.

Another objective of the Granger causality analysis was to explore the time frame that might be involved in long and short-term development outcomes. Because of the short time series available for this analysis, the possibility remains that causal relationships would be more clear using either shorter time periods (for example, quarterly data), or including more lags. Aside from the data limitations, the results we do have indicate that significant relationships for the stronger countries have shorter lag times. When relationships are significant in the weaker host countries, it takes more lags before the impact is seen.

One explanation, noted already, is that for the stronger countries, the four variables examined in this study may move together through time in a complex and interrelated process that we call development. In this case, we can argue that few relationships were significant because annual data would not capture the very short temporal links. On the other hand, weaker host countries present more opportunities for the links between and among political stability, economic growth and development to break down, or to take longer to create. Thus, significant relationships were found with more lagged periods included for the weaker countries.

To sum up, the primary result of this Granger causality analysis is that FDI is not as strong a determinant of host-country political and economic outcomes, as has been thought by previously dominant theoretical perspectives. Domestic context conditions, in many cases the putative outcomes of FDI, actually precede FDI, and this is evidence that it is useful to examine the questions using the bargaining framework. This approach allows us to explicitly model FDI as an endogenous variable and understand that the putative outcomes of FDI have much to do with the reasons foreign investors were attracted in the first place. Future statistical work on the determinants of development and FDI could incorporate these results by developing and testing a set of structural equation models, with political stability, FDI, economic growth and development as the key dependent variables. Such work may help demonstrate the indirect ways in which FDI contributes to patterns of host-country development.

6 Conclusions

In this book I have developed a qualitative framework for comparing the context and consequences of foreign direct investment in developing countries. The framework for analysis was based on the bargaining perspective, which provided theoretical and empirical links between host-country factors which draw in FDI and the results of that investment. I argued that the consequences of FDI must be examined in relationship to the factors that make a host country attractive to foreign investors. Furthermore, I maintained that those same economic and political factors are also strong determinants of future development outcomes and thus contribute to self-perpetuating development patterns.

On the basis of these propositions, I expected that host countries with strong positions on economic conditions, such as size of the domestic market and past history of economic growth, would draw in more FDI. In the presence of strong political factors, such as high state capacity to implement coherent development policies in a stable environment, the host country would be more likely to be willing and able to use FDI for domestic growth and development purposes. Host countries with weaker positions on the context factors would be less likely to draw in FDI, and also less likely to be both willing and able to use it for domestic development. I expected modernization-type results to follow from FDI in strong host countries and dependency-type outcomes to be the result of FDI in weaker host countries.

The analysis in this book indicates that general configurations of host-county context conditions are indeed associated with patterns of economic and political outcome variables. The analysis focused on six developing countries which represent variation in terms of context conditions, experiences with FDI, and the resulting economic and political development patterns. Among these six countries, those which present economic strengths relative to their neighbours were likely to draw in more FDI. This result was found in both the qualitative analysis, and the quantitative Granger causality analysis. Those countries which combine strong economies with political stability and a state that is capable of implementing coherent development policies were more likely to be able to make FDI part of a pattern of modernization-type outcomes.

Thailand, Costa Rica and Cote d'Ivoire are different in many respects, but each has demonstrated a pattern of development outcomes that has followed, more or less, the expectations of modernization and neoclassical theorists. The successes of Côte d'Ivoire, however, only look strong relative to its immediate neighbours. Mass political stability and policy stability have been high relative to other developing countries, even though in Thailand there has been much turmoil among the ruling elite. In these countries, domestic political cleavages along ethnic lines did not present as much of a potential for ongoing insurgencies that could then limit further policy options. Economic growth in these three countries was strong relative to the comparison case, although still quite low in Cote d'Ivoire. At the same time, the ruling elite has been both willing and able to use the benefits from growth for further development within the economy. In each of these countries, FDI was encouraged during the time period examined here and seemed to contribute to the positive development outcomes.

In contrast, the host country with weaker context conditions in each of the comparative case studies tended to demonstrate dependency-type outcome patterns, including slower economic growth, continued underdevelopment and high political instability. The Philippines, Ghana and Guatemala, even though they each had some strengths in the immediate post-World War II time period, exhibited dependency-type outcome patterns through time. Mass political instability and armed revolts in the Philippines and Guatemala resulted from highly unequal patterns of land and wealth distribution, and the elites were unwilling to use FDI for national development goals. Rather, FDI seemed to help the elites maintain their political and economic privilege.

In Ghana, instability among the elite produced policy instability as well, particularly in terms of economic development plans. The qualitative comparisons indicated that in each of these cases FDI may have helped the ruling elite to consolidate power, and thus contributed indirectly to a vicious cycle of economic and political decay. In each of these cases, political instability has eased recently and neoclassical development policies have been adopted. When Ghana managed to stabilize both the economy and the political situation, FDI began flowing in again, although still in very small amounts, and economic growth rates improved. Future research should be devoted to understanding how FDI interacts with these new domestic conditions.

Similarly, domestic conditions can change for the worse, and how FDI interacts in those cases is also worth examining. When economic conditions weakened in Côte d'Ivoire and political crisis deepened after the death of Houphouet, the relatively positive political pattern was interrupted. In addition, this political change came in the midst of economic turmoil. Economic growth in Cote d'Ivoire continued to be slow and economic development remained very low, despite continuing flows of FDI. All of these examples indicate that the domestic context conditions are very important for shaping the relationship between FDI and various types of development outcomes.

Thus, the primary result of this research is that FDI simply is not as important as previously suggested by development theories. FDI may interact with host country conditions, but it is not the single factor that will drive strong growth, nor is it the key factor in explaining low growth and underdevelopment. Both the qualitative comparisons and the Granger causality analysis support this conclusion. Domestic context conditions, such as the capacity of the state to formulate and implement coherent development policies, a strong history of economic growth, and higher levels of economic development, all contribute to host-country bargaining leverage because they are the drawing factors for FDI. Through time, those same factors are also both the causes and the consequences of complex political and economic processes that include FDI flows.

Indeed, the factors which contribute to bargaining power are themselves strong determinants of future outcome patterns. Economic growth yields future growth, development produces further development, and political instability is its own best predictor. But, the Granger causality analysis indicated that FDI does not generally provide a strong causal push in any one of these self-perpetuating cycles.

The conclusion that FDI is not as important as previously thought yields some important policy implications. In general, policymakers in developing countries should concentrate their efforts on creating the domestic context conditions that will allow FDI to contribute to positive rather than negative cycles, and the same prescription can be applied to aid efforts by the already industrialized and developed countries. More specifically, since FDI is drawn to stronger economies, useful host country development efforts would include human and physical capital development efforts. Similarly, policies aimed at strengthening a well-skilled bureaucracy, and policies that encourage international interactions and domestic capital accumulation would strengthen the host economy. All of these would contribute to bargaining leverage for the developing countries, and to their ability to use their resources to develop modernization-type development patterns. Perhaps more important, they are direct and important determinants of economic growth in the long run.

A reasonable objection might be that very poor countries remain poor precisely because they have been unable to generate such favourable domestic conditions. But, my analysis of these six countries indicates that change is possible, even under very difficult conditions, as in Ghana. Credible host-country efforts to improve economic conditions can be a signal to the international community that the country now has a serious commitment to development. But, this requires a strong political commitment and the political capacity to carry out the economic policies. Such commitment can perhaps be bolstered by support from connections with the international economy.

In addition to the conclusion that FDI is not a primary causal factor in domestic development, my analysis suggests that countries need not be strong on all of the variables that contribute to bargaining leverage; they can use strengths in some areas to overcome weaknesses in others. Ideally, it would be very useful to determine the relative importance of very specific context factors for their influence on both development and FDI flows. But, as demonstrated by the comparisons in this book, bargaining leverage is a complex concept. It is overdetermined by all the factors that can and do contribute at different times and on different issue areas. Thus, even after analyzing the context for FDI in six host countries, it remains impossible to distill a single and parsimonious set of bargaining conditions that are both necessary and sufficient to produce modernization-type outcomes.

Despite the lack of a single list of necessary and sufficient domestic conditions, the framework for analysis and the results of these country comparisons do provide some general conclusions that help us to understand the interaction between FDI and domestic context conditions. The first conclusion about the relative importance of context factors is that political stability is not as important as strong economic conditions for drawing in FDI. This is especially the case when political instability does not threaten foreign interests.

Cote d'Ivoire was incredibly stable politically until the late 1980s, yet it had very low levels of FDI flows during the entire time period, as did the less stable Ghana. Ghana experienced high elite and mass instability and at times it directed strong rhetoric against foreign concerns. But, in the more politically stable 1990s, Ghana has been trying to increase FDI flows and has been only marginally successful. Both Cote d'Ivoire and Ghana have small economies, with very low levels of development relative to other developing countries, they have histories of slower economic growth and they have few resources for improving the size or quality of their domestic markets. These poor economic conditions seemed to deter investors and political stability, or lack of it, was less important.

The same conclusion can be drawn based on the experiences of Thailand, the Philippines and Guatemala, where FDI flows were strong even during many periods of different types of political instability. Thailand had many coups and other abrupt changes of government, yet it was able to continue drawing in FDI. But, through time it developed a strong track record with respect to economic growth and it was able to capitalize on its relatively cheap labour.

The Philippines had a large market and a strong yet cheap labour force, and these factors drew in more foreign investment than in the poorer countries of Ghana and Côte d'Ivoire during the 1970s and 1980s; a period of insurgency and high mass political instability. The fall of the Marcos regime is a potential exception, but that was also occurring amidst economic difficulties. Similarly, even though Guatemala had very high levels of political instability, it was able to draw in FDI, especially while manufacturing was growing and exports were being diversified. During the same time period Costa Rica was economically strong and was politically stable. But, it did not have much higher levels of FDI flows than the vastly less stable Guatemala. In general, investors seemed willing to forgo some certainty about the political environment in order to obtain the benefits of investing in larger, though emerging, markets.

One interesting implication that certainly deserves further study is that it may be reasonable for policymakers in developing countries to pursue the potentially more chaotic politics of democracy than to suppress political dissent at the expense of economic growth. My qualitative analysis agrees with other studies which indicate that economic growth and development can help alleviate the underlying causes of political unrest, and that they can also help pull in outside resources to aid in the development process. The efficacy of allowing more open political processes, however, must also be examined with respect to how well the ruling regime can plan and implement development policies. Again, country-specific factors are likely to be important in this process and deserve further examination.

A second conclusion about the relative importance of context factors is that even though economic context conditions were more important for drawing in FDI, political context factors seemed to be more important for understanding the consequences of that FDI for domestic development. The ability and willingness of the host-country elites to harness the benefits of FDI for domestic purposes was critical for producing virtuous cycles of development. In some cases, changes in the political factors reshaped the economic conditions and started new patterns of economic outcomes.

For much of the time period, the elites in the Philippines and in Guatemala were unwilling to undertake policies that would allow the benefits of FDI and economic growth to spread through the economy and produce widespread development. The political incentive structure supported the pursuit of personal gain, often at the expense of national development plans. Political changes in the Philippines, Ghana, and perhaps more recently in Guatemala, have initiated new commitments to economic policies that will perhaps foster economic growth. In Ghana, the fundamental shift in policies and in elite unity during the Rawlings' regimes supports the conclusion that political context factors are very important for determining both FDI flows and the development outcomes in the country.

Political context factors can also be important for the ways they can complement, or make up for, weak economic conditions. For instance, Costa Rica was quite weak, relative to Guatemala, on background factors. It had a low population, and therefore a small labour pool, and it had a small market. But, these poor background factors were overcome by the policy decisions made by elites in Costa Rica. Economic policies that distributed the benefits of growth contributed to both political stability and further economic development. Again, in each of these poor countries, the ability and willingness of the elite to implement domestic growth and development policies was critical to the aggregate outcomes.

Unfortunately, poor economic conditions may be very difficult to ameliorate with political policies, no matter how 'right' those policies might be. Côte d'Ivoire presents a case where it has been very difficult to generate interest on the part of foreign investors and how to improve that situation significantly remains unclear. Certainly that is a point where further study could be usefully applied. Indeed, one general problem with studying how FDI contributes to economic and political development is that it usually boils down to a conclusion that the strong and rich get richer, and the poor and weak remain in that condition.

My analysis attempted to break into this tautology, and to determine whether we can specify a pattern of temporal causality among political stability, economic growth, economic development and FDI.

The qualitative comparisons suggested that political stability, along with economic growth and development drew in FDI, which then contributed to further growth. As discussed above, in countries with strong political context conditions, that growth was also used to maintain socioeconomic development.

The Granger causality analysis of data for the six countries indicated that a strong bargaining context, particularly with respect to economic growth and development, draws in FDI, but political stability does not necessarily precede the other variables. This result of the quantitative analysis is broadly consistent with the extant literature on why firms undertake direct investment overseas.

In contrast to many theories of development or underdevelopment, the Granger causality analysis indicated that FDI is not a strong causal factor in explaining growth, development, or political (in)stability in these six developing host countries. This was the case for relatively strong host countries, as well as for the weaker countries in each paired comparison. Previous changes in FDI flows simply were not statistically significant in most cases as determinants of current changes in growth, development or political outcomes. This result reemphasizes the conclusion from the qualitative studies that FDI is endogenous to the development process rather than a strong causal factor.

In contrast to my initial expectations, the Granger analysis indicated no strong evidence for the existence of cycles among the key variables, although such cycles were strongly suggested by the qualitative country comparisons. For instance, the more politically stable countries such as Cote d'Ivoire and Costa Rica seemed to have far stronger bargaining positions *vis-à-vis* foreign investors, and the political stability also seemed to contribute to relatively better economic growth and development outcomes. Similarly, Thailand was expected to demonstrate cycles in which economic growth led to development, which was then expected to contribute to continued stability.

The absence of such cycles in the quantitative analysis may be the result of problems with the data, but it may also have important substantive implications. It may be that a certain threshold level of FDI relative to the host economy must be reached before its effects will show up in aggregate analysis. Certainly this is logical, and consistent with the finding that context conditions are more important for determining outcome patterns. For example, domestic investment is one domestic factor that would be better than FDI at predicting economic growth.

Another explanation for the lack of cycles in the data is that these variables are so closely connected that a causality analysis of this sort cannot capture the nature of the relationship. The process of development, in all of its political and economic facets, is very complex. Given this, it is very possible that the simple nature of the Granger causality models used in this analysis yielded no evidence of cycles because the models were not fully specified. Future work with structural models must take into account this complexity, and must model FDI as endogenous to the process, rather than strictly exogenous.

The analysis presented in this book demonstrates that, in six developing host countries, FDI interacted with the host-country domestic context conditions in more complex ways than expected in traditional theoretical perspectives. It is possible to draw general conclusions about development outcome patterns based on the configuration of factors that contribute to host-country bargaining leverage. But, specific conclusions about which factors might be necessary or sufficient to produce modernization-type outcomes of FDI are not possible at this time. Further theoretical development must reflect the complexities pointed out by this analysis. Future quantitative and qualitative empirical work should be directed toward understanding the causal patterns that may exist in the interactions among domestic and international variables.

References

J.P. Agarwal, 'Determinants of Foreign Direct Investment: A Survey', *Weltwirtschaftliches Archiv* 116 (1980) 739–73.

J.C.W. Ahiakpor, 'The success and failure of dependency theory: the experience of Ghana', *International Organization*, 39 (1985) 535–52.

N. Akrasanee, 'Foreign Aid and Economic Development in Thailand' in U. Lele and I. Nabi, eds, *Transitions in Development: the role of aid and commercial flows* (San Francisco, CA: ICS Press, 1991) pp.75–93.

C.E. Ameringer, *Democracy in Costa Rica*, Politics in Latin America, A Hoover Institution Series (Praeger; copublished with Hoover Institution Press, Stanford University, Stanford, CA, 1982).

S. Amin, *Le Developpement du capitalisme en Côte d'Ivoire* (Paris: Editions de Minuit, 1967).

S. Amin, *Neo-Colonialism in West Africa* (New York: Penguin Books, 1973).

B. Amonoo, *Ghana 1957–1966: The Politics of Institutional Dualism* (London: George Allen and Unwin, 1981).

L. Anderson, 'Mixed Blessings: Disruption and Organization among Peasant Unions in Costa Rica', *Latin American Research Review*, 26 (1991) 111–43.

D.E. Apter, *Ghana in Transition*, 2nd edn, (Princeton, NJ: Princeton University Press, 1972).

Z. Arat, 'Democracy and Economic Development: Modernization Theory Revisited', *Comparative Politics*, 21 (1988) 21–36.

Z. Arat, *Democracy and Human Rights in Developing Countries* (Boulder and London: Lynne Rienner Publishers, 1991).

Asian Development Bank, *Key Indicators of Developing Asian and Pacific Countries*, vol. 22 (Economics and Development Resources Center, Manila, 1991).

R. Austen, *African Economic History* (London: James Currey and Portsmouth, N.H.: Heinemann, 1987).

T. Bakary, 'Elite Transformation and Political Succession' in I.W. Zartman and C. Delgado, eds, *The Political Economy of Ivory Coast* (New York: Praeger, 1984) pp.21–55.

B. Balassa, *Economic Policies in the Pacific Area Developing Countries* (New York: New York University Press, 1991).

R.J. Barro, 'Economic Growth in a Cross-Section of Countries', *Quarterly Journal of Economics*, 106 (1991) 407–43.

R. Barro and J.W. Lee, 'Sources of economic growth' in A. Meltzer and C. Plosser, eds, *Carnegie-Rochester Conference Series on Public Policy* (Amsterdam; New York: North-Holland, 1994) pp.1–46.

K.E. Bauzon and C.F. Abel, 'Dependency: History, Theory, and a Reappraisal' in M.A. Tetreault and C.F. Abel, eds, *Dependency Theory and the Return of High Politics*, Contributions in Political Science Number 140 (London: Greenwood Press, 1986; New York; Westport, CN), pp.43–69.

S. Baynham, *The Military and Politics in Nkrumah's Ghana* (London; Boulder: Westview Press, 1988).

D.C. Bennett and K.E. Sharpe, *Transnational Corporations versus the State: The Political Economy of the Mexican Auto Industry* (Princeton, NJ: Princeton University Press, 1985).

C.F. Bergsten, T. Horst, and T.H. Moran, *American Multinationals and American Interests* (Washington, D.C.: The Brookings Institution, 1978).

T.J. Biersteker, *Multinationals, the State, and Control of the Nigerian Economy* (Princeton: Princeton University Press, 1987).

A. Bing, 'Ghana' in *The Africa Review 1991/92*, 15th edn, (Edison, NJ: Hunter Publishing Inc., 1992).

J.A. Booth and M.A. Seligson, eds, *Elections and Democracy in Central America* (London: Chapel Hill: University of North Carolina Press, 1989).

J.A. Booth, and T.W. Walker, *Understanding Central America*, 2nd edn (Oxford; Boulder; San Francisco: Westview Press, 1993).

V. Bornschier, 'Dependent Industrialization in the World Economy: Some Comments and Results Concerning a Recent Debate', *Journal of Conflict Resolution*, 25 (1981) 371–400.

V. Bornschier and C. Chase-Dunn, *Transnational Corporations and Underdevelopment* (New York: Praeger, 1985).

T. Boswell and W.J. Dixon, 'Dependency and Rebellion: A Cross-National Analysis', *American Sociological Review*, 55 (1990) 540–59.

G. Bourke, 'A New Broom?' *Africa Report* 36 (1991) 13–16.

G. Bourke, 'Côte d'Ivoire' in *The Africa Review 1991/92,* 15th edn (Edison, NJ: Hunter Publishing Inc., 1992).

Y.W. Bradshaw, 'Dependent Development in Black Africa: A Cross-National Study', *American Sociological Review*, 50 (1985) 195–207.

Y.W. Bradshaw and Z. Tshandu 'Foreign Capital Penetration, State Intervention, and Development in Sub-Saharan Africa', *International Studies Quarterly*, 34 (1990) 229–51.

V. Bulmer-Thomas, *The Political Economy of Central America Since 1920* (Cambridge; New York: Cambridge University Press, 1987).

T.M. Callaghy, 'Africa and the World Economy: Caught between a Rock and a Hard Place' in J.W. Harbeson and D. Rothchild, eds, *Africa in World Politics* (Boulder: Westview Press, 1991) pp.39–68.

T. Callaghy, 'Vision and Politics in the Transformation of the Global Political Economy: Lessons from the Second and Third Worlds', in R.O. Slater, B.M. Schutz and S.R. Dorr, eds, *Global Transformation and the Third World* (London: Adamantine Press and Boulder: Lynne Rienner 1993) pp.161–257.

B. Campbell, 'The Ivory Coast' in John Dunn, ed., *West African States: Failure and Promise* (Cambridge: Cambridge University Press, 1978) pp.66–116.

J.L.V. Carballo, 'Political Parties, Party Systems and Democracy in Costa Rica' in L. Goodman, W. LeoGrande, and J.M. Forman, eds, *Political Parties and Democracy in Central America* (Oxford; Boulder; San Francisco: Westview Press, 1993) pp.203–12.

E. Cardoso, and A. Fishlow, 'Latin American Economic Development: 1950–1980', *Journal of Latin American Studies*, supplement, 24 (1992) 197–218.

F. Cardoso, 'Associated-Dependent Development: Theoretical and Practical Implications' in A. Stepan, ed., *Authoritarian Brazil: Origins, Policies, and Future* (New Haven, CT: Yale University Press, 1973) pp.142–76.

F.H. Cardoso and E. Faletto, *Dependency and Development in Latin America* (Berkeley: University of CA Press, 1979).

R.M. Carmack, ed., *Harvest of Violence: the Maya Indians and the Guatemalan Crisis* (Norman: University of Oklahoma Press, 1988).

R.E. Caves, *Multinational Enterprise and Economic Analysis* (Cambridge: Cambridge University Press, 1982).

S. Chan, 'Developing Strength from Weakness: The State in Taiwan', *Journal of Developing Societies*, 4 (1988) 38–51.

S. Chan, 'Income Inequality Among LDCs: A Comparative Analysis of Alternative Perspectives', *International Studies Quarterly*, 33 (1989) 45–65.

S. Chan and C. Clark, 'MNCs and Developmentalism: Domestic Structures as an Explanation for East Asian Dynamism' in S. Chan, ed., *Foreign Direct Investment in a Changing Global Political Economy* (London: Macmillan Press, 1995), pp.84–103.

S. Chan, C. Clark, and D. Davis, 'State Entrepreneurship, Foreign Investment, Export Expansion, and Economic Growth', *Journal of Conflict Resolution*, 34 (1990) 102–29.

N. Chazan, 'The Political Transformation of Ghana Under the PNDC' in D. Rothchild, ed., *Ghana: The Political Economy of Adjustment* (London and Boulder: Lynne Rienner Publishers, 1991) pp.21–47.

N. Chazan, 'Liberalization, Governance, and Political Space in Ghana' in G. Hyden and M. Bratton, eds, *Governance and Politics in Africa* (London and Boulder: Lynne Rienner Publishers, 1992) pp.121–41.

H. Chenery, M.S. Ahluwalia, C.L.G. Bell, J.H. Duloy, and R. Jolly, *Redistribution with Growth* (London: Oxford University Press for the World Bank and the Institute of Development Studies, University of Sussex, 1974).

F. Ching, 'The Sick Man of Asia: Ramos Moves to Reverse Philippines' Image' in *Far Eastern Economic Review*, 156, no. 44 (1993) p.51.

C. Clark and J. Lemco, 'The Strong State and Development: A Growing List of Caveats,' *Journal of Developing Societies*, 4 (1988) 1–8.

R. Coase, 'The Nature of the Firm', *Economica*, 4 (1937) 386–405.

M. Cohen, *Urban Policy and Political Conflict in Africa: A Study of the Ivory Coast* (Chicago; London: University of Chicago Press, 1974).

T.F. Cooley and S.F. LeRoy, 'Atheoretical Macroeconometrics: A Critique', *Journal of Monetary Economics*, 16 (1985) 283–308.

R. Crook, 'Politics, the Cocoa Crisis, and Administration in Côte d'Ivoire', *Journal of Modern African Studies*, 28 (1990) 649–69.

R. Crook, 'State, Society and Political Institutions in Côte d'Ivoire and Ghana' in J. Manor, ed., *Rethinking Third World Politics* (London and New York: Longman, 1991) pp. 213–41.

B. Cummings, 'The origins and development of the Northeast Asian political economy: industrial sectors, product cycles, and political consequences', *International Organization*, 38 (1984) 1–40.

S.H. Davis, 'Introduction: Sowing the Seeds of Violence' in R.M. Carmack, ed., *Harvest of Violence: The Maya Indians and the Guatemalan Crisis* (Norman, OK: University of Oklahoma Press, 1988) pp.3–36.

B. den Tuinder, *Ivory Coast: The Challenge of Success* (London and Baltimore: Johns Hopkins University Press for the World Bank, 1978).

F.C. Deyo, *Dependent Development and Industrial Order: An Asian Case Study* (New York: Praeger, 1981).

F.C. Deyo, ed, *The Political Economy of the New Asian Industrialism* (Ithaca, NY: Cornell University Press, 1987).

C.J. Dixon, *South East Asia in the World-Economy* (Cambridge: Cambridge University Press, 1991).

D. Dollar, 'Outward-oriented Developing Economies Really do Grow More Rapidly', *Economic Development and Cultural Change*, 40 (1992) 523–44.

R.F. Doner, *Driving a Bargain: Automobile Industrialization and Japanese Firms in Southeast Asia* (Oxford; Berkeley; Los Angeles: University of California Press, 1991).

T. dos Santos, 'The Structure of Dependence', *American Economic Review*, 60 (1970) 231–6.

J. Dunkerly, *Power in the Isthmus: A Political History of Modern Central America* (London; New York: Verso, 1988).

J. Dunkerly, *The Pacification of Central America* (London; New York: Verso, 1994).

J. Dunning, 'Explaining the International Direct Investment Position of Countries: Towards a Dynamic or a Developmental Approach', *Weltwirtschaftliches Archiv*, 117 (1981) 30–64.

J. Dunning, ed., *Multinational Enterprises, Economic Structure and International Competitiveness* (New York: Wiley, 1985).

R. Ebel, 'Guatemala: The Politics of Unstable Stability' in H.J. Wiarda and H.F. Kline, eds, *Latin American Politics and Development*, 3rd edn, (Boulder: Westview Press, 1990) pp.498–518.

The *Economist*, 11 April 1992, p.33.

The *Economist*, 9 May 1992, p.38.

The *Economist*, 9 August 1997, p.31.

The *Economist*, 25 October 1997, pp.39–40.

D.J. Encarnation, *Dislodging Multinationals: India's Strategy in Comparative Perspective* (London and Ithaca: Cornell University Press, 1989).

P. Evans, *Dependent Development: The Alliance of Multinational, State and Local Capital in Brazil* (Princeton, NJ: Princeton University Press, 1979).

P.M. Evans, 'Economic and Security Dimensions of the Emerging Order in the Asia Pacific', in D. Wurfel and B. Burton, eds, *Southeast Asia in the New World Order: The Political Economy of a Dynamic Region* (New York: St Martin's Press, 1996), pp. 3–16.

G. Fairclough and R. Tasker, 'Separate and Unequal', *Far Eastern Economic Review*, 157, no. 15 (1994), pp.22–3.

Y.A. Faure, 'Côte d'Ivoire: Analyzing the Crisis', in D.B.C. O'Brien, J. Dunn and R. Rathbone, eds, *Contemporary West African States* (Cambridge: Cambridge University Press, 1989) pp.59–73.

J. Feres and A. Leon, 'The magnitude of poverty in Latin America', *CEPAL Review*, 41 (1990) 133–51.

D.K. Fieldhouse, *Black Africa 1945–80: Economic Decolonization and Arrested Development* (London, Boston, Sydney: Allen and Unwin, 1986).

G. Firebaugh, 'Growth Effects of Foreign and Domestic Investment', *American Journal of Sociology*, 98 (1992) 105–30.

A.G. Frank, 'The Development of Underdevelopment', *Monthly Review*, September (1966) 17–31.

S.H. Frankel, *Capital Investment in Africa: Its Cause and Effects* (London, New York, and Toronto: Oxford University Press, 1938).

J.R. Freeman, 'Granger Causality and the Time Series Analysis of Political Relationships', *American Journal of Political Science*, 27 (1983) 359–83.

J. Freeman, and R. Duvall 'International Economic Relations and the Entrepreneurial State', *Economic Development and Cultural Change*, 32 (1984) 373–400.

J. Freeman, J.T. Williams, and T.M. Lin, 'Vector Autoregression and the Study of Politics', *American Journal of Political Science,* 33 (1989) 842–47.

H.W. French, 'Closing a Chapter', *Africa Report*, 39, no. 2 (1994) pp.19–22.

J. Friedland, 'Collateral Damage', *Far Eastern Economic Review*, 155, no.21 (1992), pp.10–12.

K. Fuentes and J. Alberto 'European investment in Latin America: an overview', *CEPAL Review*, 48 (1992) 61–81.

M. Gbetibouo and C. Delgado, 'Lessons and Constraints of Export Crop-Led Growth: Cocoa in Ivory Coast' in I.W. Zartman and C. Delgado, eds, *The Political Economy of Ivory Coast* (New York: Praeger, 1984) pp.115–47.

B. Glassburner, 'ASEAN's "Other Four": Economic Policy and Economic Performance since 1970' in R.A. Scalapino, S. Sato and J. Wanandi, eds, *Asian Economic Development – Present and Future* (Berkeley: Institute of East Asian Studies, University of California, 1985) pp.161–94.

F. Golay, *The Philippines: Public Policy and National Economic Development* (Ithaca, NY: Cornell University Press, 1961).

C. Gonzalez-Vega and V.H. Cespedes, 'Costa Rica', in S. Rottenberg, ed., *Costa Rica and Uruguay*, A World Bank Comparative Study (Oxford: Oxford University Press, 1993) pp. 15–183.

H.R. Granados, 'Parties, Transitions, and the Political System in Guatemala' in L. Goodman, W. LeoGrande and J.M. Forman, eds., *Political Parties and Democracy in Central America* (Oxford; Boulder; San Francisco: Westview Press, 1992) pp.89–110.

R.H. Green, 'Reflections on Economic Strategy: Structure, Implementation, and Necessity: Ghana and the Ivory Coast, 1957–67', in P. Foster and A.R. Zolberg, eds, *Ghana and the Ivory Coast* (London and Chicago: University of Chicago Press, 1971) pp.231–64.

J.M. Grieco, 'Between dependency and autonomy: India's experience with the international computer industry', in T.H. Moran, ed., *Multinational Corporations: The Political Economy of Foreign Direct Investment* (Lexington, MA; Toronto: Lexington Books, 1985) pp.55–82.

J.M. Grieco, 'Foreign Investment and Development: Theories and Evidence', in T. Moran, ed., *Investing in Development: New Roles for Private Capital?* (Oxford; New Brunswick: Transaction Books, 1986).

B. Grier, 'Contradiction, Crisis, and Class Conflict: The State and Capitalist Development in Ghana Prior to 1948', in I.L. Markovitz, ed. *Studies in Power and Class in Africa* (Oxford; New York: Oxford University Press, 1987) pp.27–49.

J. Grunwald and P. Musgrove, *Natural Resources in Latin American Development* (London; Baltimore: Johns Hopkins Press, 1970).

L. Gumundson, *Costa Rica Before Coffee: Society and Economy on the Eve of the Export Boom* (Baton Rouge and London: Louisiana State University Press, 1986).

E. Gyimah-Boadi, 'State Enterprises Divestiture: Recent Ghanaian Experiences', in D. Rothchild, ed., *Ghana: The Political Economy of Adjustment* (London and Boulder: Lynne Rienner Publishers, 1991) pp.193–208.

S. Haggard, 'The Newly Industrializing Countries in the International System', *World Politics*, 38 (1986) 343–70.

S. Haggard, *Pathways from the Periphery: The Politics of Growth in Newly Industrializing Countries*, (London and Ithaca: Cornell University Press, 1990).

G.B. Hainsworth, 'Economic Growth and Poverty in Southeast Asia: Malaysia, Indonesia and the Philippines', *Pacific Affairs*, 52 (1979) 5–41.

D.G.E. Hall, *A History of South-East Asia*, 4th edn (London: Macmillan Press Ltd., 1981).

G. Hawes, *The Philippine State and the Marcos Regime: The Politics of Export* (London and Ithaca: Cornell University Press, 1987).

D. Healey, *Japanese Capital Exports and Asian Economic Development* (Development Centre of the Organization for Economic Co-operation and Development, 1991).

J.M. Healey, *The Economics of Aid* (Beverley Hills, CA: Sage Publications, 1971).

R.M. Hecht, 'The Ivory Coast Economic "Miracle": What Benefits Peasant Farmers?' *Journal of Modern African Studies*, 21 (1983) 25–53.

S. Hein, 'Trade Strategy and the Dependency Hypothesis: A Comparison of Policy, Foreign Investment, and Economic Growth in Latin American and East Asia' *Economic Development and Cultural Change*, 40 (1992), 495–521.

B. Herrick, and C.P. Kindleberger, *Economic Development*, 4th edn (New York: McGraw-Hill Book Co., 1983).

K. Hewison, 'The state and capitalist development in Thailand', in R. Higgott and R. Robison, eds, *South East Asia: Essays in the Political Economy of Structural Change* (London; Boston; Melbourne; Routledge and Kegan Paul, 1985) pp.266–94.

K. Hewison, 'National interests and economic downturn: Thailand', in R. Robison, K. Hewison, and R. Higgott, eds, *Southeast Asia in the 1980s: The Politics of Economic Crisis* (London; Sydney; Boston: Allen and Unwin, 1987) pp.52–79.

H. Hill and S. Jayasuriya, 'Philippine Economic Performance in Regional Perspective', *Contemporary Southeast Asia*, 6 (1984) 135–58.

F. Hoole and C. Huang, 'The Global Conflict Process', *Journal of Conflict Resolution*, 33 (1989) 142–63.

E. Hutchful, ed., *The IMF and Ghana: The Confidential Report* (London; New Jersey: Institute for African Alternatives and Zed Books Ltd., 1987).

E. Hutchful, 'From "Revolution" to Monetarism: The Economics and Politics of the Adjustment Programme in Ghana', in B.K. Campbell and J. Loxley, eds, *Structural Adjustment in Africa* (London: Macmillan, 1989).

S. Hymer, *The International Operations of National Firms: A Study of Direct Foreign Investment* (Cambridge, MA: MIT Press, 1976).

IMF, *International Financial Statistics Yearbook* (various years).

R. Jackman, 'Dependence on Foreign Investment and Economic Growth in the Third World', *World Politics*, 34 (1982) 319–40.

R. Jackman, *Power without Force: The Political Capacity of Nation-States* (Ann Arbor: University of Michigan Press, 1993).

R. Jeffries, 'Ghana: the political economy of personal rule', in D.B.C. O'Brien, J. Dunn, and R. Rathbone, eds, *Contemporary West African States* (Cambridge: Cambridge University Press, 1989) pp.75–98.

J.C. Jenkins and A.J. Kposowa, 'The Political Origins of African Military Coups: Ethnic Competition, Military Centrality, and the Struggle Over the Postcolonial State', *International Studies Quarterly*, 36 (1992) 271–92.

R. Jenkins, *Transnational Corporations and the Latin American Automobile Industry* (Pittsburgh: University of Pittsburgh Press, 1987).

R. Jenkins, *Transnational Corporations and Uneven Development: the Internationalization of Capital and the Third World* (London and New York: Methuen, 1987).

S. Jonas, "Elections and Transitions: The Guatemalan and Nicaraguan Cases' in J. Booth and M. Seligson, eds, *Elections and Democracy in Central America* (Chapel Hill; London: University of North Carolina Press, 1989), pp.126–57.

R. Joseph, 'A Winning Formula', *Africa Report*, 38 (1993) 45–6.

P. Karp, 'Guatemala' in E. Paus, ed., *Struggle Against Dependence: Nontraditional Export Growth in Central America and the Caribbean* (London; Boulder: Westview Press, 1988), pp.65–84.

F.J. Kendrick, 'The Nonmilitary Neutrality of Costa Rica' in R.L. Woodward, Jr., ed., *Central America: Historical Perspectives on the Contemporary Crises*, (New York: Greenwood Press, 1988) pp.241–60.

T. Killick, *Development Economics in Action: A Study of Economic Policies in Ghana* (New York: St. Martin's Press, 1978).

W. Kirk, 'South East Asia in the colonial period: cores and peripheries in development processes', in D. Dwyer, ed., *South East Asian Development: Geographical Perspectives* (Essex: Longman Scientific and Technical; and New York: John Wiley and Sons, 1990) pp.15–47.

K. Kojima, *Direct Foreign Investment: A Japanese Model of Multinational Business Operations* (New York: Praeger, 1978).

J. Kraus, 'Political Change, Conflict, and Development in Ghana', in P. Foster and A.R. Zolberg, eds, *Ghana and the Ivory Coast* (London; Chicago: University of Chicago Press, 1971) pp.33–72.

J. Kraus, 'The Political Economy of Stabilization and Structural Adjustment in Ghana' in D. Rothchild, ed., *Ghana: The Political Economy of Adjustment* (London and Boulder: Lynne Rienner Publishers, 1991) pp.119–55.

J. Kraus, 'Debt, Structural Adjustment, and Private Investment in Africa' in R.A. Ahene and B.S. Katz, eds, *Privatization and Investment in Sub-Saharan Africa* (New York: Praeger, 1992) pp.73–92.

M. Krongkaew, 'The Distribution of and Access to Health Services in Thailand', in P. Richards, ed., *Basic Needs and Government Policies in Thailand* (Singapore: Maruzen Asia, 1982) pp.67–104.

A. Laothamatas, *Business Associations and the New Political Economy of Thailand: From Bureaucratic Polity to Liberal Corporatism* (Oxford; Boulder; San Francisco: Westview Press, 1992).

D.A. Lax and J.K. Sebenius, *The Manager as Negotiator: Bargaining for Cooperation and Competitive Gain* (London: Collier Macmillan; New York: Free Press, 1986).

H.P. Lehman, *Indebted Development: Strategic Bargaining and Economic Adjustment in the Third World* (New York: St. Martin's Press, 1993).

H. Lenter, *State Formation in Central America: The Struggle for Autonomy, Development and Democracy* (Westport, CN: Greenwood Press, 1993).

M.I. Lichbach, 'An Evaluation of "Does Economic Inequality Breed Conflict?" Studies' *World Politics*, 41 (1989) 431– 70.

C.W. Lindsey, 'In Search of Dynamism: Foreign Investment in the Philippines under Martial Law', *Pacific Affairs*, 56 (1983) 477–94.

C.W. Lindsey and E.M. Valencia, 'Foreign Direct Investment in the Philippines: A Review of the Literature', in *Survey of Philippines Development Research II* (Manila: Philippine Institute of Development Studies, 1982) pp.153–232.

S.M. Lipset, 'Some Social Requisites of Democracy: Economic Development and Political Legitimacy', *American Political Science Review*, 53 (1959) 69–105.

B. London and T.D. Robinson, 'The Effect of International Dependence on Income Inequality and Political Violence', *American Sociological Review*, 54 (1989) 305–8.

B. London and B.A. Williams, 'Multinational Corporate Penetration, Protest, and Basic Needs Provision in Non-Core Nations: A Cross-National Analysis', *Social Forces*, 66 (1988) 747–73.

R. Lucas, 'On the Determinants of Direct Investment: Evidence from East and South East Asia', *World Development*, 21 (1993) 391–406.

J. McBeth, 'Steady is not Enough' *Far Eastern Economic Review*, 156, no.26 (1993), 16–17.

P.J. McGowan and D.L. Smith, 'Economic Dependency in Black Africa: an analysis of competing theories', *International Organization*, 32 (1978) 179–235.

R.D. McKinlay and R. Little, 'A Foreign Policy Model of U.S. Bilateral Aid Allocation', *World Politics*, 30 (1977) 58–86.

R.D. McKinlay and T. Mughan, *Aid and Arms to the Third World* (London: F. Pinter, 1984).

S. McMillan, 'Foreign Direct Investment in Ghana and Côte d'Ivoire' in S. Chan, ed., *Foreign Direct Investment in a Changing Global Political Economy* (London; Macmillan, 1995), pp.150–65.

E.R. Mercado, 'Culture, Economics and Revolt in Mindano: The Origins of the MNLF and the Politics of Moro Separatism', in J.J. Lim and S. Vani, eds, *Armed Separatism in Southeast Asia* (Singapore: Institute of Southeast Asia Studies, 1984) pp. 151–75.

G. Michael and M. Noel, 'The Ivorian Economy and Alternative Trade Regimes', in I.W. Zartman and C. Delgado, eds, *The Political Economy of Ivory Coast* (New York: Praeger, 1984) pp. 77–114.

J.S. Migdal, 'Strong States, Weak States: Power and Accommodation', in M. Weiner and S.P. Huntington, eds, *Understanding Political Development*

(London; Glenview, II: Scott, Foresman/ Little, Brown Higher Education, 1987) pp. 391–434.

R.F. Mikesell, *U.S. Private and Government Investment Abroad* (Eugene, OR: University of Oregon Books, 1962).

R.S. Milne, 'The Role of Government Corporations in the Philippines', *Pacific Affairs*, 34 (1961) 257–70.

B.E. Moon and W.J. Dixon, 'Politics, the State, and Basic Human Needs: A Cross-National Study', *American Journal of Political Science*, 29 (1985) 661–94.

M.M. Moors, 'Indian Labor and the Guatemalan Crisis: Evidence from History and Anthropology' in R.L. Woodward, Jr., ed., *Central America: Historical Perspectives on the Contemporary Crises*, (New York: Greenwood Press, 1988) pp.67–84.

T.H. Moran, 'Multinational corporations and dependency: a dialogue for dependentistas and non-dependentistas', *International Organization*, 32 (1978) 79–100.

T.H. Moran, 'Multinational Corporations and the Developing Countries: An Analytical Overview' in T.H. Moran, ed., *Multinational Corporations: The Political Economy of Foreign Direct Investment* (Lexington, MA: Lexington Books, D.C. Heath and Co., 1985) pp.3–24.

J. Morisset, 'The Impact of Foreign Capital Inflows on Domestic Savings Reexamined: the Case of Argentina', *World Development*, 17 (1989) 1709–15.

M.D. Morris, *Measuring the Condition of the World's Poor: The Physical Quality of Life Index* (New York: Pergamon, 1979).

D.G. Morrison, R.C. Mitchell, and J.N. Paden, *Black Africa: A Comparative Handbook*, 2nd edn (New York: Paragon House, 1989).

L.K. Mytelka, 'Foreign Business and Economic Development' in I.W. Zartman and C. Delgado, eds, *The Political Economy of Ivory Coast* (New York: Praeger, 1984) pp.149–74.

National Economic and Development Authority, *National Income Accounts*, (NEDA, Manila, various years).

National Economic and Development Authority, *1990 Philippine Development Report* (NEDA: Manila, 1990).

National Economic and Development Authority, *Philippine Statistical Yearbook* (NEDA: Manila, 1987).

National Economic and Development Authority, *Statistical Yearbook of the Philippines* (NEDA: Manila, various years).

National Statistics Office, *Philippine Yearbook*, (Manila, 1989).

C.D. Neher, *Politics in Southeast Asia* (Cambridge, MA: Schenkman Publishing Co., Inc., 1981).

E.A. Nordlinger, 'Taking the State Seriously', in M. Weiner and S.P. Huntington, eds, *Understanding Political Development* (London; Glenview, II: Scott, Foresman / Little, Brown Higher Education, 1987) pp.353–90.

OECD, *Geographical Distribution of Financial Flows to Developing Countries* (various years).

C. O'Faircheallaigh, 'Foreign Investment and Development in Less Developed Countries', *Inter-American Economic Affairs*, 39 (1985) 27–35.

R. Ofori, 'Rawlings' Biggest Challenge', *Africa Report* 39 (1993) 53–5.

T. O'Hearn, 'TNCs, Intervening Mechanism and Economic Growth in Ireland: A Longitudinal Test and Extension of the Bornschier Model', *World Development*, 18 (1990) 417–29.

M. Olson, Jr., 'Rapid Growth as a Destabilizing Force', *Journal of Economic History*, 23 (1963) 529–52.

J.O.C. Onyemelukwe and M.O. Filani, *Economic Geography of West Africa* (London; Lagos; New York: Longman, 1983).

P. Osei-Kwame and P.J.Taylor, 'A Politics of Failure: The Political Geography of Ghanaian Elections, 1954–1979', *Annals of the Association of American Geographers*, 7 (1984) 574–89.

E. Pantojas-Garcia, *Development Strategies as Ideology: Puerto Rico's Export-Led Industrialization Experience* (London and Boulder: Lynne Rienner Publishers, 1990).

D. Pellow and N. Chazan, *Ghana: Coping with Uncertainty* (Boulder: Westview Press, 1986).

W. Pelupessy and J. Weeks, eds, *Economic Maladjustment in Central America* (New York: St. Martin's Press, 1993).

V. Perara, *Unfinished Conquest: The Guatemalan Tragedy* (London; Berkeley; Los Angeles: University of California Press, 1993).

D. Pierce and L. Haugh, 'Causality in Temporal Systems: Characterizations and a Survey', *Journal of Econometrics*, 5 (1977) 265–93.

R. Ram, 'Government Size and Economic Growth: A New Framework and Some Evidence from Cross-Section and Time-Series Data', *American Economic Review*, 76 (1986) 191–203.

R. Ramsaran, *US Investment in Latin America and the Caribbean: Trends and Issues* (New York: St. Martin's Press, 1985).

R. Rathbone, 'Ghana' in J. Dunn, ed., *West African States: Failure and Promise* (Cambridge: Cambridge University Press, 1978) pp.22–35.

J. Ravenhill, 'Inequality in the Third World: A Reexamination', *Comparative Political Studies*, 19 (1986) 259–68.

H.V. Richter and C.T. Edwards, 'Recent Economic Developments in Thailand', in R. Ho and E.C. Chapman, eds, *Studies of Contemporary Thailand* (Canberra: Australian National University, 1973) pp.17–65.

F.W. Riggs, *Thailand: The Modernization of a Bureaucratic Polity* (Honolulu: East-West Center Press, 1966).

D. Rimmer, *Staying Poor: Ghana's Political Economy 1950–1990* (Oxford; New York; Seoul; Tokyo: Pergamon Press, 1992).

J. Rippy, *British Investments in Latin America, 1822 -1949* (Minneapolis: University of Minnesota Press, 1959).

D.A. Rondinelli, *Spatial Analysis for Regional Development: A Case Study in the Bicol River Basin of the Philippines* (Tokyo: The United Nations University, 1980).

L.L. Rood, 'Foreign Investment in African Manufacturing' *Journal of Modern African Studies*, 13 (1975) 19–34.

W.W. Rostow, *Politics and the Stages of Growth* (Cambridge: Cambridge University Press, 1971).

D. Rothchild and E. Gyimah-Boadi 'Ghana's Economic Decline and Development Strategies' in J. Ravenhill, ed., *Africa in Economic Crisis* (New York: Columbia University Press, 1986) pp.254–85.

J.M. Rothgeb, Jr., *Myths and Realities of Foreign Investment in Poor Countries: the Modern Leviathan of the Third World* (New York: Praeger, 1989).

D. Rueschemeyer and P.B. Evans, 'The State and Economic Transformation: Toward an Analysis of the Conditions Underlying Effective Intervention', in P.B. Evans, D. Rueschemeyer, and T. Skocpol eds, *Bringing the State Back In* (Cambridge: Cambridge University Press, 1985) pp.44–77.

D.R. SarDesai, *Southeast Asia: Past and Present* (Boulder; San Francisco: Westview Press, 1981).

D.R. SarDesai, *Southeast Asia: Past and Present,* 2nd edn (Boulder; San Francisco: Westview Press, 1989).

S. Schlesinger and S. Kinzer, *Bitter Fruit: The Untold Story of the American Coup in Guatemala* (Garden City, NY: Doubleday, 1982).

F. Schneider and B.S. Frey, 'Economic and Political Determinants of Foreign Direct Investment', *World Development*, 13 (1985) 161–75.

H. Schneider, *Adjustment and Equity in Côte d'Ivoire* (Paris: OECD, 1992).

R.W. Scofield, 'Land Reform in Central America' in R. Prosterman, M. Temple, and T. Hanstad, eds, *Agrarian Reform and Grassroots Development: Ten Case Studies* (London; Boulder: Lynne Rienner, 1990).

Seligson, Mitchell (1980) *Peasants of Costa Rica and the Development of Agrarian Capitalism* (Madison, WI: University of Wisconsin Press).

Seligson, Mitchell (1990) 'Costa Rica' in Howard J. Wiarda and Harvey F. Kline, eds, *Latin American Politics and Development*, 3rd edition (Boulder: Westview Press), pp.455–66.

T.H. Silcock, *Thailand: Social and Economic Studies in Development* (Canberra: Australian National University Press, 1967).

C.A. Sims, 'Money Income and Causality' *American Economic Review*, 62 (1972) 540–52.

T. Skocpol, 'Bringing the State Back In: Strategies of Analysis in Current Research' in P.B. Evans, D. Rueschemeyer, and T. Skocpol eds, *Bringing the State Back In* (Cambridge: Cambridge University Press, 1985) pp.3–43.

H. Starr, F. Hoole, and J. Hart 'The Relationship between Defense Spending and Inflation', *Journal of Conflict Resolution*, 28 (1984) 103–22.

Statistical Yearbook Thailand.

R.B. Stauffer, 'The Philippine Political Economy: (dependent) state capitalism in the corporatist mode', in R. Higgott and R. Robison, eds, *Southeast Asia: Essays in the Political Economy of Structural Change* (London; Boston; Melbourne; Henley: Routledge and Kegan Paul, 1985) pp.241–65.

J. Stowe, *Siam Becomes Thailand: A Story of Intrigue* (London: Hurst and Company, 1991).

A. Suehiro, *Capital Accumulation in Thailand, 1855–1985* (Tokyo: The Centre for East Asian Cultural Studies, 1989).

R. Summers and A. Heston, 'The Penn World Table (Mark 5): An Expanded Set of International Comparisons, 1950–88' *Quarterly Journal of Economics*, (1991) 327–68.

C. Taylor and M. Hudson, with K. Dolan, *World Handbook of Political and Social Indicators*, 2nd edn (New Haven: Yale University Press, 1972).

C. Taylor and D. Jodice, *World Handbook of Political and Social Indicators, vols 1 and 2*, 3rd edn (London and New Haven: Yale University Press, 1983).

K.P. Thomas, *Capital Beyond Borders: States and Firms in the Auto Industry, 1960–94* (London: Macmillan Press).

R. Tiglao, 'Issues Held at Ransom: Crime, Power Struggles Lead Political Agenda' *Far Eastern Economic Review* 155, no. 37 (1992) p.17.

R. Tiglao, 'Paralyzed by Politics' *Far Eastern Economic Review* 157, no.19, (1994) 22–5.

M. Todaro, *Economic Development in the Third World* 3rd edn (New York: Longman, 1985).

E. Torres Rivas, *History and Society in Central America*, translated by Douglass Sullivan-Gonzalez, Translations from Latin America Series (Austin: University of Texas Press, 1993).

R.H. Trudeau, 'The Guatemalan Election of 1985: Prospects for Democracy' in J. Booth and M. Seligson, eds., *Elections and Democracy in Central America* (London; Chapel Hill, NC: University of North Carolina Press, 1989), pp.93–125.

R.H. Trudeau, *Guatemalan Politics: The Popular Struggle for Democracy* (London; Boulder: Lynne Rienner Publishers, 1993).

F. Tugwell, 'Petroleum Policy in Venezuela: Lessons in the Politics of Dependence Management', *Studies in Comparative International Development*, 9 (1974) 84–120.

United Nations, *Government Finance Statistics Yearbook* (United Nations: New York, various years).

United Nations, *National Accounts Statistics: Compendium of Income Distribution Statistics* (United Nations: New York, 1985).

United Nations, *Statistical Yearbook for Asia and the Pacific, 1996* (UN: Bangkok, Thailand, 1996).

United Nations Council on Trade and Development, *Handbook of International Trade and Development Statistics, 1994* (New York and Geneva, UN, 1994).

United Nations Centre on Transnational Corporations, *Salient Features and Trends in Foreign Direct Investment* (United Nations: New York, 1983a).

United Nations Centre on Transnational Corporations, *Transnational Corporations in World Development: Third Survey* (United Nations: New York, 1983b).

United Nations Centre on Transnational Corporations, *World Investment Report 1991: The Triad in Foreign Direct Investment* (New York, 1991).

United Nations Centre on Transnational Corporations, *World Investment Report: Transnational Corporations as Engines of Growth*, (New York, 1992).

United Nations Centre on Transnational Corporations, *Transnational Corporations and Integrated International Production*, (New York, 1993).

United Nations Centre on Transnational Corporations, *World Investment Report* (New York, 1996).

United Nations Conference on Trade and Development *The Least Developed Countries 1987 Report* (New York: United Nations, 1988).

UN Economic Commission for Latin America and the Caribbean, *Statistical Yearbook for Latin America and the Caribbean* (New York: United Nations, 1991).

UNESCO, *Statistical Yearbook* (United Nations: New York, various years).

UNESCO, *Literacy Situation in Asia and the Pacific, Country Studies: Thailand* (Bangkok: UNESCO Regional Office for Education in Asia and the Pacific, 1984).

U.S. Department of Commerce, *U.S. Business Investments in Foreign Countries: A Supplement to the Survey of Current Business* (Washington, D.C., 1960).

R. Vernon, 'International Investment and International Trade in the Product Cycle', *Quarterly Journal of Economics*, May, 1966 pp.190–207.

R. Vernon, *Sovereignty at Bay* (New York: Basic Books, 1971).

R. Vernon, *Storm over the Multinationals* (Cambridge, MA: Harvard University Press, 1977).

C.M. Vilas, *Between Earthquakes and Volcanoes* (New York: Monthly Reveiw Press, 1995), translated by Ted Kuster.

M.J. Watts and T.J. Bassett, 'Politics, the State and Agrarian Development: a comparative study of Nigeria and the Ivory Coast', *Political Geography Quarterly*, 5 (1986) 103–25.

B. Wawm, *The Economies of the ASEAN Countries: Indonesia, Malaysia, Philippines, Singapore and Thailand* (London: Macmillan, 1982).

F.S. Weaver, *Inside the Volcano: The History and Political Economy of Central America*, Series in Political Economy and Economic Development in Latin America (Boulder: Westview Press, 1994).

J. Weeks, *The Economies of Central America* (New York; London: Holmes & Meier, 1985).

D. Wheeler and A. Mody 'International investment location decisions, the case of U.S. firms,' *Journal of International Economics*, 33 (1992) 57–76.

J. Wilkie, ed., *Statistical Abstract of Latin America*, vol.29, part 2 (Los Angeles: UCLA Latin American Center Publications, 1992).

J. Wilkie, C.A. Contreras and C.A. Weber, *Statistical Abstract of Latin America*, vol.30, parts 1 and 2 (Los Angeles: UCLA Latin American Center Publications, 1993).

R.G. Williams, *Export Agriculture and the Crisis in Central America* (London; Chapel Hill: University of North Carolina Press, 1986).

O. Williamson, *Markets and Hierarchies* (New York: Free Press, 1975).

L. Willmore, 'Direct Foreign Investment in Central American Manufacturing', *World Development* 4 (1976), 499–517.

L. Willmore, 'Industrial policy in Central America', *CEPAL Review* 48 (1992) 95–105.

D. Woods, 'State Action and Class Interests in the Ivory Coast', *African Studies Review*, 31 (1988) 93–116.

R.L. Woodward, Jr, *Central America: A Nation Divided* (New York; Oxford: Oxford University Press, 1985).

World Bank, *World Tables* (London; Baltimore: Johns Hopkins University Press for the World Bank, various years).

World Bank, *Ghana: Policies and Program for Adjustment* (Washington, D.C.: World Bank, 1984a).

World Bank, *World Development Report* (Oxford; New York: Oxford University Press, 1988 and 1996).

World Bank, *Sub-Saharan Africa: From Crisis to Sustainable Growth* (Washington, D.C.: World Bank, 1989).

World Bank, *Trends in Developing Economies 1991* (Washington, D.C.: World Bank, 1991).

World Bank, *Ghana: 2000 and Beyond* (Washington, D.C.: World Bank, 1993).

M. Wubneh, 'Patterns of Foreign Investment in Africa, 1970–1988', in R.A. Ahene and B.S. Katz, eds, *Privatization and Investment in Sub-Saharan Africa* (New York: Praeger, 1992) pp.55–72.

D.K. Wyatt, *Thailand: A Short History* (London; New Haven: Yale University Press, 1984).

A.Y. Yansane, *Decolonization in West African States with French Colonial Legacy: Comparison and Contrast, Development in Guinea, the Ivory Coast, and Senegal (1945–1980)* (Cambridge, MA: Schenkman Publishing Co., Inc., 1984).

K. Yoshihara, *Philippine Industrialization: Foreign and Domestic Capital* (Oxford; Manila: Ateneo de Manila University Press; Singapore: Oxford University Press, 1985).

I.W. Zartman and C. Delgado, eds., *The Political Economy of Ivory Coast* (New York: Praeger, 1984).

A.R. Zolberg, *One-Party Government in the Ivory Coast* (Princeton, NJ: Princeton University Press, 1969).

A.R. Zolberg, 'Political Development in the Ivory Coast Since Independence', in P. Foster and A.R. Zolberg, eds, *Ghana and the Ivory Coast* (Chicago; London: University of Chicago Press, 1971) pp.9–31.

Bibliography

I. Adelman and C. Taft Morris, *Economic Growth and Social Equity in Developing Countries* (Stanford: Stanford University Press, 1973).

R.A. Ahene and B.S. Katz, eds, *Privatization and Investment in Sub-Saharan Africa* (New York: Praeger, 1992).

N. Ahmad, *Deficit Financing, Inflation and Capital Formation: The Ghanian Experience, 1960–65* (Munchen: Weltforum Verlag, 1970).

A.H. Amsden, 'The State and Taiwan's Economic Development' in P.B. Evans, D. Rueschemeyer, and T. Skocpol eds, *Bringing the State Back In* (Cambridge: Cambridge University Press, 1985) pp.78–106.

T.P. Anderson, *Politics in Central America*, rev. edn (London; New York; Westport: Praeger, 1988).

A. Armstrong, 'The Political Consequences of Economic Dependence', *Journal of Conflict Resolution*, 25 (1981) 401–28.

E. Azar, 'Analysis of International Events', *Peace Research Reviews*, 4 (1970).

B. Balassa and Associates, *Development Strategies in Semi-Industrial Economies* (Baltimore: Johns Hopkins University Press, 1982).

W.L. Baldwin and W.D. Maxwell, eds, *The Role of Foreign Financial Assistance to Thailand in the 1980s*, (London: Lexington, MA: Toronto; Lexington Books, D.C. Heath and Company, 1975).

Bank of Ghana, *Annual Report* (various years).

Bank of Ghana, *Quarterly Economic Bulletin* (various years).

M. Beenstock, (1980) 'Political Econometry of Official Development Assistance', *World Development*, 8 (1980) 137–44.

R. Benjamin and R. Duvall, 'The Capitalist State in Context' in R. Benjamin and S. Elkin, eds, *The Democratic State* (University of Kansas Press, 1985) pp.19–57.

R.J. Berg and D.F. Gordon, eds, *Cooperation for International Development: The United States and the Third World in the 1990s* (Boulder: Lynne Rienner Publishers, 1989).

H.S. Bienen and M. Gersovitz, 'Economic Stabilization, Conditionality, and Political Stability', *International Organization*, 39 (1985) 729–54.

T.J. Biersteker, *Distortion or Development? Contending Perspectives on the Multinational Corporation* (Cambridge, MA: The MIT Press, 1978).

K.A. Bollen, 'Issues in the Comparative Measurement of Political Democracy', *American Sociological Review*, 45 (1980) 370–90.

K.A. Bollen, 'World System Position, Dependency, and Democracy: The Cross-National Evidence', *American Sociological Review*, 48 (1983) 468–79.

K.A. Bollen and R.W. Jackman, 'Political Democracy and the Size Distribution of Income', *American Sociological Review*, 50 (1985) 438–57.

K.A. Bollen and R.W. Jackman, 'Democracy, Stability and Dichotomies', *American Sociological Review*, 54 (1989) 612–22.

J.A. Booth, 'Socioeconomic and Political Roots of National Revolts in Central America', *Latin American Research Review*, 26 (1991) 33–73.

V. Bornschier, 'Multinational Corporations and Economic Growth: a Cross-National Test of the Decapitalization Thesis', *Journal of Development Economics*, 7 (1980) 191–210.

V. Bornschier, *Comparative World Data: A Statistical handbook for the Social Sciences* (Baltimore: Johns Hopkins University Press, 1988).

V. Bornschier and T.H. Ballmer-Cao, 'Income Inequality: A Cross-National Study of the Relationships Between MNC-Penetration, Dimensions of the Power Structure and Income Distribution', *American Sociological Review*, 44 (1979) 487–506.

V. Bornschier, C. Chase-Dunn and R. Rubinson, 'Cross-National Evidence of the Effects of Foreign Investment and Aid on Economic Growth and Inequality: A Survey of Findings and a Reanalysis', *American Journal of Sociology*, 84 (1978) 651–83.

P. Bowles, 'Foreign Aid and Domestic Savings in Less Developed Countries: Some Tests for Causality' *World Development*, 15 (1987) 789–96.

M.M. Burdette, *Zambia: Between Two Worlds* (Boulder: Westview Press, 1988).

J.A. Caporaso, 'Introduction to the Special Issue of International Organization on Dependence and Dependency in the Global System', *International Organization*, 32 (1978) 1–12.

J.A. Caporaso, 'Dependency Theory: Continuities and Discontinuities in Development Studies', *International Organization*, 34 (1980) 605–28.

J.A. Caporaso, 'Industrialization in the Periphery: The Evolving Global Division of Labor', *International Studies Quarterly*, 25 (1981) 347–84.

J.A. Caporaso, 'Introduction to a Special Issue on the State in Comparative International Perspective', *Comparative Political Studies*, 21 (1988) 3–12.

F. Cardoso, 'The Consumption of Dependency Theory in the United States', *Latin American Research Review*, 12 (1977) 7–24.

C.C. Carvounis, *The Debt Dilemma of Developing Nations: Issues and Cases* (Westport, Connecticut: Quorum Books, 1984).

R. Cassen, R. Jolly, J. Sewell and R. Wood, eds, *Rich Country Interests and Third World Development* (London: Croom Helm, 1982).

Central Bureau of Statistics, *Economic Survey* (Accra, Ghana, various years).

S. Chan, *East Asian Dynamics: Growth, Order and Security in the Pacific Region* (Boulder; San Francisco: Westview Press, 1990).

S. Chan, ed., *Foreign Direct Investment in a Changing Global Political Economy*, (London: Macmillan, 1995).

N. Chazan, *An Anatomy of Ghanaian Politics: Managing Political Recession, 1969–1982* (Boulder, CO: Westview Press, 1983).

H. Chenery, M.S. Ahluwalia, C.L.G. Bell, J.H. Duloy and R. Jolly, *Redistribution with Growth* (London: Oxford University Press for the World Bank and the Institute of Development Studies, University of Sussex, 1974).

H. Chenery and N.G. Carter, 'Foreign Assistance and Development Performance', *American Economic Review*, 63 (1973) 459–69.

H. Chenery and A. Strout, 'Foreign Assistance and Economic Development', *American Economic Review*, September 1966.

H. Chenery and M. Syrquin, *Patterns of Development, 1950–1970* (Oxford and New York: Oxford University Press 1975).

Y.A. Choong, 'Foreign Investment and Trade Promotion Schemes: with some Comparisons between Korea and Latin American Countries', *Journal of Development Economics*, 13 (1988) 163–79.

C. Clark, 'The Taiwan Exception: Implications for Contending Political Economy Paradigms', *International Studies Quarterly*, 31 (1987) 327–56.

B.J. Cohen, 'International Debt and linkage Strategies: Some Foreign-Policy Implications for the United States', *International Organization*, 39 (1985) 699–727.

B.J. Cohen, 'The political economy of international trade', *International Organization*, 44 (1990) 261–81.

J.M. Cohen, M.S. Grindle, and S.T. Walker, 'Foreign Aid and Conditions Precedent: Political and Bureaucratic Dimensions', *World Development*, 13 (1985) 1211–30.

D.C. Colander, ed., *Neoclassical Political Economy: The Analysis of Rent-Seeking and DUP Activities* (Cambridge, MA: Ballinger Publishing Company, 1984).

D.C. Dacy, 'Foreign Aid, Government Consumption, Saving and Growth in Less-developed Countries', *Economic Journal*, 85 (1975) 548–61.

J. Delacroix, 'The Export of Raw Materials and Economic Growth: A Cross-National Study', *American Sociological Review*, 42 (1977) 795–808.

J. Delacroix, 'The Distributive State in the World System', *Studies in Comparative International Development*, 15 (1980) 3–21.

J. Delacroix and C. Ragin, 'Structural Blockage: A Cross-national Study of Economic Dependency, State Efficacy, and Underdevelopment', *American Journal of Sociology*, 86 (1981) 1311–47.

H. de Soto, *The Other Path: The Invisible Revolution in the Third World* (New York: Harper & Row, 1989; translated by June Abbott).

G. Di Palma and L. Whitehead, eds, *The Central American Impasse* (New York: St. Martin's Press, 1986).

M.B. Dolan and B.W. Tomlin, 'First World-Third World Linkages: External Relations and Economic Development', *International Organization*, 34 (1980) 41–64.

C. Doran, G. Modelski, and C. Clark, *North/South Relations: Studies of Dependency Reversal* (New York: Praeger, 1983).

J.M. Dowling, and U. Hiemenz, 'Biases in the Allocation of Foreign Aid: Some New Evidence', *World Development*, 13 (1985) 535–41.

R. Duvall, 'Dependence and Dependicia Theory: Notes Toward Precision of Concept and Argument', *International Organization*, 32 (1978) 51–78.

R. Duvall and J.R. Freeman, 'The State and Dependent Development', *International Studies Quarterly*, 25 (1981) 99–118.

R. Duvall and J.R. Freeman, 'The Techno-Bureaucratic Elite and the Entrepreneurial State in Dependent Industrialization', *American Political Science Review*, 77 (1983) 469–587.

R.L. Merritt and B.M. Russett eds, *National Development to Global Community: Essays in Honor of Karl W. Deutsch* (London: George Allen and Unwin, 1981).

W.N. Eskridge, Jr., ed., *A Dance Along the Precipice: The Political and Economic Dimensions of the International Debt Problem* (Lexington, MA: Lexington Books, 1985) pp.xv–xxvii.

P. Evans, 'Multinationals, State-Owned Corporations, and the Transformation of Imperialism: A Brazilian Case Study', *Economic Development and Cultural Change*, 26 (1977) 43–64.

P.B. Evans, D. Rueschemeyer, T. Skocpol, eds, *Bringing the State Back In* (Cambridge; New York: Cambridge University Press, 1985).

I.K. Feierabend and R.L. Feierabend, 'Aggressive Behaviors within Polities, 1948–1962: A Cross-National Study', *Journal of Conflict Resolution*, 10 (1966) 249–71.

R. Fiala, 'Labor Force Structure and the Size Distribution of Income Within Countries, 1960–80', *International Studies Quarterly*, 31 (1987) 403–22.

G.S. Fields, *Poverty, Inequality and Development* (Cambridge; New York: Cambridge University Press, 1980).

P. Foster and A.R. Zolberg, eds, *Ghana and the Ivory Coast* (London; Chicago; University of Chicago Press, 1971).

C.R. Frank and R.C. Webb, eds, *Income Distribution and Growth in the Less-Developed Countries* (Washington, D.C.: Brookings Institution, 1977).

M. Fransman, ed., *Industry and Accumulation in Africa* (London: Heinemann, 1982).

A. Gerschenkron, *Economic Backwardness in Historical Perspective* (Cambridge, MA: Harvard University Press, 1966).

R. Gilpin, *The Political Economy of International Relations* (Princeton: Princeton University Press, 1987).

R. Gilpin, *U.S. Power and the Multinational Corporation: The Political Economy of Foreign Direct Investment* (New York: Basic Books, 1975).

G. Goertz, 'Contextual Theories and Indicators in World Politics', *International Interactions*, 17 (1992) 285–303.

W. Grabendorff, H.W. Krumwiede and J. Todt, eds, *Political Change in Central America: Internal and External Dimensions*, Westview Special Studies on Latin America and the Caribbean (London; Boulder: Westview Press, 1984).

C.W.J. Granger, 'Investigating Causal Relations by Econometric Models and Cross-Spectral Methods', *Econometrica*, 37 (1969) 424–38.

N. Grimwade, *International Trade: New Patterns of Trade, Production and Investment* (London; New York: Routledge, 1989).

J. Grunwald and K. Flamm, *The Global Factory: Foreign Assembly in International Trade* (Washington, D.C.: Brookings Institution, 1985).

D.K. Gupta, *The Economics of Political Violence: The Effect of Political Instability on Growth* (New York: Praeger, 1990).

K.L. Gupta. and M.A. Islam, *Foreign Capital, Savings, and Growth: An International Cross-Sectional Study* (Dordrect, Holland; Boston: D. Reidel Publishing Co., 1983).

N. Hicks, 'Growth vs. Basic Needs: Is there a Trade-Off?' *World Development*, 7 (1979) 985–94.

C. Holtsberg, 'Rice Pricing Policy' in P. Richards, ed., *Basic Needs and Government Policies in Thailand* (Singapore: Maruzen Asia, 1982) pp.161–81.

A. Hopkins, *An Economic History of West Africa* (New York: Columbia University Press, 1973).

R.E. Huke, *Shadows on the Land: an Economic Geography of the Philippines* (Manila: Bookmark, 1963).

S.P. Huntington, *Political Order in Changing Societies* (London; New Haven: Yale University Press, 1968).

IMF, *Surveys of African Economies Volume 6: The Gambia, Ghana, Liberia, Nigeria, and Sierra Leone* (1975).

IMF, *Surveys of African Economies Volume 3: Dahomey, Ivory Coast, Mauritania, Niger, Senegal, Togo, and Upper Volta* (1970).

J.C. Ingram, *Economic Change in Thailand, 1850–1970* (Stanford: Stanford University Press, 1971).

D.A. Jodice, 'Sources of change in Third World regimes for foreign direct investment, 1968–1976', *International Organization*, 34 (1980) 177–206.

C. Johnson, 'Introduction – The Taiwan Model' in J.C. Hsiung, ed., *Contemporary Republic of China: The Taiwan Experience 1950–1980* (New York: Praeger, 1981) pp.9–18.

C. Johnson, *MITI and the Japanese Miracle: The Growth of Industrial Policy* (Stanford, CA: Stanford University Press, 1982).

P.J. Katzenstein, ed., *Between Power and Plenty: Foreign Economic Policies of Advanced Industrial States* (Madison, WI: University of Wisconsin Press, 1978).

R.M. Kavoussi, 'International Trade and Economic Development: The Recent Experience of Developing Countries', *Journal of Developing Areas*, April (1985), pp.379–92.

H.G. Kebschull, ed., *Politics in Transitional Societies: The Challenge of Change in Asia, Africa and Latin America* (New York: Appleton-Century-Crofts, 1968).

R. Keohane and J. Nye, *Power and Interdependence: World Politics in Transition* (Boston: Little Brown, 1977).

G.B. Key, ed., *The Political Economy of Colonialism in Ghana: A Collection of Documents and Statistics, 1900–1960* (Cambridge: Cambridge University Press, 1972).

C.P. Kindleberger, *Manias, Panics, and Crises* (New York: Basic Books, 1978).

C.P. Kindleberger, *The World in Depression, 1929–1939* (Berkeley: University of California Press, 1973).

A. Kohli, M.F. Altfeld, S. Lotfian, and R. Mardon, 'Inequality in the Third World: An Assessment of Competing Explanations', *Comparative Political Studies*, 17 (1984) 283–318.

D. Kowalewski, *Global Establishment: The Political Economy of North/Asian Networks* (New York: St Martin's Press, 1997).

S.D. Krasner, 'State Power and the Structure of International Trade', *World Politics*, 28 (1976) 317–47.

S.D. Krasner, 'Approaches to the State: Alternative Conceptions and Historical Dynamics', *Comparative Politics*, 16 (1984) 223–46.

A.O. Krueger, *et al., Aid and Development* (Baltimore: Johns Hopkins University Press, 1989).

S. Kuznets, 'Economic Growth and Income Inequality', *American Economic Review*, (1955) pp.1–28.

S. Kuznets, 'Quantitative Aspects of the Economic Growth of Nations: VIII Distribution of Income by Size', *Economic Development and Cultural Change*, 11 (1963) 1–80.

S. Kuznets, *Toward a Theory of Economic Growth* (1968).

D.A. Lake, *Power, Protection, and Free Trade: International Sources of U.S. Commercial Strategy* (Ithaca, NY: Cornell University Press, 1988).

D. Lal, 'The Misconceptions of "Development Economics"', in C.K. Wilber, ed., *The Political Economy of Development and Underdevelopment*, 4th edn (New York: Random House, 1988) pp.28–36.

S. Lall and F. Stewart, eds, *Theory and Reality in Development* (New York: Macmillan, 1986).

R.J. Langhammer, 'Competition Among Developing Countries for Foreign Investment in the Eighties – Whom did OECD investors Prefer?' *Weltwirtschaftliches Archiv*, 127 (1991) 390–403.

L. Laudan, *Progress and its Problems* (Berkeley: University of California Press, 1977).

C. Legum, *et al.*, *Africa in the 1980s* (New York: McGraw-Hill, 1979).

U. Lele and I. Nabi, eds, *Transitions in Development: the role of aid and commercial flows* (San Francisco, CA: ICS Press, 1991).

R.T. Libby, 'External Co-optation of a Less Developed Country's Policy Making: The Case of Ghana, 1969–1972', *World Politics*, 29 (1976) 67–89.

D. Lim, 'Fiscal Incentives and Direct Foreign Investment in Less Developed Countries', *Journal of Development Studies*, 19 (1983) 207–12.

J.J. Lim and S. Vani, eds, *Armed Separatism in Southeast Asia* (Singapore: Institute of Southeast Asia Studies, 1984) pp.217–33.

L.Y.C. Lim and P.E. Fong, *Foreign Direct Investment and Industrialization in Malaysia, Singapore, Taiwan and Thailand* (Paris: OECD, 1991).

L. Macdonald, *Supporting Civil Society: The Political Role of Non-Governmental Organizations in Central America*, (London: Macmillan and New York: St Martin's Press, 1997).

V. Mahler, *Dependency Approaches to International Political Economy: A Cross-National Study* (New York: Columbia University Press, 1980).

V. Mahler, 'Mining, Agriculture, and Manufacturing: The Impact of Foreign Investment on Social Distribution in Third World Countries', *Comparative Political Studies*, 14 (1981) 267–97.

J. Masini, *et al.*, *Multinationals and Development in Black Africa: A Case Study in the Ivory Coast* (New York: Praeger, 1979).

S.D. McDowell, *Globalization, Liberalization and Policy Change: A Political Economy of India's Communications Sector*, (London: Macmillan and New York: St Martin's Press, 1997).

M.C. McGuire, 'Foreign Assistance, Investment, and Defense: A Methodological Study with an Application to Israel, 1960–1979', *Economic Development and Cultural Change*, 35 (1987) 847–73.

C. Michalopoulos, 'Private Direct Investment, Finance and Development', *Asian Development Review*, 3 (1985) 59–71.

J.S. Migdal, 'A Model of State-Society Relations', in H.J. Wiarda, ed., *New Directions in Comparative Politics* (London; Boulder: Westview Press, 1985) pp.41–55.

R.F. Mikesell, W. Bartsch, J. Behrman, P. Church and others, *Foreign Investment in Petroleum and Mineral Industries: Case Studies of Investor-Host Country Relations* (London; Baltimore: Johns Hopkins University Press, 1971).

K.A. Mingst, 'The Ivory Coast at the Semi-Periphery of the World-Economy', *International Studies Quarterly*, 32 (1988) 259–74.

J.H. Mittelman and M.K. Pasha, *Out from Underdevelopment Revisited: Changing Global Structures and the Remaking of the Third World* (New York: St Martin's Press, 1997).

D. Morawetz, *Twenty-five Years of Economic Development, 1950–1975* (Johns Hopkins University Press for the World Bank, 1977).

B.A. Most. and H. Starr, *Inquiry, Logic and International Politics* (Columbia, South Carolina: University of South Carolina Press, 1989).

E.N. Muller, 'Democracy, Economic Development, and Income Inequality', *American Sociological Review*, 51 (1988) 441–45.

E.N. Muller and M. Seligson, 'Inequality and Insurgency', *American Political Science Review*, 81 (1987) 425–51.

G.P. Muller with V. Bornschier, *Comparative World Data: A Statistical Handbook for Social Science* (London and Baltimore: Johns Hopkins University Press for the World Bank, 1988).

E.W. Nafziger, *The Economics of Political Instability: The Nigerian-Biafran War* (Boulder, CO: Westview Press, 1984).

J.M. Nelson, ed., *Economic Crisis and Policy Choice: The Politics of Adjustment in the Third World* (Princeton, NJ: Princeton University Press, 1990) pp.113–67.

D.C. North and R.P. Thomas, 'An Economic Theory of Growth in the Western World', *The Economic History Review*, 2nd series, 23 (1970) 1–17.

J. O'Loughlin and L. Anselin, 'Bringing Geography Back to the Study of International Relations: Spatial Dependence and Regional Context in Africa, 1966–1978', *International Interactions*, 17 (1991) 29–61.

M. Olson, Jr., *The Rise and Decline of Nations: Economic Growth, Stagflation, and Social Rigidities* (London and New Haven: Yale University Press, 1982).

B. Onimode, *A Political Economy of the African Crisis* (London; New Jersey: Institute for African Alternatives, Zed Books, Ltd., 1988).

R.A. Packenham, *Liberal America and the Third World: Political Development Ideas in Foreign Aid and Social Science* (Princeton, NJ: Princeton University Press, 1973).

R.A. Packenham, 'Political Development Doctrines in the American Foreign Aid Program', *World Politics*, 18 (1966) 194–235.

G. Palma, 'Dependency: A Formal Theory of Underdevelopment or a Methodology for the Analysis of Concrete Situations of Development?' *World Development*, 6 (1978) 881–924.

M. Parvin, 'Economic Determinants of Political Unrest: An Econometric Approach', *Journal of Conflict Resolution*, 17 (1973) 271–96.

F. Paukert, 'Income Distribution at Different Levels of Development: A Survey of Evidence', *International Labour Review*, 108 (1973) 97–125.

E. Paus, 'Direct Foreign Investment and Economic Development in Latin America: Perspectives for the Future', *Journal of Latin American Studies*, 21 (1989) 221–39.

E. Paus, ed., *Struggle Against Dependence: Nontraditional Export Growth in Central America and the Caribbean* (London; Boulder: Westview Press, 1988).

W. Pelupessy and J. Weeks, eds, *Economic Maladjustment in Central America* (New York: St. Martin's Press, 1993).

G.A. Petrochilos, *Foreign Direct Investment and the Development Process: The Case of Greece* (Aldershot; Brookfield USA; Hong Kong; Singapore; Sydney: Avebury, 1989).

T. Porter, *States, Markets and Regimes in Global Finance*, (New York: St Martin's Press, 1993).

T.A. Poynter, *Multinational Enterprises and Government Intervention* (London: Croom Helm, 1985).

J. Ravenhill, ed., *Africa in Economic Crisis* (New York: Columbia University Press, 1986).

P. Richards, ed., *Basic Needs and Government Policies in Thailand* (Singapore: Maruzen Asia, 1982).

D. Rimmer, *The Economies of West Africa* (London: Weidenfeld and Nicolson, 1984).

R. Robison, K. Hewison, and R. Higgott, eds, *Southeast Asia in the 1980s: The Politics of Economic Crisis* (London; Sydney; Boston: Allen and Unwin, 1987) pp.80–112.

S.C. Ropp and J.A. Morris, eds, *Central America: Crisis and Adaptation* (Albuquerque, NM: University of New Mexico Press, 1984).

D. Rothchild and N. Chazan, eds, *The Precarious Balance: State and Society in Africa* (Boulder: Westview Press, 1988).

J.M. Rothgeb, Jr., 'The Effects of Foreign Investment on Overall and Sectoral Growth in Third World States', *Journal of Peace Research*, 21 (1984) 5–15.

J.M. Rothgeb, Jr., 'Trojan Horse, Scapegoat, or Non-Foreign Entity', *Journal of Conflict Resolution*, 31 (1987) 227–65.

J.M. Rothgeb, Jr., 'Direct Foreign Investment in Mining and Manufacturing in Underdeveloped States', *Social Science Journal*, 25 (1988) 24–43.

J.M. Rothgeb, Jr., 'Investment Dependence and Political Conflict in Third World Countries', *Journal of Peace Research*, 27 (1990) 255–72.

J.M. Rothgeb, Jr., 'The Effects of Foreign Investment Upon Political Protest and Violence in Underdeveloped Societies', *Western Political Quarterly*, 44 (1991) 9–38.

S. Rottenberg, ed., *The Political Economy of Poverty, Equity and Growth Costa Rica and Uruguay* (London: Oxford University Press for the World Bank, 1993).

R. Rubinson, 'Dependence, Government Revenue, and Economic Growth, 1955–1970', *Studies in Comparative International Development*, 12 (1977) 3–28.

R. Rubinson, ed., *Dynamics of World Development* (London and Beverly Hills: Sage, 1981).

R. Rubinson and D. Holtzman 'Comparative Dependence and Economic Development', *International Journal of Comparative Sociology*, 22 (1981) 86–101.

V.W. Ruttan, 'What Happened to Political Development?' *Economic Development and Cultural Change*, 39 (1991) 265–92.

J.D. Sachs, ed., *Developing Country Debt and the World Economy* (Chicago: University of Chicago Press, 1989) pp.263–74.

D. Sanders, *Patterns of Political Instability* (New York: St. Martin's Press, 1981).

C.E. Santiago, 'The Impact of Foreign Direct Investment on Export Structure and Employment Generation', *World Development*, 15 (1987) 317–28.

A. Sen, 'Development: Which Way Now?' in C.K. Wilber, ed., *The Political Economy of Development and Underdevelopment*, 4th edn (New York: Random House, 1988) pp.37–58.

B. Sharma, 'Multinational Corporations and Industrialization in Southeast Asia', *Contemporary Southeast Asia*, 6 (1984) 159–71.

L. Sigelman and M. Simpson, 'A Cross-National Test of the Linkage Between Economic Inequality and Political Violence', *Journal of Conflict Resolution*, 21 (1977) 105–28.

T.H. Silcock, ed., *Thailand: Social and Economic Studies in Development* (Durham, N.C.: Duke University in Association with Australian National University Press, 1967).

H.W. Singer, 'The World Development Report 1987 on the Blessings of "Outward Orientation": A Necessary Correction', *Journal of Development Studies*, 24 (1988) 232–6.

H.W. Singer, *The Strategy of International Development: Essays in the Economics of Backwardness* (White Plains, NY: International Arts and Sciences Press, 1975).

R.D. Singh, 'The Multinationals' Economic Penetration, Growth, Industrial Output, and Domestic Savings in Developing Countries: Another Look', *Journal of Development Studies*, 25 (1988) 55–82.

R.D. Singh, 'State Intervention, Foreign Economic Aid, Savings and Growth in LDCs: Some Recent Evidence', *Kyklos*, 38 (1985) 216–32.

D. Snyder and E.L. Kick, 'Structural Position in the World System and Economic Growth, 1955–1970: A Multiple-Network Analysis of Transnational Interactions', *American Journal of Sociology*, 84 (1979) 1096–126.

T.N. Srinivasan, 'Neoclassical Political Economy: The State and Economic Development', *Asian Development Review*, 3 (1985) 38–58.

H. Stein, ed., *Asian Industrialization and Africa: Studies in Policy Alternatives to Structural Adjustments* (London: Macmillan and New York: St Martin's Press, 1995).

A. Stepan, ed., *Authoritarian Brazil: Origins, Policies, and Future* (New Haven, CT: Yale University Press, 1973).

W.A. Stoever, 'The Stages of Developing Country Policy Toward Foreign Investment', *The Columbia Journal of World Business*, 20 (1985) 3–11.

C. Stoneman, 'Foreign Capital and Economic Growth', *World Development*, 3 (1975) 11–26.

J. Stopford and S. Strange with J. Henley, *Rival states, rival firms: Competition for world market shares* (Cambridge; New York; Port Chester; Melbourne; Sydney: Cambridge University Press 1991).

P. Streeten with S.J. Burki, M. Haq, N. Hicks, and F. Stewart, *First Things First: Meeting Basic Human Needs in the Developing Countries* (Oxford; New York: Oxford University Press for the World Bank, 1981).

P. Streeten, 'Accelerating Development in the Poorest Countries', in R.J. Berg and D.F. Gordon, eds, *Cooperation for International Development: The United States and the Third World in the 1990s* (Boulder: Lynne Rienner Publishers, 1989) pp.142–63.

L. Swatuk and T. Shaw, eds, *The South at the End of the Twentieth Century: Rethinking the Political Economy of Foreign Policy in Africa, Asia, the Caribbean and Latin America* (London: Macmillan, 1994).

H.B. Thorelli and G.D. Sentell, *Consumer Emancipation and Economic Development: The Case of Thailand* (London; Greenwich, Connecticut: JAI Press, 1982).

M. Timberlake and K.R. Williams, 'Dependence, Political Exclusion, and Government Repression: Some Cross-National Evidence', *American Sociological Review*, 49 (1984) 141–46.

M. Timberlake and K.R. Williams, 'Structural Position in the World-System, Inequality, and Political Violence', *Journal of Political and Military Sociology*, 15 (1987) 1–15.

P.L. Tsai, 'Determinants of Foreign Direct Investment in Taiwan: An Alternative Approach with Time-Series Data', *World Development*, 19 (1991) 275–85.

J.E. Uba, *The Awakening Frontier* (Houston, TX: Pratt and Hall, 1990).

G. Underhill, ed., *The New World Order in International Finance*, (New York: St Martin's Press, 1997).

U.S. Department of Commerce International Trade Administration, *International Direct Investment: Global Trends and the U.S. Role* (Washington, D.C.: U.S. Government Printing Office, 1988).

P. Uri, *Development without Dependence* (New York: Praeger, for the Atlantic Institute for International Affairs, 1976).

A. Varas, ed., *Democracy Under Siege: New Military Power in Latin America* (New York: Greenwood Press, 1989).

E.M. Villegas, *Studies in Philippine Political Economy* (Manila: Silangan Publishers, 1983).

I. Wallerstein, *Politics of the World-Economy* (Cambridge; New York: Cambridge University Press, 1984).

I. Wallerstein, 'The Capitalist World-Economy: Middle-Run Prospects', *Alternatives*, 14 (1989) 279–88.

P. Weber-Schafer, *et al.*, China – NICs – ASEAN: Competition or Cooperation?, vol. 4 of *East Asia: International Review of Economic, Political, and Social Development* (Frankfurt: Campus Verlag and Boulder: Westview Press, 1987).

C.K. Wilber, ed., *The Political Economy of Development and Underdevelopment* 4th edn (New York: Random House, 1988).

O. Williamson, *The Economic Institutions of Capitalism: Firms, Markets and Relational Contracting* (New York: Free Press, 1985).

World Bank, *World Debt Tables* (Washington, D.C: World Bank, various years).

World Bank, *Aspects of Poverty in the Philippines* (Washington, D.C.: World Bank, 1980a).

World Bank, *Thailand: Income Growth and Poverty Alleviation* (Washington, D.C.: World Bank, 1980b).

World Bank, *Accelerated Development in Sub-Saharan Africa* (Washington, D.C.: World Bank, 1981a).

World Bank, *The Philippines: Priorities and Prospects for Development* (Washington, D.C.: World Bank, 1981b).

World Bank, *Toward Sustained Development in Sub-Saharan Africa* (Washington, D.C.: World Bank, 1984).

World Bank, *Financing Adjustment with Growth* (Washington, D.C.: World Bank, 1986).

J. Woronoff, *West African Wager: Houphouet versus Nkrumah* (Methuchen, NJ: The Scarecrow Press, Inc., 1972).

D. Wurfel and B. Burton, eds, *Southeast Asia in the New World Order: The Political Economy of a Dynamic Region*, (New York: St Martin's Press, 1996).

Index

AӨΛESH 11.